Public Money
and
the Muse

THE AMERICAN ASSEMBLY was established by Dwight D. Eisenhower at Columbia University in 1950. Each year it holds at least two nonpartisan meetings that give rise to authoritative books that illuminate issues of United States policy.

An affiliate of Columbia, with offices at Barnard College, the Assembly is a national, educational institution incorporated in the state of New York.

The Assembly seeks to provide information, stimulate discussion, and evoke independent conclusions on matters of vital public interest.

CONTRIBUTORS

STEPHEN BENEDICT

MARY BURGER, Harvard University

MILTON C. CUMMINGS JR., Johns Hopkins
University

PAUL J. DIMAGGIO, Yale University

ROBERT GARFIAS, University of California, Irvine

JOAN JEFFRI, Columbia University

ARTHUR LEVITT JR., Levitt Media Company

KATHLEEN M. SULLIVAN, Harvard Law School

STEPHEN E. WEIL, Smithsonian Institution

DENNIE PALMER WOLF, Harvard University

GERALD D. YOSHITOMI, Japanese American
Culture and Community Center

THE AMERICAN ASSEMBLY
Columbia University

Public Money
and
the Muse

Essays on Government Funding for the Arts

STEPHEN BENEDICT
Editor

W · W · NORTON & COMPANY
New York   London

The text of this book is composed in Baskerville.
Composition and Manufacturing by the Haddon Craftsmen, Inc.

First Edition.

ISBN 0-393-03015-6 (cloth)

ISBN 0-393-96135-4 (paper)

W.W. Norton & Company, Inc., 500 Fifth Avenue, New York, N.Y. 10110
W.W. Norton & Company, Ltd., 10 Coptic Street, London WC1A 1PU

1 2 3 4 5 6 7 8 9 0

Contents

Public Money
and
the Muse

Preface

An unprecedented national debate commenced in the latter part of 1989 about the role of the arts in American life. As a result, initially, of the controversy surrounding two visual arts exhibitions, funded with federal monies, the Congress and public groups engaged in examining and questioning the processes, standards, and the enabling legislation of the National Endowment for the Arts (NEA). The debate extended to more general issues regarding the arts and artists. What appeared to be missing from the discussions was an informed analysis of the role of the arts in national life, and of the appropriate sources of support for them.

The American Assembly saw an opportunity to contribute to a broader and more informal national discussion about the arts, American society, and the government. It became the Assembly's objective to assist in the development of a broad, positive agenda for this decade for the arts in relationship to government, an agenda that would go beyond the role of the NEA and encompass all the main elements of government policies affecting the arts. Eight regional Dialogues were first held in Kansas City, Pittsburgh, Minneapolis, Chicago, Los

Angeles, Dallas, Miami, and Atlanta to help shape the issues and to involve community and national leaders. The Assembly asked Stephen Benedict, founder and former director of the Graduate Program in Arts Administration at Columbia University, to direct this series of regional Dialogues. These meetings were held amidst the turbulent developments of the year, including the criminal prosecution of a museum director for exhibiting Robert Mapplethorpe photographs, state and local government budget cuts around the country adversely affecting support of arts institutions, and a bruising but successful battle in the Congress to reauthorize the NEA. The results of the Assembly regional meetings were reported in my testimony before the Independent Commission, which had been set up by Congress and the White House to examine the procedures of the NEA.

Against this background a national American Assembly convened on November 8-11, 1990 at Arden House in Harriman, New York. Entitled *The Arts and Government: Questions for the Nineties,* this American Assembly brought together seventy-one distinguished Americans from around the country representing various sectors of our society. Many of the differing points of view about the arts and government prevalent in the ongoing national debate were represented at Arden House. Background papers on aspects of the intersection of the arts and government were prepared under the editorial supervision of Mr. Benedict. Participants discussed an agenda prepared by Mr. Benedict and Steven Lavine, president of the California Institute of the Arts, who served as co-directors of the meeting.

After their deliberations, the Assembly participants issued a report of findings and recommendations with respect to the role of public support of the arts, the NEA, state and local involvement, advocacy by the arts, issues of cultural diversity, U.S. international cultural policy, tax policy, and the role of arts in education. Copies of the report can be obtained by writing directly to: The American Assembly, 412 Altschul Hall, Barnard College, Columbia University, New York, NY 10027-6598. The full report is also included in this volume.

The background papers used by the participants have been compiled into the present volume, which is published as a stimulus to further thinking and discussion about this subject. We hope that this book will provoke a broader understanding of these issues.

Funding for this project was provided by The Rockefeller Foundation and the AT&T Foundation. The opinions expressed in this volume are those of the individual authors and not necessarily those of the sponsors nor of The American Assembly, which does not take stands on issues it presents for public discussion.

Stephen Stamas
Chairman
The American Assembly

Foreword

STEPHEN BENEDICT

W hen the American Assembly project on "The Arts and Government" was planned in the fall of 1989, it was clear that 1990 would be a lively time for the chosen subject. But could anyone then have fully anticipated how lively? Soon after, the issue of public arts funding, specifically in the context of reauthorizing the National Endowment for the Arts, came to dominate discussion in the arts—and other—worlds during the following twelve months.

A qualitative change seemed to have taken place during the year in the way the American public perceived the issue of government funding. For the first time, a substantial portion

---

STEPHEN BENEDICT founded the Graduate Program in Arts Administration at Columbia University and directed it from 1979–89. Prior to that, from 1975–78, he directed the Project in the Arts for the Council on Foundations and the National Endowment for the Arts. From 1959–74 he was program officer, with responsibility for the arts, for the Rockefeller Brothers Fund. He is also a founder and past president of the Theatre Development Fund and has served on the board of numerous arts institutions in New York City.

of the electorate had come to feel it had a personal stake in the expenditure of government arts dollars. The road to this new level of attention was not one that anybody in the arts would have chosen to take, but the new awareness was here, not likely to go away, and had to be dealt with. It could be argued that this outcome will ultimately benefit the arts and help generate a larger audience if it causes artists and other art professionals to address the question seriously and to explore new ideas and methods for reaching a broader public for the arts of every culture and genre.

The challenge to those guiding the American Assembly arts and government project was to train its focus on questions that would outlive the ones that commanded immediate attention in an excited political climate. Also, on a much larger canvas, during this same period, world-altering events were unfolding in Eastern Europe and the Soviet Union and, later on, in the Middle East. The onset of dark economic clouds at home only sharpened the problematic character of the questions that faced every domestic social activity for which tax derived funding is important. Thus the arts and government project found itself taking place in a turbulent and uncertain atmosphere, domestic and foreign.

Against this backdrop, the issues we have chosen to highlight by commissioning these chapters from a group of distinguished men and women are subjects we believe will continue to be on the agenda of all those concerned with helping shape the future of the arts in America, whatever the external obstacles. They provide a wealth of good information and opinion and a distinctive point of view on each of the topics they address.

This is not a book that takes up the issue of whether or not it is government's proper business to aid the arts. That question will always be a legitimate one, but the proponents of a negative view are, at this stage, a dwindling band. To the extent the House of Representatives provides a rough barometer of public opinion on issues of public policy, it did so in this case during the 1990 debate. An amendment to the NEA reauthorization bill by Representative Philip Crane to abolish the National Endowment for the Arts was defeated by a margin of more than 5 to 1. The vote was 361–64. If the issue is not quite dead, it is moribund.

The authors of this book all believe that public arts funding, in some fashion, is a justifiable activity for government to take on. They locate the genuine controversies within the parameters of each specific issue, e.g.: what *kind* of arts education should every child receive and how can government help? What approaches to the support of the individual artist work and what don't? What are the implications of providing more federal arts funds to the states? Does government have a special responsibility for helping achieve cultural democracy?

Because of the close and often overlapping nature of these issues, there is a degree of duplication in the chapters that we have chosen to retain. In some instances, it serves to expose different perspectives on the same events or ideas; in others, it highlights the common body of information and events that every serious arts policy analyst must consider.

Not all of the major issues are addressed here in depth. Of particular importance—as the Report of the American Assembly acknowledges—is the question of international cultural policy. World events of the past year have opened up a kaleidoscope of possibilities and imperatives that could easily provide the basis for another American Assembly and collection of essays devoted exclusively to the topic.

The papers that *are* included represent a broad spectrum of lay and academic reflection on subjects we believe will be central in the decade of the nineties. Arthur Levitt Jr. draws analogies between the role of research and development in the progressive business corporation and the arts. He also suggests that more energetic and sophisticated political action by the business community is imperative.

Milton C. Cummings Jr. surveys the history of the arts and government relationship in this country and finds illuminating parallels in our past with the political frenzies of the last year. *Plus ça change* in many respects, though not all.

Kathleen Sullivan explores the First Amendment aspects of content restrictions on the grant-making process and other constitutional issues raised by the NEA controversy. Stephen E. Weil, approaching some of the same questions from the standpoint of tax policy, draws a sharp distinction between change oriented art and art that reinforces public stability. His analysis suggests why the arts community was often so divided in its time of troubles.

Joan Jeffri, utilizing fresh research on the life patterns and needs of individual creative artists, discusses the new relationships that have evolved in recent years between the artist and the public and the consequences for both parties.

Robert Garfias and Gerald D. Yoshitomi set forth two perspectives on cultural democracy and the actions necessary if the phrase is to be realized in public policy. In a related essay, Paul J. DiMaggio reflects on the increasingly decentralized structure for public arts funding that has emerged in recent years. What does it imply and what new choices does it present?

Dennie Wolf and Mary Burger, addressing the arts and education, trace the evolution from a utilitarian rationale to the contemporary view of the arts as a cognitive discipline. They outline the critical leadership role they believe that federal, state, and local government can play in promoting a more informed and lasting integration of the arts into the educational system.

Finally, there is the report of the American Assembly, November 8–11, 1990, for which the essays in this book were prepared. Each participant received them prior to the meeting as background reading. In one respect or another, all of the chapters find some reflection in the Report, which sought to sum up, in a general way, the conclusions and recommendations that emerged from the three days of discussion.

Introduction

ARTHUR LEVITT JR.

The year 1990 saw a rapid succession of startling events that together challenged and changed the relationship between government and the arts.

For the first time in history, an American museum and its director were brought to trial on criminal charges of pandering obscenity. No matter what one may think about the subject matter of the *XYZ Portfolio* by noted, and now infamous, photographer Robert Mapplethorpe, the Cincinnati Contemporary Arts Center and Dennis Barrie were brought to trial for what one museum director described as "doing its job, which is exhibiting art by artists."

For the first time in the history of the National Endowment for the Arts (NEA), that agency's survival was seriously and

ARTHUR LEVITT JR. is chairman of the Levitt Media Company in New York City. From 1978–1989 he served as chairman and chief executive officer of the American Stock Exchange, Inc. Mr. Levitt has served on numerous boards, including the Rockefeller Foundation, the Solomon R. Guggenheim Foundation, the Williams College Board of Trustees, and the New York State Council on the Arts.

dangerously threatened because of the content and type of art it supported. The NEA's battle—unlike anything the arts world had ever experienced, at least on a national level—was marked by distortions, heated and emotional debate, divisive actions, and inflammatory rhetoric.

The situation became so dire that the National Endowment could not be assured of reauthorization or appropriation until the eleventh hour because it lacked basic support from enough members of Congress. The buffeted National Endowment lost its favored status with elected officials and perhaps with a significant segment of the American people. There is no doubt that the agency was left with a seriously damaged image.

For the first time, the arts' lack of political know-how became its donnybrook, and its political clout was found to be ineffective at best. Even the arts boards of directors, usually the trump card of arts institutions, found the controversy "too hot to handle."

In yet another first, the NEA's relationship with its own constituency—the arts community itself—was eroded and jeopardized because of the required signing of "obscenity oaths" by grantees and other actions by the newly appointed National Endowment chair, John Frohnmayer. For the first time, artists and mainstream arts institutions sued their government patron. Still more refused to accept much-needed grants.

The arts and government relationship has been forever changed by these events. In my mind one thing above all stands out: the need for effective political action has catapulted its way to the top of the agenda of urgent needs in the arts.

Top-line Thinking

While 1990's political controversy had a negative impact on national attitudes towards the arts, what should not be overlooked, and what we who support the arts should not be afraid to assert, is the usefulness of controversial art, indeed its essential importance. To quote Edson Spencer, chair of the Ford Foundation and former CEO of Honeywell, Inc., "The creation of controversy and the clash of ideas are among those forces that help democracy flourish. The arts and humanities are precisely where those controversies and ideas are born and grown."

While others share Spencer's view, there is something intrinsic to the arts that interests me, as a businessman, even more. If one steps back and views the arts and the National Endowment for the Arts without the distorting white heat generated during 1990, one can find some useful lessons for business, among them the true value of risk taking.

American business is beset with major problems, which have become readily apparent through the litmus test of global competitiveness. Today the ten largest banks in the world are Japanese; twenty years ago they were all American. A recent list of the ten most powerful brands in the world marketplace is headed by Japanese and German names, although a handful of American companies remain on the list.

Those American corporations that suffer the most in world markets have a few things in common: short-term focus, bottom-line-only decision making, inability to adapt to change, avoidance of long-range commitments like research and development, and fear of risk taking. These traits are so abundant in American business as to become almost synonymous in some circles with the phrase "American management style." Such an approach cripples the competitive abilities of these companies far more than foreign trade barriers.

On the other hand, those companies that have performed the best in today's fiercely competitive environment are comfortable with risks, tend to spend more on research and development, and oppose protectionist policies that interfere with the market process. Their decisions are based not just on bottom-line considerations, but also on what I call top-line values, the most important of which is an obsessive devotion to quality and a total responsiveness to the needs and attitudes of their customers.

These successful companies have something in common with the arts. The arts, too, are driven by top-line thinking: quality comes first. Quality is what endures in art and what artists strive for above all else. And, until recently at least,

quality was the deciding factor in the National Endowment for
the Arts' grant making. Its peer panels have demonstrated a
remarkable instinct for recognizing and supporting quality, as
well as the promise of quality.

For example, this benchmark directed NEA support to an
enviable list of artists and arts organizations that began with
the American Ballet Theater (the NEA's first grant recipient)
and extends to John Irving, who wrote *The World According to
Garp* with an NEA literature fellowship. There were also grants
to Alice Walker, Billy Taylor, Alvin Ailey, Twyla Tharp, the St.
Louis Symphony, the Houston Opera, Nam June Paik, and
even the Cowboy Poetry Gathering in Elko, Nevada, to name
just a few of the 85,000 grant recipients that have caught my
eye.

The NEA has made certain, too, that it provided support for
emerging artists, its version of research and development. It is
no accident that all four Pulitzer Prize winners in 1990 received NEA funds at important junctures in their careers: Mel
Powell for music, Oscar Hijuelos for fiction, Charles Simic for
poetry, and August Wilson for playwriting. In fact, every Pulitzer Prize–winning play *since 1976* received its premiere production at a nonprofit theater, with NEA support.

Finally, the NEA has not shied away from risk taking or from
experimentation. It was a risk to support the fledgling Dance
Theater of Harlem, first funded through a category called expansion arts, but that company went on to achieve national
and international acclaim. The Vietnam War Memorial, one of
the most visited monuments in Washington, resulted from an
NEA design competition, and this monumental piece initially
received a significant amount of controversy. Likewise, the
Calder sculpture in Grand Rapids, Michigan, was criticized in
its early years but has endured and become a symbol of civic
pride.

It is an extraordinary record, one that many businesses
might try to emulate. But what about the failures? Did the NEA
also fund artists or arts organizations whose work was disappointing or even disastrous? Definitely. Sometimes the bet was
placed and was lost. Sometimes the bet should not have ever

been placed. But it is through the courage to fail that success is eventually achieved—whether in art or in business. Artists have that courage; so do scientists; so have the greatest leaders of corporations, most of whom have gone broke or come close to it sometime during their corporate careers.

Arts Integral to Economy

As I travel throughout America talking to hundreds of business people and visiting the best and worst of those communities that either spawn or spurn growth, creativity, and improved living standards, I recognize an important economic issue that has not been sufficiently explored. It is that the arts and economic vitality are linked in powerful ways. Almost without exception, I have found that the best places for locating businesses, for job growth, for commercial viability, are those communities that support their cultural institutions.

Likewise, the poorest choices for economic growth potential are invariably those places that cannot or do not nurture the development of the arts.

Examples of this phenomenon abound. They can be found in Minneapolis, one of the nation's most vibrant arts communities; in Houston, whose cultural growth literally put that city on the map; and in Miami and Seattle, to name a few.

Business and culture are two integral, interdependent systems that are part and parcel of a thriving community. Without one, the other does not function optimally. Without both in place and working, the community is incomplete, in a sense handicapped.

The National Endowment for the Arts, during its first twenty-five years, played a vital part in the cultural growth of countless cities and small towns across America. By so doing, it became an important contributor not only to our cultural life but also to this nation's economic vitality.

An Easy Target

So why were the attackers of the National Endowment able to wreak such havoc? There were, of course, many complex factors at play. But a key element was that the political far right, strengthened and highly organized during the eighties, found itself without a unifying issue. Communism was on the wane worldwide, lower taxes in the face of intolerable deficits had become an impossibility, and even abortion had lost its previous political currency.

The arts—decentralized, unprepared, and politically innocent—provided a convenient, and juicy, target. As one political commentator said, "It was a situation made in heaven. It had sex, religion, and politics, all wrapped up into one. The National Endowment became a clear, easy target."

The controversy tapped a rich vein of social unrest that included the AIDS epidemic and its underbelly: an increase in the fear of and disdain for homosexuals. Though the arts had flourished with NEA support, their growth throughout the country was still fresh and young, their many friends too new and not yet committed to its fundamental causes.

Some of the charges by critics contained an element of truth, like elitism and the "private club" atmosphere that still exists in some arts organizations. To Marvin Sloves, an advertising executive who serves on several arts boards, this charge is a vestige of times past. "Cultural institutions can no longer be clubs because of the growth of public support," he has insisted. But the truth is, some still are elitist and many others are still perceived that way. It is an issue that needs to be faced and seriously addressed because as Sloves admits, "Where there is still, to some extent, a club mentality, it is in conflict with a strong need by the arts for public support in order to survive."

A related issue is what has come to be described as multiculturalism. Changing demographic, social, and linguistic processes are transforming this country, affecting all segments of American life. These changes are being reflected in the arts and were an essentially undiscussed aspect of the controversies in 1990.

Cultural pluralism has become an organizing principle of our society. In contrast to the melting pot, which promised to erase ethnic and group differences, the United States—as a haven for many different groups—has allowed each group to maintain its cultural heritage, to assimilate, or to do both. Our common culture is now being formed by the interaction of our diverse, multiple cultures.

Artist Guillermo Gomez-Pena describes this new common culture as "border culture." "Today," he says, "if there is a dominant culture, it is border culture. The border is all we share." This pluralistic interaction can be, in my mind, an exciting prospect.

But while artists and their work may be reflecting multicultural changes, our arts institutions, by and large, are not. The boards and staffs of arts organizations all too often are woefully lacking in minority representation.

The need for minority staff is not a new one. In the early 1970s, Theater Communications Group helped to identify black individuals for positions with arts organizations in Los Angeles. Today several foundations, like the Rockefeller Foundation, the Pittsburg Foundation, and the Howard Heinz Endowment, are exploring projects that focus on the training and development of culturally diverse staff. But one does not get a sense that dramatic changes in staff composition are occurring, and we would do well to examine why.

The same is true for board representation. If one believes that cultural institutions are important to the well-being of communities, then they must be managed with skill and creativity *guided by and representing their multicultural communities.* It is a risk-taking idea. It means sharing power and decisions. It means accepting change. But aren't risk taking and change intrinsic to the nature of the arts?

Identifying minority board member candidates can be an obstacle to otherwise willing organizations who neither have access, nor know how to obtain access to minority individuals with the skills they need. But this is, of course, solvable. A few forward-looking service organizations have new multicultural programs that identify potential African-American, Latino, and Asian board members for arts organizations. Both the

Toledo Symphony and the Cleveland Opera, with grants from the Ohio Arts Council, have launched outreach projects that include the recruitment of black board members.

A number of those groups that have addressed this issue, though, are not truly getting to the inner core of their communities. Thus in major urban areas we see boards, with minority representation, selecting individuals who are more assimilated into the establishment, and therefore not really in touch with the soul of the community from which they came. This approach results in a missed opportunity, and these organizations, besides missing the point, are the poorer for it.

Cultural pluralism is one of the norms of a free society, and this can be a resource, particularly for the arts, rather than a problem to be solved. For culture is fundamentally a form of communication. Cultures are constantly influencing one another, exchanging ideas about art, technology, and society—and the exchange is usually enriching, not depleting.

The arts can take a leadership role in the arena of multiculturalism, and in some ways they are beginning to. When Gomez-Pena speaks of "border culture," the point where America's diverse cultures intersect, he says, "Cultures are not closed systems. In order to dialogue, we must learn each other's languages, history, art, literature and political ideas. It is mostly writers, artists, arts administrators—not politicians, scientists or religious leaders—who are leading this effort."

The Arts and Politics

If the arts are to continue to open new avenues of cultural communication, to grow and expand, indeed even to survive in some form similar to their present level of activity, then the reality and importance of politics to our future must be recognized. Among our highest priorities must be to succeed in the political arena.

We have to ask the hard questions of ourselves. Why is it that America's cultural institutions, managed by the most visible and influential business, academic, and social leaders, have been so ineffective in defining an arts agenda or persuading the legislative and executive branches that the arts and their survival are vital to our society? Why were Jesse Helms et al. able to be so effective?

When Helms threw down the gauntlet by opposing government funding for the arts and denouncing the type of art supported by the NEA, his accusations generated an outpouring of letters to members of Congress nearly sixteen to one against the NEA. As the debate grew more strident and pro-NEA forces began to write letters, testify, and editorialize in favor of reauthorization, the public's response began to shift. A number of senators and representatives, however, viewed that shift with cynicism. One member quipped, "Most of my favorable letters are coming from actors and artists and very few from real people." This is a view we should not let stand.

The arts have lost touch with those in society who have a say about their future and their economic vitality. This means they have lost touch with elected officials. The days are gone when a few people in Washington could shield the arts from "getting their hands dirty" with politics. As in all other sectors of American life, ignoring Washington is done at one's peril, whether one is an educator, a small business, a truck driver, a farmer, or a corporation. Today, even clothes designers have a trade union in Washington.

This issue goes beyond simple monetary support through the National Endowment for the Arts. Federal support is an indication of the national importance of the arts in our society. It is recognition that is worth preserving and fighting for.

The NEA's decline or demise would have far-reaching effects beyond its multimillion dollar appropriation. Just as its grant making leverages billions of private support dollars, so too its decline would create a ripple effect on private giving. "If the NEA is unwilling and unable to fill the role it had in the past of taking risks and providing support for emerging new artists," says Spencer of the Ford Foundation, "public and corporate foundations are going to be even less inclined to do so."

Among the places hardest hit would be not New York, Chicago, Los Angeles, or other major urban centers, but cities and towns like Phoenix, Arizona; Portland, Oregon; Boise, Idaho; St. Louis, Missouri; Austin, Texas; Richmond, Virginia; and Santa Fe, New Mexico. These are places where an NEA grant has been crucial, giving arts organizations the leverage and the endorsement they need to raise private funds and to enrich the life of their communities.

One of the most striking examples of the reach of the National Endowment can be found in a tiny town in New Mexico, southeast of Santa Fe. A Hispanic hill town of only a few hundred population, Villa Nueva's last major civic event was when the railroads were built. Until, that is, the women's sewing circle received a grant from the folk art program of the NEA (rumor has it that one of the women's husbands filled out the application). People from all over the country visit Villa Nueva to see the colcha embroidery tapestry that rings the inside of the parish church. (If you go, ask at the country store for Stella. She has the key to the church.) Made up of over fifty panels, the tapestry tells the history of the Pecos Valley, which was settled in the late 1600s by the Spanish. To the people of Villa Nueva a grant from the U.S. government was an honor and a godsend.

There are many other issues in government that impact the arts beyond those surrounding the National Endowment. The Tax Reform Act of 1986, for example, has had a deleterious effect on individual giving, and there has been little interest on the part of Congress to ameliorate these disincentives. The reforms have also had a severe impact on contributions of appreciated property, in particular donations of works of art. A tax on the earned income of nonprofit organizations, such as museum gift shop receipts, could easily gain momentum again. And on and on.

Leaders in the arts must mobilize resources, scarce though they might be, to change the present negative views held by Congress. It will not be an easy task. Besides money, it will require some new skills: wisdom and savvy, courage and guts, managing risks and making hard choices. It means spending a lot of time in political trenches.

There are some, maybe many, in the arts who shun the very

idea. The arts are and should be essentially apolitical or beyond politics, they say.

Such attitudes are understandable. Art should not be subject to political influence in this country. That was certainly the intention of the framers of the legislation that created the National Endowment for the Arts. The only way to stop political interference, however, is to be politically active and, more importantly, to be politically astute.

The key to any effort to alter congressional attitudes is the breadth of appeal from constituents. The fact is that there are not enough votes or money represented by all the artists and arts organizations in this country to sway many congressional votes. Chances are that a member representing Fort Wayne, Indiana or Watertown, New York will not be sympathetic to funding the arts when his or her district endures a 15 percent unemployment rate.

How then do we reach policy makers who, over the next ten years, will have an increasingly important say about government funding, program content, and public perception of America's cultural landscape? The answer, I suggest, relates to how our institutions are governed, the relevance of their programs to their communities, and how we define and articulate the arts' key relationship to quality of life, job creation, economic vitality, education, and the enhancement of national values.

No one organization can do this job alone, but the work must be cohesive, thorough, and politically sophisticated. We need to develop strong coalitions with groups outside the arts who might be enlisted to join us in standing up to critics, so that small (but dazzlingly effective) pressure groups are not given inappropriate influence.

Such an effort should command the attention of the boards of directors of arts institutions. No longer can we leave this responsibility to executive staffs who must continue to focus on the survival and growth of the arts in their communities. No longer can our boards beg off political involvement because it may conflict with corporate legislative agendas. The people who create the jobs and socialize with elected officials are the

best ones, perhaps the only ones, who can counter the sophisticated efforts of the religious right and others who have recently given the issue of cultural funding such a political cast.
As leaders in their communities, the boards' voices will be
heard.

I would go so far as to suggest that the board chairs of one
hundred of America's arts organizations consider creating a
powerful lobbying organization. This cultural council of CEOs
could engage high-level lobbyists, keep a legislative score
card, testify regularly before congressional oversight committees, and address legislative, legal, and tax issues that adversely affect artists and the arts. Their actions would be of
great value to other organizations in Washington involved in
arts advocacy.

"It is time to begin broadcasting the truth and it is this,"
proclaimed Garland Wright, artistic director of the Guthrie
Theater, "no matter how provocative, the arts stand for a system of ethical values. We stand for the dignity of the individual
and for each individual's freedom to exercise imagination."
Wright gives us three very good reasons why the arts and their
leaders must demonstrate political as well as intellectual merit.

The chapters in this volume seek to define some of the most
critical issues in this high-stakes encounter between government and the arts.

1

Government and the Arts: An Overview

MILTON C. CUMMINGS JR.

W e may sometimes forget the fact, but the United States of America was 176 years old before it committed itself to a program of sustained, direct financial support for the arts by the national government. Throughout that long period, this American practice of leaving the arts largely to fend for themselves was frequently contrasted with what was called "The European Tradition"—substantial and sometimes lavish state support for the arts.

Actually, during these years there really were at least *two* European traditions concerning arts support, one lavish, the other much less so. On the one hand, there were the formerly

MILTON C. CUMMINGS JR. is professor of political science at Johns Hopkins University. Dr. Cummings is the author of many articles and books, including *The Patron State: Government and the Arts in Europe, North America, and Japan,* coedited with Richard S. Katz; and *Who's to Pay for the Arts? The International Search for Models of Support,* coedited with J. Mark Davidson Schuster. Dr. Cummings wishes to thank Matthew C. Price for research assistance in the preparation of this chapter.

royal, absolutist states of continental Europe, such as Austria and France, where for centuries there has been a sustained and enormously rich tradition of government patronage of the arts. In these countries it has simply been assumed that patronage of the arts is a normal government responsibility. On the other hand, there were the more plutocratic, mercantilist states with more limited monarchies, such as England and the Netherlands. These countries historically have had a much less lavish government patronage of the arts.[1]

We in the United States inherited primarily this latter, English tradition—one with relatively little direct government patronage of the arts. Moreover, in the late eighteenth and early nineteenth centuries, as they tried to forge a new nation on the edge of a vast wilderness, many Americans were preoccupied with other things. As John Adams put it, in a famous ordering of national priorities: he had to study politics and war, so that his sons could study mathematics and philosophy, in order to give their children a right to study painting, poetry, music, and architecture.

In addition, some early American statesmen, John Adams among them, worried that a strong focus on the fine arts might be linked with an excess of luxury, a trend Adams felt he had observed in France during diplomatic service at the Court of Versailles. For this reason Adams worried that too great an interest in the fine arts might corrupt his fellow citizens in the new American nation.

Even so, very shortly after the founding of the American republic, certain forms of art attracted considerable attention from American government leaders. There were, first of all, practical problems of architecture and city planning—designing a new capital city in Washington, D.C. Furthermore, early government leaders were aristocrats, by American standards, with considerable knowledge of the arts.

George Washington, John Adams, Benjamin Franklin, Thomas Jefferson, James Madison, James Monroe, and John Quincy Adams were remarkable political leaders, by any measure—large in their view of America and the world, and large in their view of the importance of the arts. The Constitution itself, in Article I, Section 8, stipulated that: "Congress shall have the Power . . . To promote the Progress of Science and useful Arts, by securing . . . to Authors and Inventors the exclusive Right to their respective Writings and Discoveries. . . ." Thomas Jefferson personally submitted two entries in the design competition for the new Capitol building. (Jefferson lost. The competition winner was William Thornton.) And it was George Washington's belief that "the Arts and Sciences essential to the prosperity of the State and to the ornament and happiness of human life have a primary claim to the encouragement of every lover of his Country and mankind."

John Quincy Adams put the case for active promotion of the arts by the government most strongly of all. In his first annual message as president, the younger Adams defined the "great object" of government as "the improvement of the condition of those who are parties to the social compact," and called for "laws promoting . . . the cultivation and encouragement of the mechanic and of the elegant arts, the advancement of literature, and the progress of the sciences." Failure to exercise constitutional powers for the elevation of the people, John Quincy Adams said, "would be treachery to the most sacred of trusts."[2]

In addition to planning the design for a new capital city, American government leaders became involved in decorating the new public buildings that were being constructed in Washington, especially the Capitol—filling them with statues, paintings, and other ornaments. Here, when it commissioned specific artists to do the work, the government often got into trouble.

In 1817 the American artist John Trumbull was commissioned to paint four monumental pictures commemorating the Revolutionary War, to be hung in the rotunda of the Capitol. For his four paintings—*The Surrender of General Burgoyne at Saratoga, The Surrender of Lord Cornwallis at Yorktown, The Declaration of Independence,* and *The Resignation of Washington*—Trumbull was paid $32,000, a large sum of money for the time. The cost of the project was sharply criticized by several members of Congress, but an even greater controversy erupted over the quality of Trumbull's work, when government officials and members of the public were able to see the paintings.

In the late summer of 1818, John Quincy Adams paid a visit to Trumbull's studio to see how the work was progressing. The future president recorded in his diary that although his expectations for the pictures had always been very low, the paintings were even worse than he had expected. Trumbull's *Declaration of Independence,* the younger Adams wrote, was "immeasurably below the dignity of the subject."[3] Nor was the controversy quickly forgotten. Several years later, when Congress was debating whether to purchase portraits of General Washington, General Lafayette, and other Revolutionary War officers, Senator Holmes of Maine took the floor to oppose the purchase. In buying Trumbull's paintings, Senator Holmes contended, Congress "had been abominably taken in. Those paintings, which cost thirty-two thousand dollars, were not worth thirty-two cents."[4]

The most serious consequence of the controversy over the merits of Trumbull's paintings, however, was its effect on the willingness of members of Congress to support any additional public project that involved the arts. Half a century later, the authors of a detailed congressional report on *Art in the District of Columbia* declared, "The prejudice excited against these pictures" had a "damaging effect on American art." It "served to defeat all attempts to afford it government patronage, or even to call in the aid of American artists to decorate the Capitol."[5]

George Washington as "Venus of the Bath"

In fact, however, the spirited controversy over the John Trumbull commission did not stop all further involvements of the national government with the arts; just a few years after the Trumbull paintings were completed, the Congress tried again. As the centennial of George Washington's 1732 birth year approached, pressures began to mount for some form of tribute to the nation's first president. Among the members of Congress who were in favor of honoring Washington, some opposed the installation of another painting or sculpture in the Capitol. Instead they favored something that could reach a larger cross section of the American people, such as a biography of the first president that could be read in "the pine hills in North Carolina . . . the Western forests, and every portion of this Union."[6] But in 1832, partially as a result of the lobbying efforts of James Fenimore Cooper, a commission for a statue of Washington was awarded to the young American sculptor Horatio Greenough.

The cosponsor of the resolution authorizing the commission was Representative Leonard Jarvis, chair of the House Committee on Public Buildings and a former Harvard College classmate of the painter Washington Allston. Jarvis had consulted Allston over the years on a variety of arts issues that concerned the government. So when Allston suggested that Greenough was the person to do the statue of Washington, Jarvis was responsive.

The commission that Jarvis cosponsored placed few restrictions on the artist. In later resolutions Congress agreed to pay Greenough a fee of $20,000, and to cover the cost of transporting the statue from Greenough's studio in Italy to the United States. It was the largest sum for a single piece of art ever awarded by the United States government up to that time.

Horatio Greenough was just twenty-seven-years old when he received his commission to execute a monumental statue of George Washington. After graduating from Harvard in 1825, Greenough had gone almost immediately to Rome, and then somewhat later had settled in Florence, where he came under the influence of Lorenzo Bartolini, a sculptor who was notable for "combining ideality of intent with a faithful study of nature."[7]

When Greenough received his commission from Congress to prepare a statue of Washington, he felt that he had been blessed with a remarkable opportunity. As the art historian Joshua Taylor noted: "He saw it as a chance to consolidate the likeness of Washington the man with that of Washington as the personification of the republic." For Greenough, "the truth of Washington lay not in his physical lineaments but in his symbolic existence as father of his country. The form, then, should follow the symbolic function."[8]

The statue that Greenough executed had Washington seated, assuming a godlike pose. His right hand extended upward and in his lower hand he held his sword. But probably most shocking to many of the statue's nineteenth-century American viewers, the lower half of Washington's body was covered only by a large drapery and the upper half was naked. When the statue finally arrived in the capital city in 1841, it touched off a controversy that made the public reaction to Trumbull's paintings seem mild by comparison.

The statue, wrote Philip Hone of New York, "looks like a great Herculean warrior—like *Venus of the bath* . . . undressed with a huge napkin lying on his lap and covering his lower extremities, and he, preparing to perform his ablutions, is in the act of consigning his sword to the care of his attendant." Other viewers of the statue echoed this theme. Greenough's conception of Washington, Charles Bulfinch declared, had the first president looking as if he were "entering or leaving a bath." According to another joke that circulated in the capital in later years, what the statue really represented was "Washington reaching out his hand for his clothes, which were on exhibition in a case at the Patent Office."[9]

The "naked statue" was also heatedly denounced by Representative Henry Wise of Virginia. Wise told the House that the head of the statue should be preserved, but that the body should be thrown into the Potomac River, "to hide it from the eyes of the world, lest the world should think that that was the people's conception of the nation's founder." In 1852 Senator John Parker Hale of New Hampshire had a request for the Senator's Library Committee. Would the committee "inquire," he asked, "into the expediency of removing that thing in the east yard called 'Greenough's Washington.' "[10] In time the statue was moved from the Capitol and its surrounding grounds—to be stored with the collections of the Smithsonian Institution.

There were, to be sure, some critics of art both inside and outside the Congress who were less severe than Representative Wise or Senator Hale. Edward Everett, the former Whig governor of Massachusetts, diplomat, and member of Congress, as well as a connoisseur of the arts, regarded the statue as "one of the greatest works of sculpture of modern times." George Henry Calvert, the editor of a Baltimore newspaper, took issue with his countrymen's preference for a Washington in full dress and approved of the artist's refusal to stoop to "uncultivated tastes" in order to popularize his art. "By presenting [the statue] to the general gaze in its severe simplicity, and thus, through grandeur and beauty of form, lifting the beholder up into the ideal region of art," Calvert asserted, Greenough would eventually make his art popular.[11]

Nevertheless, some twelve years after Greenough's Washington first appeared in the United States, Captain Montgomery Meigs, the superintendent of new extensions to the Capitol building, probably accurately summarized the dominant reaction of the American public to the statue. Americans, Meigs declared, did not "appreciate too refined and intricate allegorical representations and while the naked Washington of Greenough is the theme of admiration to the few scholars, it is unsparingly denounced by the less refined multitude...."[12]

"God Help the Government that Meddles with Art"

The commissioning of paintings by John Trumbull and the selection of Horatio Greenough to execute a monumental statue of George Washington are two of the most celebrated examples of government patronage of the arts in the early years of the American republic. But there were other forays by the government into the arts as well, and their outcome often seemed to reinforce the dictum of the British prime minister of the 1830s, Lord Melbourne: "God help the government that meddles with art."[13] From the beginning, the involvements of the American national government with the arts were often fraught with controversy; and from the beginning that controversy tended to center around two basic questions:

1. Should the government be spending *any* public money to aid the arts?

2. If and when the government did spend money on art, did the people—both government decision makers and the general public—like the art they got?

Aside from a series of practical, and not altogether happy, involvements, however, the government in early nineteenth-century America generally left the arts alone. Moreover, a concern for "things that were useful" prevailed. Alexis de Tocqueville commented on this in 1835, in his influential book *Democracy in America.* He also gave reasons for this characteristic American attitude.

In a chapter entitled "In What Spirit the Americans Cultivate the Arts," de Tocqueville wrote:

It would . . . waste the time of my readers and my own if I strove to demonstrate how the general mediocrity of fortunes, the absence of superfluous wealth, the universal desire for comfort, and the constant efforts by which everyone attempts to procure it make the taste for the useful predominate over the love of the beautiful in the heart of man. Democratic nations, among whom all these things exist, will therefore cultivate the arts that serve to render life easy in preference to those whose object is to adorn it. They will habitually prefer the useful to the beautiful, and they will require that the beautiful should be useful.

In such a climate of opinion, American artists had to make their way on their own.

The Climate Changes

In the years after de Tocqueville wrote these lines, however, several developments in American society began to occur that ultimately would affect—and change profoundly—the relations between government and the arts. First, a number of Americans began to record some achievements in the arts that were world class in their stature. An early breakthrough for Americans was in the field of literature. Nathaniel Hawthorne, Herman Melville, Ralph Waldo Emerson, and others won international recognition of a sort that in time Americans would achieve in other forms of art. These achievements by American writers and other artists began to attract the attention of their fellow citizens. Americans have always admired success. A second major development was the gift of £100,000 left to the United States in 1835 by an English man of science, James Smithson, whose will stipulated that it should be used "for the increase and diffusion of knowledge among men." The initial response of America's political leaders to this remarkable bequest by a foreign citizen was less than enthralling. President Jackson ignored it; and several senators, including Calhoun, declared that it was unconstitutional.[14] But in the end, after a ten-year battle, former President John Quincy Adams, now a member of the United States House of Representatives from Massachusetts, persuaded the Congress to accept it. The Smithsonian Institution, which was thus created, began to include cultivation of the arts along with the institution's well-known scientific objectives.

A third important development in American society took even longer to unfold. Before the Civil War, but especially after that struggle was over, the great family fortunes of America began to accumulate. (Had Alexis de Tocqueville been able to visit the United States in 1881, instead of 1831, he no longer would have been struck by a "general mediocrity of fortunes.") This, in turn, led to the development of great private art collections, and to the establishment of great public or quasi-public museums to which eventually the great collectors began to leave those collections. The Metropolitan Museum of Art was founded in New York in 1870, and major art museums were established in other cities—including Boston, Philadelphia, Chicago, and Cleveland—soon thereafter. In a number of cities where art museums were founded, moreover, there was important municipal government funding from the local city government.

Philanthropy, Postal Rates, and Tax Policy

As the nation's great art museums were being established, another major trend in American society began to be increasingly evident. In the latter decades of the nineteenth century, a remarkable system of private philanthropy for the arts began to develop in the United States. Often this was the result of private giving by individual Americans, who gave financial support for specific arts activities that they enjoyed. For several decades, for example, the box seat holders of the Metropolitan Opera were able to write personal checks that would cover any "earnings gap" between the opera company's annual expenditures and its revenues.

Finally, particularly after the Civil War, great new waves of immigrants came into the country, and brought with them interests in specific forms of art. In a number of cities, for example, German-Americans played an important role in the establishment of symphony orchestras. In some cities, Italian-Americans were leading boosters of the opera. In addition, some of the newer immigrants to America brought with them new attitudes. Some were more favorably disposed toward the principle of government support for the arts than the earlier English settlers had been. Nevertheless, a more general support for that principle in the American public as a whole was still far in the future.

Throughout the nineteenth century, certain policies of the United States government did have an impact on the nation's literature and other forms of art. Yet throughout this period, the *indirect effects* of policies designed primarily for other purposes were often more important for the arts world than were government actions that were consciously designed for their impact on the arts.

American copyright law had a major influence on the development of American literature in the nineteenth century. Before 1891 only American authors could copyright their work in the United States. This profoundly irritated Charles Dickens, but it also had the curious effect of hurting American writers, who had to compete with royalty-free editions of the works of established British authors such as Scott, Dickens, and Thackeray.

The establishment of the second-class postal rate in 1879 was another policy decision that was profoundly important for American literature. The second-class postal rate was a major cause of the subsequent rapid growth of American magazines that provided, among other things, a commercial outlet for the short story. Had Edgar Allen Poe lived forty years later, he might not have starved.[15]

The national government thus played an important role in maintaining the legal framework within which the arts in America operated. Nevertheless, by the beginning of the twentieth century, although there was some government financial aid for the arts at the municipal level, in terms of direct subsidy and promotion of the arts, the national government's policy was still one of nearly complete laissez faire.

Then came three events with enormous implications for the future. The first was the passage of the Federal Income Tax Law of 1916; the second was the advent of the Federal Inheritance Tax in 1918; and the third was the subsequent establishment of the principle that contributions to arts organizations would be tax deductible like contributions to hospitals, educational institutions, and welfare agencies. When federal tax rates were moderate, as they were in the 1920s, they provided some additional incentive for private giving to the arts. But when marginal federal tax rates shot up to very high levels—in World War II and thereafter—they provided a very powerful incentive for private giving for the arts.

The WPA: A Radical Departure

Fifteen years or so after the Federal Income Tax and the Federal Inheritance Tax came the Great Depression, and the extraordinary and totally unprecedented arts program of the New Deal, the first comprehensive federal arts program of the national government of the United States. The program was initially prompted by a 1933 letter from the painter George Biddle to his former roommate in prep school, the new President Franklin D. Roosevelt. Biddle's letter specifically cited the Mexican mural movement and the important role the government of Mexico had played in supporting it. At their peak, between 1935 and 1938, the arts initiatives of the New Deal were the largest public arts program in the history of the world. More than 40,000 artists were directly employed by the government; there were 1,371 commissions for murals in post offices and other public buildings; there was a Federal Theater Project and a Federal Writers Project; there were symphony orchestras; and much, much more.

These New Deal arts programs were also a radical departure from previous government relations with the arts. In a sense, they were the closest the United States has come to a socialist arts program. The major impetus for the programs was to provide employment for artists in the midst of the depression. The federal government hired artists directly. The government, through its Federal Theater Project, presented plays directly. A few of the Federal Theater Project's productions attacked the capitalist system; and some murals supported by the Federal Arts Project, including work by communist artists, aroused fierce public controversy. And the New Deal arts programs began to draw heavy political fire.

In 1938 there was a widely publicized investigation of some of the programs by the House Committee on Un-American Activities. That same year, the proposed Coffee-Pepper bill, which would have given some of the New Deal arts programs permanent status, failed to gain sufficient support in the House and the Senate. In 1939 the New Deal arts programs were cut back sharply by the Congress. The nation began to prepare for the war against the Axis Powers that eventually came in December 1941, and by January 1943, the first federal arts program was dead.

A Wartime Rescue Operation

During World War II, Chief Justice Harlan Fiske Stone and Justice Owen J. Roberts of the United States Supreme Court played a major role in one of the most benign and effective initiatives concerning the arts ever conducted by the American government. In 1942 Chief Justice Stone was approached by several leading figures in the American arts world—Francis Henry Taylor, director of the Metropolitan Museum of Art; Sumner McKnight Crosby, president of the College Art Association; William B. Dinsmoor, president of the Archeological

Institute of America; and David E. Finley, director of the National Gallery of Art. The four men explained to Stone that the Nazi government of Germany had systematically pillaged major art collections from other European countries that were occupied by Germany during the war. A number of these stolen art objects were now in the personal art collections of Nazi government officials; many others were held in German museums or in hideaways in the German countryside. Chief Justice Stone immediately took a personal interest in the problem and, in turn, asked President Roosevelt for his support.

Within government circles in Washington, Stone began to argue strongly that American military forces should be organized and prepared to protect these collections when American military forces entered Germany. He also argued that there should be orderly procedures for returning the art collections to the previous owners. After extensive discussions among several government agencies, including the Joint Chiefs of Staff, in August 1943 the Department of State announced the establishment of an American Commission for the Protection and Salvage of Artistic and Historic Monuments in War Areas. The chairman of the commission was Justice Owen J. Roberts, and it was this commission that worked with the War Department to plan for what was to come when Germany was occupied. In one of the most successful operations of the war, the great majority of the stolen art collections were saved and returned to the museums from which they had come, in 1945 and 1946.[16]

World War II also led to another federal government initiative that affected the arts. Working within the State Department, Nelson Rockefeller developed a program to promote closer cultural relations with Latin America, especially Brazil, Argentina, and Mexico. Rockefeller's efforts led to exhibits at the Museum of Modern Art in New York of the work of leading artists from those countries, and the State Department program also sent art exhibitions and performing arts groups from the United States to Latin America.

After World War II, a Limited Federal Presence

After World War II, several supporters in Congress of government aid for the arts, most notably Representative Charles Howell of New Jersey, tried to get a comprehensive and ambitious federal arts bill passed. These efforts drew only limited support in the Congress as a whole. In addition, in the late 1940s and early 1950s, another series of widely publicized congressional investigations of arts figures for alleged subversive activities widened the gulf between the government and the arts. During these years, in fact, many artists themselves were opposed to a larger federal government role in the arts. As the painter John Sloan once put it, he would welcome a United States Ministry of Culture; then he would know where the enemy was.

As a result of these and other factors, artistic activities in the United States in the 1950s continued to be supported primarily at the box office or in the marketplace, and by a truly remarkable (and tax deductible) system of private patronage. This private patronage was provided mainly by individual donors, but it also came from private foundations, including the Ford Foundation beginning in 1957, and from some business corporations.

Nevertheless, by the 1950s there were four general types of arts activities in which the federal government had a continuing interest: international cultural exchanges; the design and decoration of public buildings; government collections such as the National Gallery of Art; and the design of coins and stamps. During the 1950s the role of the national government in several of these spheres increased. Part of this growth came from an increasing use of art as an instrument of United States foreign policy in the Cold War. Under International Cultural Exchange legislation passed in 1954 and 1956, 111 attractions, ranging from Dizzy Gillespie to the New York Philharmonic, were sent to eighty-nine countries in the program's first four years. In 1954 the Office of Foreign Buildings of the

Department of State launched a ten-year $200 million program to build new embassies and consulates on four continents. Using an advisory committee of three leading architects appointed on a rotating basis, the State Department tried with considerable success to ensure that the new embassies abroad would be distinguished buildings.

Initiatives were also taken that would have a direct impact on the arts at home. In March 1958 a bill to save the Patent Office Building in Washington for an art museum became law. The Patent Office Building had been designed by Robert Mills (who also designed the Washington Monument) during the administration of Andrew Jackson. The bill to save it was backed by Representative Frank Thompson of New Jersey and Senators Hubert Humphrey of Minnesota and Clinton P. Anderson of New Mexico. In September 1958 Congress authorized the building of a National Cultural Center on the banks of the Potomac River in Washington. Under the act, cosponsored by Senator J. William Fulbright of Arkansas and Congressman Thompson, the federal government was to donate the land if private funds could be raised to build the center within five years.[17]

These government initiatives that had an impact on the arts were significant, and in time they became more so. But compared with every major country in Europe, the involvement of the American government in the arts in the 1950s was very limited. There was still no equivalent of the Arts Council of Great Britain, and the arts legislation that was passed by the federal government in the 1950s was often cautious and tentative. Above all, there was no large-scale and continuous tradition of direct subsidy by the government, such as was common in Europe. Direct federal government support for the arts was still not part of the prevailing public ideology in the United States.

The case against federal aid for the arts had several components:

1. *Indifference.* The view that the arts were not important enough to justify spending public tax dollars for them. In

vast sections of the country, many rural areas, and much of the territory between the East Coast and the West Coast, there were almost no year-round theater companies, and few other strong arts organizations. It showed when there were votes on proposed arts legislation in Congress.

2. *Philosophical opposition* to government involvement and possible government interference in the arts. Many thoughtful Americans feared that government funds would mean that there would be government rules and government strings attached and that artistic freedom would suffer.

3. Finally, there was a *practical basis for opposition.* Some American political leaders who were potentially receptive to the concept of federal aid for the arts, President Kennedy among them, worried about how such a program would be administered. How, they asked, would the government decide *which* arts organizations and which artists to support?

1959: A New Model Emerges

By 1959, however, there was a small but committed group of senators and representatives in the Congress who favored a new federal arts program: Representative John Lindsay and Senator Jacob Javits from New York; Representative Frank Thompson of New Jersey; and, after the 1960 election, Senator Claiborne Pell of Rhode Island. Gradually, a new model for a federal government arts program began to emerge, a model that was radically different from the arts program model of the New Deal. Instead of having the government running theater projects and symphonies and employing artists directly, supporters of a new government arts program now argued that a federal government arts foundation should be created, much like the National Science Foundation, the extramural program units of the National Institutes of Health, or the Arts Council of Great Britain. This government arts foundation, they argued, should make grants to existing private arts organizations or to individual artists, with the decisions as to who should receive a grant being made by panels of experts in various art fields, exercising peer review.

While this consensus about how to administer a new government arts program was developing, the American arts world itself was undergoing rapid change. The scope of organized professional arts activities in the country was growing, and struggling new arts organizations began to appear more frequently between the East Coast and the West Coast. In addition, arts organizations that had been in existence for some time, like the nation's major symphony orchestras, were expanding their seasons and in some cases providing year-round contracts for their musicians or other performing artists. The Ford Foundation's arts program, which had been started in 1957 but was greatly expanded in 1962, began to have a significant impact. And in the six years following 1959, the federal government's policy toward the arts was turned around.

The administration of John F. Kennedy, which came to power in January 1961, made the rhetorical case for a greater federal government role in the arts, even though Kennedy himself did not actively push for the establishment of a government arts foundation during the three brief years he was president. Kennedy did approach Roger Stevens, the New York theater producer and real estate investor, and Stevens was given the assignment of raising the necessary private funds to start building a National Cultural Center. The president's wife, Jacqueline Kennedy, made her own interest in the arts clear in a number of ways, and the president appointed Harvard historian Arthur M. Schlesinger Jr. to serve on his White House staff. Schlesinger was a strong supporter of federal aid for the arts.

Kennedy was cautious about getting too far ahead of opinion in the Congress on arts policy issues. But with the help of others in the administration, Schlesinger began to encourage the president to take several concrete steps toward a greater government role in the arts. On November 13, 1961, a glittering state dinner took place at the White House in honor of Pablo Casals. With many luminaries from the arts world in attendance, the great cellist gave a concert in the East Room. It was the first time Casals had played at the White House since 1904, during the administration of President Theodore Roosevelt.

The enormously favorable public reaction to the Casals evening persuaded Arthur Schlesinger that the time was ripe to try to persuade the president to take another step forward in developing a federal government cultural policy. On November 22nd he wrote Kennedy a two-page memorandum on "Moving Ahead on the Cultural Front."

> The Casals evening has had an extraordinary effect in the artistic world. On the next day, when the advisory council for the National Cultural Center met, a number of people said to me in the most heartfelt way how much the Administration's evident desire to recognize artistic and intellectual distinction meant to the whole intellectual community. You probably saw John Crosby's column this morning ("President Kennedy is the best friend culture . . . has had in the White House since Jefferson").
>
> All this is of obvious importance, not only in attaching a potent opinion-making group to the Administration, but in transforming the world's impression of the United States as a nation of money-grubbing materialists. And it is notable that all this has taken place without any criticism, so far as I am aware. Contrary to the expectations reported by Crosby, no editorial writer has used the Casals dinner to accuse you of fiddling while Berlin burns.
>
> I wonder whether this might not be an appropriate time to carry the matter a step further. . . .[18]

Schlesinger then spelled out what he felt the next step by the administration should be, and this time Schlesinger's proposal fell on receptive ears. In February 1962 the *New York Times* broke a front page news story that concerned the arts. August Heckscher, the director of the Twentieth Century Fund, would become the first special consultant to the president for the arts. The new post would be established on a part-time basis, and in the months that followed, Heckscher normally devoted three days a week to his job as special consultant.

When August Heckscher took on his new assignment, he hoped to achieve three main goals during his stay in Washington. He wanted to contribute to the establishment of a Federal Advisory Council on the Arts; he planned to prepare a report, which would include policy recommendations for the future, on the arts and the national government; and he hoped to obtain a permanent successor, thereby institutionalizing the role of a special assistant to the president for the arts.

By early 1963 Heckscher had completed a draft of his report on *The Arts and the National Government.* It was released to the public in May. In June 1963, after considerable delay, Kennedy announced that he was establishing an Advisory Council on the Arts by executive order. (There was still probably not sufficient support in the Congress to create an advisory council by legislation, the route that President Kennedy would have preferred.) On the morning of November 22nd, the *New York Times* announced that Richard Goodwin, a presidential advisor and speechwriter, would be appointed as a full-time special assistant to the president for the arts and ran a profile of Goodwin. Early that afternoon, John F. Kennedy was assassinated in Dallas.

The specific list of names John F. Kennedy had approved for what would have been the first Federal Advisory Council on the Arts was not acted upon. But in the twenty-two months that followed, under President Lyndon B. Johnson, federal action and legislation to assist the arts moved forward at a rate that would have seemed unthinkable in the early Kennedy years.

In the immediate aftermath of Kennedy's death, there was apprehension in the arts world that the new president, Lyndon B. Johnson, might not give the arts the same emphasis that Kennedy had. On November 29th, one week after the assassination, Arthur Schlesinger wrote Johnson a two-page memorandum entitled the "Future of the Arts Program." After detailing what had happened since Heckscher was appointed in March 1962, Schlesinger said: "The question is whether you will want to go ahead with this effort. I hope very much that you will. . . ." After indicating what the program could do that would be of benefit to the arts, Schlesinger also added a practical political argument: "It can strengthen the connections between the Administration and the intellectual and artistic community—something not to be dismissed when victory or defeat next fall will probably depend on who carried New York, Pennsylvania, California, Illinois, and Michigan."[19]

Very soon after the assassination, Johnson supported legislation renaming the National Cultural Center the John F. Kennedy Center for the Performing Arts and providing up to $15 million in federal matching-grant funds for its construction. Then for a while the administration, faced with the staggering task of taking over the reins of power and with the presidential election less than a year away, did little on the arts front. But in May 1964, Roger Stevens was appointed as a special assistant to the president for the arts, and later that summer, in part because of skillful lobbying by Stevens, legislation creating a Federal Advisory Council on the Arts was finally passed by Congress.

In June 1964 another event that was eventually to be of importance for the arts took place. A special nongovernmental commission of scholars in the humanities released a report on the status of the humanities in American life. The commission had been created by the American Council of Graduate Schools, the American Council of Learned Societies, and Phi Beta Kappa. Dr. Barnaby Keeney, the president of Brown University, was its chair. In its report, the commission called for the establishment of a National Foundation for the Humanities with broad similarities to the National Science Foundation.

On September 29, 1964, while on a tumultuous campaign tour of Rhode Island and the rest of New England, President Johnson gave a major speech on education policy at Brown University. Looking directly at the university's president, Dr. Keeney, who shared the podium with him, Johnson declared that he looked "with the greatest of favor" on the Keeney commission's proposal for a National Foundation for the Humanities. The establishment of a humanities foundation had become a presidential campaign pledge.[20]

The National Foundation
on the Arts and Humanities

In November Johnson was elected to a full four-year presidential term by an enormous majority over Barry Goldwater.

At the same time there was a Democratic landslide for Congress that decisively altered the balance of power in the House of Representatives. Many members of Congress who had opposed federal arts legislation were defeated. In early 1965 a political compromise was worked out whereby the supporters of arts legislation and the supporters of humanities legislation joined forces to work for passage of legislation creating a National Foundation on the Arts and Humanities. The foundation was to have a National Endowment for each field. This alliance added to the forces that had been working for an arts bill much of the political constituency for higher education, which then had nearly 5 million students; several hundred thousand faculty members; and colleges, universities, or junior colleges in every congressional district in the country.

As the spring of 1965 approached, the chances of passing a major arts bill in Congress seemed far, far better than they had just four years earlier, when a relatively modest bill to create a Federal Advisory Council on the Arts by legislation had been decisively defeated in the House of Representatives. The support in the country for an expansion of the scope of government activity in many fields was rising, and was probably greater than it had been at any time since the early days of the New Deal. The civil rights movement was bringing about far-reaching changes in American society and American politics. And black voters, who in the 1960 presidential election had given nearly a third of their votes to Richard Nixon, the Republican, had moved overwhelmingly into Lyndon Johnson's electoral coalition against Goldwater, further swelling the ranks of those who were committed to change.

On March 10, 1965, the administration submitted its legislative proposal to create a National Foundation on the Arts and Humanities. In September, after a spirited floor fight in which many Republicans and some Democrats opposed the measure in the House of Representatives, the bill was passed. Included in the legislative provisions for the Arts Endowment was a very important provision first proposed by Senator Joseph Clark of Pennsylvania. Of the National Endowment's total budget, 20 percent of the funds were to "pass through" directly to the states—if they chose to establish their own state arts council. Within two years, every state in the nation had an arts council; and state legislatures began to vote state funds for their state's arts council, to be added to the funds from the national government.

Once the bill creating the twin Endowments had been signed, President Johnson appointed Roger Stevens to serve as the first chair of the National Endowment for the Arts. Johnson also picked Dr. Barnaby Keeney to head the Humanities Endowment. In its first full year of operations (fiscal year 1967), the Arts Endowment received an appropriation of $8 million from Congress. But in the next two years, as the Johnson administration increasingly became bogged down in the bitterly divisive war in Vietnam, funding for both the arts and the humanities remained stagnant. Both Roger Stevens and Barnaby Keeney attempted to obtain increased financial support for their agencies. Barnaby Keeney, for example, appealed for an increase in the humanities budget every time he was able to get a few minutes alone with the president. But Keeney's appeals were unsuccessful and the president's answer was always the same: "This war, Doctor. This war, Doctor."[21] On March 31, 1968, Lyndon B. Johnson startled the nation by announcing that he would not seek another term as president.

An Unanticipated Champion: Richard Nixon

The close, hard-fought 1968 presidential election campaign gave the voters a choice among three candidates who drew significant political support: Hubert Humphrey, Lyndon Johnson's vice president, running on the Democratic ticket; Richard Nixon, the Republican; and Governor George Wallace of Alabama, running on the American Independent party ticket. Hubert Humphrey was known as a strong supporter of the federal government's arts program, but the arts community was not so sure about the man who won the 1968 election—Richard M. Nixon. As it turned out, however, Nixon as president began to double and redouble the budget of the Arts and Humanities Endowments, with the result that within a fairly short time the National Endowment for the Arts was able to make a significant impact on the arts in America.

One of the first important decisions of the Nixon administration that affected the arts was the appointment of Nancy Hanks, president of the Associated Councils on the Arts, to serve as chair of the National Endowment for the Arts. A second major decision was to entrust responsibility for arts and humanities policy issues to Leonard Garment on the White House staff. Garment was a former law partner of the president in New York; and by late 1969 Garment was encouraging President Nixon to move forward on arts legislation much as Arthur Schlesinger Jr. had encouraged President Kennedy eight years before.

Meanwhile, Nancy Hanks went to work at the Endowment. Even before she began her duties as chair, Nancy Hanks knew that the budget of the Arts Endowment would have to be expanded dramatically if the agency's programs were to have any significant effect on the arts. Once she became chair, she prepared a lengthy memorandum for the president, in which she asked him to support a $40 million appropriation for the arts and the humanities for the next fiscal year. As she told the president:

This is a substantial increase over sums available to the Endowment for expenditure this year. . . . However, the increase would not basically affect the federal budget. And the increase would be essential to the Administration's ability to have any impact.[22]

Once Nancy Hanks had completed her memorandum, Leonard Garment also went to work. In a memorandum of his own to the president, Garment put the case for a budget increase even more strongly than Hanks had done:

It is important that the administration be identified forcefully with increased support for the arts and humanities. In a message to the OMB you [should] indicate your strong desire to ask for the same appropriation as you are requesting in the authorizing legislation. . . .

At least two extremely powerful, and emotionally persuasive groups are standing by to put great pressure on the committees and the Congress for considerable increases (the symphony orchestras and the museums). In each of these two cases, we are assured by private conference if your message holds a hope for some assistance, no great effort to criticize the effort will be made.

For an amount of money which is minuscule in terms of the total federal budget, you can demonstrate your commitment to "reordering national priorities to emphasize the quality of life in our society."

Garment added some powerful political arguments for President Nixon to take the lead as a patron of the arts:

The amount proposed . . . would have high impact among opinion formers. It is, on the merits, justified, i.e., the budget for the arts and humanities is now completely inadequate. Support for the arts is, increasingly, good politics. By providing substantially increased support for cultural activities, you will gain support from groups which have not been favorable to this administration.[23]

For Richard Nixon, the arguments that Nancy Hanks and Leonard Garment advanced were decisive. On December 10, 1969, the president sent a message to Capitol Hill calling on the Congress to double the budgets of both the humanities and the arts endowments. The president had now done his part, but whether the Congress would support a dramatic increase in funding for the arts and humanities was an open question. As Michael Straight, who had become deputy chair of the Arts Endowment, later noted: "The Congress at that moment was hostile to the President's request. We knew that we had six months hard work ahead of us before our budget request came to a vote."[24]

Nancy Hanks and Michael Straight began the job of trying to enlist support for the arts program on Capitol Hill. Their task was not made any easier when the legislative assistant of an Iowa representative who opposed the Arts Endowment made an unannounced visit to Michael Straight's office and seized a volume of Endowment funded poetry. The anthology contained a one-word poem for which the author had received a $500 grant.[25] Nevertheless, between the two of them, sometimes together, sometimes separately, Nancy Hanks and Michael Straight visited the offices of more than 200 members of Congress in order to urge support for the Endowment's programs. On June 30, 1970, the arts and humanities appropriations bill went to the floor of the House of Representatives. Michael Straight later recorded the events of that afternoon:

We sat in the gallery, a team from the Arts Endowment and a team from the humanities, looking down on that chaotic arena. By then, we had broken down the House of Representatives into friends, fence-sitters, and forget-thems. Each of us clutched a list of friends whom we were to summon when the vote was imminent. On a signal from our floor leader, we rushed out, made our calls, and hurried back. The Congressmen sauntered in, in a manner that seemed to us unbearably casual; the late arrivals crowded in the well to record their votes; the clerk read out the tally: 262 for the bill, 78 against it. Our friends on the floor looked up at us grinning; we looked at each other, halfway between laughter and tears. We had carried Georgia and Alabama, Kansas and Nebraska, Ohio and Indiana, Iowa and the Dakotas. We were part of a national movement and we were moving ahead.[26]

Among those on the floor of the House were a substantial number of Republican members of Congress who had voted against the establishment of the National Endowment for the Arts in 1965 but who now supported this 1970 proposal by a Republican president for increased arts funding. In that group of Republicans was the minority leader of the House of Representatives, Gerald R. Ford of Michigan.

Under Nancy Hanks's leadership, there followed an extraordinary growth in the scope and range of the Arts Endowment's programs. During the Nixon years, the annual budget for the Endowment increased from $8.3 million for the fiscal year 1970 to $80 million for fiscal 1975. When President Nixon was forced to resign in the political upheaval caused by the Watergate scandal, the man Nixon had nominated to become an unelected vice president, Gerald Ford, became president. The Ford administration also provided budget increases for the arts program, and the president's wife, Betty Ford, who had studied dance under Martha Graham, was regarded as a particular friend of the arts. Nevertheless, her husband's commitment was now also solid. As President Ford put it when he addressed an arts gathering less than four weeks after he assumed the presidency: "Converts are known sometimes as better advocates than those brought up in the religion."[27]

Four days after Ford made that speech, he granted Richard Nixon a "full, free and absolute pardon" for any federal crimes that Nixon had "committed or may have committed" while he was president.

The political backlash was intense. There was a Democratic landslide in the midterm congressional elections in November 1974, and two years later, in a very close election, Gerald Ford lost his bid for a full four-year presidential term in his own right. Jimmy Carter, a Democrat and the former governor of Georgia, became president. When Nancy Hanks's term as chair of the Arts Endowment expired in 1977, President Carter selected Livingston Biddle to be the new chair. Biddle, as legislative assistant to Senator Claiborne Pell, had played a major role in shaping the Arts Endowment legislation in 1965. Now, as head of the agency he had helped to create, he presided over a further expansion of the Endowment's programs. During the Carter years there were two annual budget increases that brought the Endowment's budget from $100 million in fiscal 1977 to $149 million in fiscal 1979. In absolute terms, those were the largest budget increases in the history of the National Endowment for the Arts.

The NEA: Assault and Vindication

Then came the election year of 1980. Public confidence in the Carter administration had been seriously undermined by two major problems that President Carter seemed unable to solve—widespread economic distress in the wake of two consecutive years of double-digit inflation and the holding of American hostages by the revolutionary government of Iran. Carter's electoral vulnerability was underscored when he was forced to make a major fight within his own party to get renominated, in the face of a serious challenge from Senator

Edward Kennedy of Massachusetts. Meanwhile, on the Republican side, the preferred presidential choice of many moderate and liberal Republicans, George Bush, was defeated for the nomination by the decidedly more conservative candidate, Ronald Reagan. During the fall campaign, substantial voter dissatisfaction with both major party candidates was reflected in significant support for an independent presidential nominee, John Anderson of Illinois.

In the November general election, Reagan won by a decisive margin, opening up a lead of ten percentage points over Jimmy Carter, and carrying forty-four of the fifty states. In the elections for Congress, where the Republican party also made sweeping gains and captured control of the Senate, two leading Democratic supporters of the arts program in the House of Representatives, Frank Thompson and John Brademas, went down to defeat. Included in Reagan's successful electoral coalition were some Reagan supporters who, echoing what had been the dominant view in the 1950s, were opposed to the basic principle of government support for the arts. That viewpoint did not become dominant in the new Reagan administration, but when President Reagan and his budget director, David Stockman, proposed their first full-year budget, for fiscal year 1982, it called for a cut of 50 percent in the budgets of both the Arts and the Humanities Endowments.

The Stockman-Reagan budget proposals evoked consternation in the arts community. Some supporters of federal aid for the arts who had long memories worried that they were but a first step toward a complete dismantling of the programs built over the previous fifteen years. Was it 1939 all over again? Some members of the arts community were also disquieted when President Reagan selected Frank Hodsoll to become Livingston Biddle's successor as chair of the National Endowment for the Arts. Hodsoll had personal ties with the president, and had worked actively in Reagan's 1980 presidential campaign. There were fears that he might be taking the leadership of the arts program in order to preside over the liquidation of the National Endowment for the Arts.

What followed was a classic political battle throughout

1981, in which members of the arts community, like many other interest groups who were threatened by proposed Reagan budget cuts, organized their political defenses. In the House of Representatives, Sidney Yates of Chicago led the defense of the National Endowment's budget in the House Appropriations Subcommittee, which he chaired. Members of the boards of major arts organizations, many of them Republicans, spoke out in favor of the arts program. Supporters of the National Endowment for the Arts began to show considerable skill in making use of the news media. Prominent American singers and actors testified on behalf of the arts program, and their statements were heard nationwide on the evening television news broadcasts.

Faced with more political opposition over the arts budget than it had anticipated, the administration in the spring of 1981 appointed a special blue-ribbon President's Commission on the Arts and the Humanities, to review the entire structuring and operation of the two Endowments programs. The co-chairs of the commission were the Hollywood actor Charlton Heston, a personal friend of President Reagan, and Dr. Hanna Holborn Gray, the president of the University of Chicago. In October the commission issued a report that was generally supportive of the way the Endowments were currently operating.

Meanwhile, congressional supporters of the arts program held the cuts in the National Endowment for the Arts budget to 10 percent. (The following year, in 1982, when the administration again proposed drastic reductions, they were held to zero.) Frank Hodsoll, while publicly supporting the administration's budget recommendations for his agency, began to make it clear that he was generally supportive of the purposes and procedures of the National Endowment for the Arts. Some observers began to feel that Hodsoll's status as a "Reagan insider" may have been a source of protection for the arts program during the Reagan years. Hodsoll had credibility within the Reagan White House; with him as the head of the arts agency, the acceptability of the entire program to the administration was enhanced. In any event, the National Endowment for the Arts survived the battles of the budget of 1981 and 1982. By October 1984, shortly before President Reagan was reelected to a second term by a near-landslide margin, the budgets for nearly all of the federal government's cultural programs were back to what they had been at the end of the Carter years.

Other Issues of the 1980s

During the 1980s, a number of other public policy issues that concerned the arts were actively debated both inside and outside the arts community. By 1983 the major cuts in income tax rates that had been enacted in 1981 were fully in place, effectively putting the top rate at 28 percent (with a 33 percent "bubble" on income between certain specified levels). Some observers feared that the lower marginal income tax rates, with their attendant lower tax deductions, might discourage private giving for arts activities. But it was the Tax Reform Act of 1986 that most deeply affected the arts. That legislation affected donations of artworks to museums by sharply curtailing deductions for charitable donations of artworks that had appreciated in value, at a time when art prices themselves were skyrocketing.

Nathan Leventhal, the president of Lincoln Center for the Performing Arts, spoke for many in the arts community when he declared: "It seems a little inconsistent to me for the Administration to be continually emphasizing the importance of private voluntary support of the arts, while at the same time reducing tax incentives for that private support. Arts organizations will feel the pinch of this whipsaw action." And so they did. Some estimates put the decline in the value of donations at 33 percent in the year after the tax bill went into effect.[28]

The need for a greater emphasis on arts education was also discussed frequently in the 1980s, especially within the arts community. This resulted, in 1986, in the creation of a new National Endowment program, arts in education, designed to promote instruction in the arts from kindergarten through the twelfth grade. The program was a significant policy innovation, for it was the first time the Endowment had sought to play a major role in promoting curriculum change throughout the nation's schools. As Hodsoll said, "Our emphasis has always been on artists and art institutions, but in this case we are putting the emphasis on the kids. Our premise is that arts education, to be meaningful, must be made an integral part of basic education. It must be serious, it must be systematic, and it must be sequential."[29] In addition, a 182-page Arts Endowment report, *Toward Civilization,* issued in May 1988, argued that basic arts education was suffering from serious neglect in the United States. Unless substantial progress were made in this area, the report warned, "the artistic heritage that is ours, and the opportunities to contribute significantly to its evolution, are being lost to our young people."[30]

Questions of cultural equity also became increasingly salient in the 1980s, as many artists grew concerned that the arts programs being supported by public funds tended to reflect the social and artistic values of mainstream, upper status, white America, while neglecting the artistic needs of minority communities. Gradually the National Endowment for the Arts began to give greater attention to this issue. In localities across the country, from Los Angeles to Chicago, and New York to Miami, steps were taken independently to promote the arts and access to the arts in communities where arts activities had previously had little support.

While some members of the arts community were attempting to expand the reach of the arts into areas of the United States where they had not previously been adequately supported, others were arguing for greater help from the national government to send American art and American artists overseas. As we have seen, this concern of arts policy makers dates back at least to the 1940s. Nevertheless, many continued to fear that the arts in America were being poorly represented internationally, and that the cultural image of the United States abroad was suffering as a result of it. Thus in 1983, Charles Reinhart, the director of the American Dance Festival, took note of the fact that the total budget of the United States Information Agency (USIA) for sending artists and exhibitions overseas was $2 million. Appealing for greater federal funding for the program, he called the USIA budget figure "an embarrassment."[31]

While these debates over broad issues of arts policy were taking place, some members of the arts community were showing considerable skill in the narrower, relatively invisible arena of Washington interest group politics where so many small and middle-sized political decisions are made. One consequence of the 1986 Tax Reform Act was that income tax deductions for artists' expenses were to be allowed only when an artistic product produced income. In response to this, sixty-nine arts organizations formed a group called Artists for Tax Equity to lobby for reform of the legislation and its implementation. After intense Capitol Hill lobbying by the arts coalition, the Internal Revenue Service agreed in May 1988 to allow artists to deduct their expenses over a three-year period, 50 percent in the first year, and 25 percent in each of the two subsequent years.

But opponents of this aspect of the 1986 tax bill did not stop there. In November, continued artist lobbying resulted in passage by Congress of the Technical and Miscellaneous Act of 1988, allowing freelance authors, writers, and photographers to deduct artistic expenses in the same year they were accrued. Paul Battista, executive director of the Graphic Artists Guild and coordinator of Artists for Tax Equity, expressed satisfaction that the political power of the artists had been able to prevail: "When you raise your voice in a democracy, you really can make changes."[32]

The Bush Era Begins

Meanwhile, there were important events in the larger political arena that would affect the development of public policy for the arts. In November 1988 Ronald Reagan's vice president, George Bush, won the presidential election, defeating the Democratic candidate, Governor Michael Dukakis of Massachusetts. On February 15, 1989, President Bush announced that Frank Hodsoll would step down from his post as chair of the National Endowment for the Arts to assume a senior position at the Office of Management and Budget. Hodsoll had served as chief of the Endowment for more than seven years. Only Nancy Hanks had served longer.

The ensuing scramble for the vacated chair was indicative of the prestige and prerogatives now associated with the office. Livingston Biddle, the Arts Endowment chair under Carter, explained why the $82,500 a year position attracted so much attention in the spring of 1989: "The person who holds the job is at once regarded as Santa Claus by the whole arts community, whenever the season, or Scrooge, hoarding his resources. He is also regarded as the Oracle of Delphi when it comes to the arts."[33]

On July 6, 1989, the White House announced that John Frohnmayer had been selected chair of the National Endowment for the Arts. Frohnmayer was picked from a strong field of candidates that was said to have included Schuyler Chapin, formerly the dean of the School of the Arts at Columbia University and former general manager of the Metropolitan Opera; Louise Burke Shepard, director of the Institute of Museum Services; Milton Rhodes, president of the American Council for the Arts; Alberta Arthurs, director for arts and humanities at the Rockefeller Foundation; and Barnabas McHenry, former executive of the Readers Digest.

Frohnmayer, then relatively unknown in national arts circles, was an Oregon attorney and arts activist who had worked in the Bush campaign in 1988. He had been chair of the Oregon State Arts Commission, where he instituted a tax checkoff system that would allow taxpayers to donate part of their refunds to arts programs in the state. Frohnmayer was the first chair of the National Endowment for the Arts to come from west of the Mississippi River, and he had won high marks for his service on behalf of the arts in the relatively consensual politics of Oregon. He arrived in Washington just as a controversy involving the Arts Endowment was erupting that would make all of the previous arts policy issues of the 1980s seem gentle by comparison.

Mapplethorpe: "The Conflagration Begins"

The first sparks of what would become a political conflagration were ignited in May 1989, when it became public knowledge that a traveling exhibition of works of Andres Serrano contained a photograph of a crucifix submerged in urine. Almost immediately, the National Endowment for the Arts and Serrano came to be linked in the public mind. The Endowment had given financial support to the Southeastern Center for Contemporary Art in Winston-Salem, North Carolina; and the Southeastern Center in turn had given part of a $15,000 grant to Serrano. The Serrano photograph was deeply offensive to many, and both the photograph and the use of public funds for a grant to Serrano were denounced by Senator Alfonse D'Amato of New York and Senator Jesse Helms of North Carolina. In the period after the two Republican senators raised the issue, close to fifty senators and 150 representatives, responding to mail and phone calls from their constituents, contacted the National Endowment with queries about the agency's funding procedures. On June 6th, the acting chair of the Endowment, Hugh Southern, acknowledged that the criticism was legitimate, and reported that the National Endowment was "discussing this matter with our congressional oversight committees and [we] have agreed that, together, we will review our process to ensure that Endowment processes are effective and maintain the highest artistic integrity and quality."[34]

Six days later, on June 12th, the Corcoran Gallery of Art in Washington announced the cancellation of a scheduled exhibit entitled "Robert Mapplethorpe: The Perfect Moment," which contained a number of homoerotic photographs among the 150-piece retrospective. During the preceding weeks, the Corcoran's director, Christina Orr-Cahall, had been quietly advised that it might hurt the cause of government support for the arts if a controversial art exhibition were held in Washington while the scheduled consideration by Congress of a five-year reauthorization for the National Endowment for the Arts was approaching. As the Corcoran director explained her decision: the scheduled exhibit was "at the wrong place at the wrong time," and the discussion belonged "with the NEA and Congress to resolve. We would not and could not allow ourselves to be drawn into the debate."[35]

It is almost certain that neither Christina Orr-Cahall nor those who advised her to cancel the Mapplethorpe exhibit fully anticipated what the ensuing reaction would be. In the succeeding days and weeks, rhetoric mounted upon rhetoric, with angry demonstrations by members of the arts community in reaction to the cancellation, and statements of indignation by members of Congress in reaction to the content of the exhibition, which by this time had become highly publicized. (Although the Corcoran had not received any National Endowment funding for the show, the Endowment had made a grant of $30,000 to the Institute of Contemporary Art at the University of Pennsylvania, which organized the traveling exhibition of the Mapplethorpe work.)

One month after the cancellation of the Mapplethorpe exhibit at the Corcoran, the House of Representatives acted on the first of a series of proposed legislative retaliations against the National Endowment for the Arts. When the Endowment's budget appropriation for fiscal year 1990 came to the House floor, Representative Dana Rohrabacher (R-Ca.) offered an amendment that would have cut the agency's budget to zero. Later that afternoon, two other budget cuts for the Arts Endowment—one for 10 percent, the other 5 percent—were also proposed. The House of Representatives did not pass any of these measures, but it did adopt a far milder amendment proposed by Representative Charles W. Stenholm (D-Tx.). By a vote of 361 to 65, the House voted to reduce the funding the House Appropriations Committee had recommended for the Arts Endowment by $45,000, the amount of Endowment funds that were linked with the Serrano and Mapplethorpe exhibitions. While this figure represented a fraction of the Endowment's $171.4 million budget, the reduction was designed, said its advocates, to serve as a reminder that the agency would be held accountable for its grant-making decisions.[36] And other legislative battles over the Arts Endowment, both in the

House and in the Senate, were yet to come.

In a season of rough-and-tumble politics, public arts questions were further politicized when Ed Rollins, the chair of the
National Republican Congressional Committee, released a
press memo. The memorandum suggested that all Democrats
who opposed budget cuts in response to the Arts Endowment's funding of offensive art could be targeted at election
time as having supported "sexually explicit and anti-religious
works of art that are offensive to millions of Americans."[37] The
arts program was becoming a high-visibility issue with a potential impact on the general voting public.

Enter Jesse Helms

On July 26, 1989, two weeks after the House vote on the
Arts Endowment budget, Senator Jesse Helms entered the
battle. The Senate was considering the $10.9 billion appro-
priations bill for the Department of the Interior and related
agencies, which included the National Endowment for the
Arts. Near the end of the debate, after most of the senators had
retired for the evening, and at a time when all were preparing
to adjourn for the August recess, Senator Helms proposed a
last-minute amendment to the huge appropriations bill. The
amendment, which passed with little debate on a voice vote by
the few senators present, forbade the use of federal funds for
"promoting, disseminating, or producing" the following:

1. Obscene or indecent materials, including but not limited to
   depictions of sadomasochism, homoeroticism, the exploitation of children, or individuals engaged in sex acts; or

2. material which denigrates the objects or beliefs of the ad-
   herents of a particular religion or nonreligion; or

3. material which denigrates, debases, or reviles a person,
   group, or class of citizens on the basis of race, creed, sex,
   handicap, age, or national origin.[38]

The ensuing political uproar lasted through the summer.
On one side, a number of conservative members of Congress

supported the constraints, and condemned the National Endowment for the Arts for funding with taxpayers' money art that most taxpayers consider objectionable. On the other side, many members of the arts community grew increasingly concerned, and increasingly vocal, about any efforts to limit the content of art.

Supporters of the National Endowment for the Arts in the Senate determined not to fight the issue on the floor, fearing that prolonged debate would only incite even greater public agitation, and thereby serve Helms's purposes. Moreover, like the Arts Endowment's supporters in the House, the Endowment supporters in the Senate hoped to avoid a roll call vote against the Helms amendment, which might be portrayed to the voters back home as a vote for pornographic art at the taxpayers' expense. So the Endowment's Senate supporters planned to wait until the House-Senate conference committee meeting, when they hoped they could quietly strike the language of the Helms amendment.

Meanwhile, in the House of Representatives, the showdown came on September 13th. Supporters of the Arts Endowment, led by the eighty-year-old Interior Appropriations Subcommittee Chair Sidney Yates and Representative Ralph Regula of Ohio, the ranking subcommittee Republican, faced off against those favoring legislative restraints on the agency, led by Representative Rohrabacher of California. Rohrabacher intended to call for a roll call vote to instruct the House conferees who would be attending the upcoming House-Senate conference committee meeting to adopt the Helms amendment. This would force each member of the House to go on public record on a delicate issue that could be readily exploited at election time.

Representative Regula spoke first and moved that the House conferees be instructed to support an amendment that had been offered in the Senate by Senator Robert Byrd of West Virginia, which would result in an investigation of the process that had led up to the Mapplethorpe and Serrano grants. (No member of Congress wanted to go on record as having favored those grants. "Two out of 85,000 is still too many, and let us not let this happen again," Regula declared.)

Then, after having refused to yield the floor to Representative Rohrabacher, Regula "moved the previous question," thus cutting off debate and preventing Rohrabacher from ever offering his amendment. The vote in favor of Regula's motion was 264 to 153.[39]

Although the day marked a victory for the supporters of the National Endowment for the Arts, it also pointed toward greater political tumult and politicization that lay ahead. In preparing for the September 13th debate, Rohrabacher worked closely with Representative William Dannemeyer, a member of Congress noted for what he calls "legislative guerilla warfare." One of Dannemeyer's staff members said that the aim was to characterize the issue as one in which a few out-of-touch artists and bureaucrats were making decisions with taxpayer funds that the general public found offensive: "Mom and apple pie against perversity. It's us against a bunch of smug Ph.D. types telling us what art is." Shortly after losing the vote, Rohrabacher declared: "I'm sure the debate is going to leave the floor of the House of Representatives and is heading for the hinterlands of America, where I think the people will have more common sense on this matter."[40]

Once again the spotlight shifted to the United States Senate—and to Senator Jesse Helms of North Carolina. Himself at the beginning of what some observers felt might become a tight Senate race in 1990, Helms had found an issue that, whatever the specific policy outcome for the National Endowment for the Arts, could be used to bolster his image back home as a prime supporter of traditional American values. His objective, then, was to frame the political question in such a way that to support the Arts Endowment's position was to oppose the moral sentiments of many Americans. Furthermore, he was determined to force his Senate colleagues to vote on the issue. As they approached the impending arts policy debate, Helms's Senate opponents may well have felt toward Helms as Henry Labouchere had felt toward William Ewart Gladstone: he did not object to Gladstone's always having the ace of trumps up his sleeve, but he did object to his pretense that God had put it there.

On September 28, 1989, and into the early hours of the next

day, the Senate debated the amendment, which Helms had offered again as a "sense of the Senate" resolution instructing conferees to adhere to the language the Senate passed a month earlier. The frustration of the senators, forced by Helms to deal with an issue they would have preferred to avoid, was palpable. Declared Senator Helms:

The House of Representatives ducked a vote and the conferees are tied up trying to decide how they can avoid taking a stand on this important issue. . . . There have been all sorts of declarations by various House members as well as the liberal news media of this country, saying that this is censorship, which is not true. The people who are saying that know it is not the case. The Senate should stick by its amendment. Therefore, I want the Senate to vote on it.[41]

Helms ambled through the Senate chamber, showing photos of the Mapplethorpe collection to anyone who cared to look. "See for yourself what the NEA calls art worthy of tax-payer support." Most did not care to look.

Supporters of the amendment, such as Senator Phil Gramm of Texas, stressed that the amendment applied only to publicly funded works, and argued that "taxpayers should not pay for things that basically represent what is considered by the great majority of taxpayers to be pornography or offensive."

Senator Patrick Leahy of Vermont brought up the unspoken concern that lurked not far beneath the surface of the entire debate:

. . . someday, if you vote against this amendment and do the right thing, if you protect the NEA, then somebody is going to run that 30-second ad and say, "Senator so-and-so wants your tax dollars spent for pornography."

Senator Claiborne Pell, the only member of Congress remaining from the principal sponsors of the legislation that created the National Endowment for the Arts in 1965, remembered that earlier day. At that time, he said, one of the chief fears of the National Endowment's founders had been the potential problem of government censorship and interference:

As it is now, if the amendment passed, if it is followed literally, we would find sculpture like Rodin's *The Kiss* or Michaelangelo's figures in the Sistine Chapel forbidden. I do not think we mean to do that. So my hope is that we should defeat the pending legislation.

The tension of politicians dealing with a no-win issue filled the air; and tempers flared. Senator Wyche Fowler (D-Ga.) tried to turn Helms's moral appeal on its head, and argued that parts of the amendment could be interpreted to restrict artwork and literature that many Christians held dear:

Would not the Senator admit that the Holy Scripture itself, that the words of Jesus in the Sermon on the Mount, in all the Gospels, Matthew, Mark, Luke and John, depictions in the Bible, in any written work, much less 700 years of Christian art, can be conceived as being offensive to Jews. . . .

If . . . we cannot disseminate any material which offends the beliefs of any religion, or nonreligion—I will not even get into that. Jesus said, "Go ye therefore into all the world, teach in the name of the Father, the Son and the Holy Ghost."

Senator Fowler then engaged in a face-to-face dialogue with Senator Helms:

Fowler: Would the Senator from North Carolina consider modifying his amendment by dropping section 2?

Helms: No, because not until tonight did I realize that Matthew, Mark, Luke, and John might be applying for Federal funds.

Fowler: It is the depiction of what happened in Matthew, Mark, Luke and John, and art and literature, I say to the Senator, that are subject to the amendment.

Helms: I thought I answered the Senator's question. . . .

On and on the words flew, into the night. After extensive debate, Senate Majority Leader George Mitchell of Maine moved to table the Helms amendment, and by a 62 to 35 roll call vote, the motion to table the amendment was approved. Clearly, the majority of members in both houses of Congress supported the Endowment's position. But many feared that it was becoming politically risky to do so.

The next day the House-Senate conference committee came to a compromise designed to reduce the political heat emitted by the issue for a while. On September 29, 1989, it barred the

funding of art that is "obscene," as defined by the Supreme
Court's 1973 *Miller v. California* decision. No other new restrictions were placed on the National Endowment for the Arts.
Three tests for what constituted obscenity were specified:
works that were lacking in serious literary, artistic, political, or
scientific value; works appealing to prurient interests; or works
containing patently offensive portrayals of specific sexual conduct.[42] This language would be included in the terms and conditions of each grant made, leading many in the arts community to denounce the statement as a required "anti-obscenity
pledge." (Frohnmayer would later argue that it was not a
pledge or oath, maintaining that it was simply a statement of
the principles entailed in the grant-making process, of which
the artist should be made aware.)

The Independent Commission Reports

The House-Senate conference committee also called for the
establishment of a special commission to review the entire process by which the Arts Endowment distributed grants. This
Independent Commission would consist of twelve members,
four appointed by the president of the United States, four by
the speaker of the House, and four by the president pro tem-
pore of the Senate. When the commission began its work in
the spring of 1990, its cochairs were John Brademas, now the
president of New York University, and Leonard Garment, now
practicing law in Washington, D.C.

The spring of 1990 saw another important aspect of the
relationship between government and the arts again come to
the fore, the issue of what kinds of art might be censored by
governments when public funding of the arts was not involved.
In Cincinnati, Ohio, the director of the Contemporary Arts
Center, Dennis Barrie, made sure that his gallery did not currently have any federal, state, or local government funding. He
then proceeded to present an exhibit of the photographs of
Robert Mapplethorpe. On April 7, 1990, the day the exhibit
opened, Barrie and his gallery were indicted by city authorities
on charges that they were pandering obscenity by showing the

exhibit. The gallery and its director also faced charges that they had violated a state law against the use of materials depicting nude minors. The case was the first in American history in which an art gallery was to be tried on obscenity charges. The trial itself would begin in the late summer.

By the time the Cincinnati indictments were handed down, it had been almost a year since the controversy over the proper content of art had erupted over the work of Andres Serrano and Robert Mapplethorpe. The debate had sometimes been shrill, and much of the time both sides had talked past each other. Nevertheless, a number of important questions had been raised, questions that reflected fundamental issues concerning the relationship between government and the arts in America. The Cincinnati case raised two of the most critical questions: what kind of artwork would the government be justified in censoring, and what kind of artwork might be judged to be obscene.

But the debate had also opened up a deeply divisive cluster of issues relating to government support of the arts; and these were issues on which many members of the public at large, not just people involved in the arts, had strong views. Critics of certain National Endowment grants felt that a government grant was not a right, and that it was not improper for some restrictions to be attached to their issuance. The critics also argued that there was a problem when art supported by the entire community, through public tax monies, was deeply offensive to parts of the community. At the individual level, many taxpayers who wrote and telephoned their members of Congress resented having their tax money going for art or art activities that they *did* regard as deeply offensive.

Moreover, these concerns raised additional questions. Should the standard for publicly funded art go beyond the standard for privately funded art? Were there some kinds of artistic expression that should not be funded at the taxpayers' expense, even though they should be free to flourish without public support? In the debate that was taking place, were members of the arts community giving adequate attention to the rights of the general public to have their values and viewpoints reflected in a publicly funded program for the arts? Should the voice of the public weigh more heavily in the decision making of the National Endowment for the Arts by, for example, the appointment of strong "public members" to the panels that considered the applications for arts grants? Now that government aid for the arts had become a mass public issue, did the supporters of government arts programs need to develop a new rationale for public support? And what direction should public policy take on some of the other issues that had risen to prominence in the 1980s—tax policies that affect the arts, art education, cultural equity, and the effective presentation of America's artistic achievements in the rest of the world?

In September and early October of 1990, some of the responses of the government on arts policy issues began to become clearer. On September 11th the bipartisan Independent Commission issued its long-awaited report. The commission began by underscoring some of the dilemmas that are inherent in relations between government and the arts:

> The Endowment is charged with one of the most complex and delicate tasks that an agency of government can perform in a democracy. On the one hand, it must seek to offer a spacious sense of freedom to the artists and the arts institutions it assists; from such freedom grows the capacity of the arts to expand our horizons. At the same time, the NEA must, if it is to maintain public confidence in its stewardship of public funds, be accountable to all of the American people.
>
> With its discretion to spend public money, the Endowment must make sure that its policies and procedures are fair, reasonable and efficient. Insuring the freedom of expression necessary to nourish the arts while bearing in mind limits of public understanding and tolerance requires unusual wisdom, prudence, and most of all, common sense.

The commission unanimously recommended "against legislative changes to impose specific restrictions on the content of works of art supported by the Endowment," adding that "content restrictions may raise serious constitutional issues, would be inherently ambiguous and would almost certainly involve the Endowment and the Department of Justice in costly and unproductive lawsuits." At the same time, the commission declared that it recognized "that obscenity is not protected speech and that the National Endowment for the Arts is prohibited from funding the production of works which are obscene or otherwise illegal." Three days after the commission report was issued, Leonard Garment underscored this point in a letter to the editor of the *Washington Post*—the inclusion of anti-obscenity language in the authorizing legislation for the National Endowment for the Arts was not necessary because the funding of obscene material was already illegal. Garment wrote that because "obscenity is not protected under the First Amendment" in any case, "the agency obviously has to consider this requirement of law, as it does other statutory criteria, in determining whether or not to make a grant."[43]

The commission also stressed that the first priority in making grants remained artistic excellence, but it added that "the standard for publicly funded art must go beyond the standard for privately funded art . . . to support art from public funds entails considerations that go beyond artistic excellence. Publicly funded art must take into account the conditions that traditionally govern the use of public money."

The commission then stressed the need for changes in the operation of the Arts Endowment in order to strengthen its accountability to the public. Declared the commission:

To assure that the NEA operate in a manner accountable to the President, Congress and the American people, the Endowment's procedures for scrutiny and evaluation of applications for grants must be reformed.

Among the major reforms the Commission believes necessary are: (1) strengthening the authority of the Chairperson—the sole authority of the Chairperson to make grants [should] be made explicit in legislation; (2) making the National Council more active; (3) eliminating real or perceived conflicts of interest; (4) assuring that evaluation of grant applications be fair, accountable and thorough; (5) clarifying the function of the grant advisory panels and broadening their membership to make them more representative; and (6) making clear that the National Endowment for the Arts belongs not solely to those who receive its grants but to all the people of the United States.[44]

The Senate and House Committees Act

Shortly after the Independent Commission report was made public, the arts legislation that the Congress had been shaping during the summer was reported out of committee. On September 13, 1990, the Senate Labor and Human Resources Committee voted fifteen to one in favor of a five-year reauthorization bill that would leave the question of obscenity up to the courts (an artist who received a grant but was then convicted of obscenity would have to return the public funds), but otherwise left the Endowment unchanged. The strategy of backers of the Endowment seemed to have become one of full legislative support tempered by mediated political responsibility. Perhaps the legislators hoped that the issue might be defused somewhat, just as the question of abortion had lost some of its political volatility when it was understood to be a question in the hands of the courts. Nevertheless, when asked whether he believed the Senate committee bill would end the year-long struggle over the Endowment, Senator Orrin Hatch (R-Utah) reflected the frustration that many felt in dealing with the issue. "Who knows? It's a very politically charged issue and some people around here are afraid of their own shadows."[45]

Meanwhile, on October 4, 1990, members of the House Postsecondary Education Subcommittee announced that they, too, had reached a bipartisan compromise on reauthorization legislation for the National Endowment for the Arts. Like the Senate bill, it dealt with the question of obscenity in works funded by federal grants by leaving it up to the courts. But it also differed in some important respects from the Senate bill.[46] After a conference committee met to reconcile the differences between the House and Senate bills, the will of the Congress finally became clearer on October 27, 1990, when the House and the Senate approved the conference committee report. The final legislation included a number of provisions that were in the House bill. It called for a substantial increase in the portion of National Endowment funds that go directly to the states—from 20 percent to 35 percent between 1990 and

1993. It reauthorized the National Endowment for the Arts for three years rather than five years. It called for broader representation of diverse artistic and cultural points of view on the grant-recommending panels, including the addition of knowledgeable "lay persons" to the panels. It required the Endowment to monitor more closely how artists were using their grants. And it required the chair of the National Endowment to ensure that grants were awarded while taking into consideration "general standards of decency and respect for the diverse beliefs and values of the American public."

Two other decisions involving relations between government and the arts also were made in October 1990. On October 5th, the court case in Cincinnati was decided. A jury of four men and four women found the Contemporary Arts Center and its director, Dennis Barrie, not guilty on charges that they had pandered obscenity by displaying an exhibit of photographs by Robert Mapplethorpe. Both defendants were also acquitted on charges that they had violated a state law against the use of materials depicting nude minors. The jury took less than two hours to reach its verdict.[47]

In addition, during the hectic final budget negotiations before Congress adjourned, the 101st Congress passed a tax measure designed to aid the nation's museums and other cultural institutions—a restoration of tax deductions for the full market value of donated works of art. As passed, the tax provision permitted the larger deductions for one year only, 1991. The measure's chief legislative sponsor was Senator Daniel Patrick Moynihan (D-NY).

In Conclusion:
Assessing the Relationship

The bruising political battles of 1989 and 1990 underscored how fragile and potentially tempestuous the relationship between government and the arts can be. Nor were the events of 1989 and 1990 entirely new. From the political uproar over the quality of John Trumbull's paintings for the Capitol, through the public reaction to Horatio Greenough's "naked Washington," the controversies over the arts programs of the New Deal, and the political battle over the Helms amendment, the relationship between government and the arts in America often has been an uneasy one. In the apt phrase of Joan Simpson Burns, it has been an "awkward embrace."[48]

At the same time, the battle joined in 1989 and 1990 should not obscure the fact that a major change has taken place in the relations between government and the arts in the United States since 1960. A remarkable system of government aid for the arts has been fashioned over the last thirty years. First, it builds on, and supplements, the extraordinary preexisting system of private philanthropy for the arts in America. Moreover, by matching grants, challenge grants, and other devices, the government programs aim to stimulate additional private giving. The provision of tax deductions that are relatively easy to claim for charitable donations is probably still the most important public policy of the national government that affects the arts in America. In 1989 tax deductions for contributions to the arts probably exceeded $1 billion. The total budget for the National Endowment for the Arts was $169 million.

Second, by 1990 government involvement with the arts contained a considerable range of other federal programs in addition to the National Endowment for the Arts—the Institute of Museum Services, programs to send American artists overseas, the arts programs of the Smithsonian Institution, Department of Education grants for art education in the schools, the American Film Institute, funds administered by the General Services Administration for artwork in public buildings, and numerous other government programs that affect the arts.

Third, since the mid-1970s, the funding for the National Endowment for the Arts has been large enough that its programs alone have had a major impact on the development of the arts in America. The appropriations of public money that the National Endowment has received since 1965 now total close to $2.5 billion. At the same time, money from the Endowment has never been large enough that artists and art institutions could relax their efforts to raise money in many other ways; and they have shown remarkable skill in raising money on their own. Grants from the National Endowment for the Arts have seldom accounted for more than 5 percent of any single art institution's budget.

Finally, the relationship that has evolved between government and the arts in the United States is a highly pluralistic system. Fifty states, the District of Columbia, and five territories or special jurisdictions have state arts councils or their equivalent, and the public funds that state legislators have been voting for their state arts councils have been growing. By 1986 the total public funding for state arts councils exceeded the total budget of the National Endowment for the Arts. By 1990 state arts funding had reached $285 million, compared with $171.2 million for the National Endowment. (Chapter 7 examines this subject in detail.)

In addition, there are expenditures on behalf of the arts by city and other local governments—the *terra incognita* of government support for the arts. The full amount of these public funds is yet to be precisely counted. They are widely scattered in grants to city and county arts councils; direct budget line items for museums, symphonies, and other arts organizations; grants for arts purposes in parks and recreation department budgets; and funds that affect the arts in many other programs that local governments undertake. Expenditures for the arts by local governments clearly exceed $300 million a year, and the full amount spent for the arts at the local level may well be far above that figure.

Taken together, the scope and depth of government programs to promote the arts are of a magnitude that would have been undreamed of just thirty years ago. At their outer edges, those involvements of the government with the arts continue to draw intense political fire, as they often have ever since the founding of the republic. But the programs have taken root; American artists and American arts institutions and their leaders are a resourceful and hardy lot; and the American government—in fact, American governments—have played an important role in the remarkable flowering of the arts that has occurred in the United States over the last generation.

Notes

[1] Cummings and Katz (1987), pp. 5–7.

[2] Quoted and summarized in Arthur M. Schlesinger Jr., "America, the Arts and the Future," the Nancy Hanks Lecture on the Arts and Public Policy, Washington, D.C., April 13, 1988, pp. 4–5.

[3] Quoted in Purcell (1956), pp. 15–16.

[4] Purcell (1956), p. 16.

[5] U.S. House of Representatives, 41st Congress, 2nd session, *Art in the District of Columbia,* Executive Document 315 (1871), p. 727.

[6] *Register of Debates,* 18th Congress, 2nd session, Vol. I., pp. 638–639.

[7] Taylor (1979), pp. 60–61.

[8] Taylor (1979), p. 61.

[9] Miller (1966), pp. 61–62.

[10] Miller (1966), p. 63.

[11] Miller (1966), p. 64.

[12] Miller (1966), p. 63.

[13] Quoted in Harris (1970), p. 13.

[14] Morison (1965), p. 536.

[15] Cummings (1982), p. 141.

[16] Ginsberg (1987). See also Roxan and Wanstall (1964) and the *Report of the American Commission for the Protection and Salvage of Artistic and Historic Monuments in War Areas,* U.S. Government Printing Office, 1946.

[17] Cummings (1982), pp. 142–143.

[18] Cummings (1982), p. 151.

[19] Cummings (1982), p. 160.

[20] Cummings (1982), p. 161.

[21] Interview with Barnaby Keeney, Little Compton, Rhode Island, November 11, 1978.

[22] Swaim (1982), p. 184.

[23] Swaim (1982), p. 185.

[24] Straight (1979), p. 21.

[25] Straight (1979), p. 21.

[26] Straight (1979), pp. 22–23.

[27] *Washington Post,* September 5, 1974, p. C1.

[28] *New York Times,* June 17, 1986, p. C13; and *Washington Post,* May 20, 1989, p. A24.

[29] *New York Times,* May 19, 1986, p. C14.

[30] *New York Times,* May 4, 1988, Section 2, p. 10.

[31] *Washington Post,* January 19, 1983, p. B4.

[32] *New York Times,* May 14, 1988, Section 1, p. 1; and *Washington Post,* February 13, 1989, Section 4, p. 36.

[33] *New York Times,* March 20, 1989, Section 1, p. 1.

[34] *Washington Post,* June 7, 1989, p. C1.

[35] *Washington Post,* June 13, 1989, Section 1, p. 18.

[36] *New York Times,* July 13, 1989, Section 1, p. 18.

[37] *Washington Post,* July 19, 1989, p. A6.

[38] *Washington Post,* July 27, 1989, p. C1; and *New York Times,* July 27, 1989, p. A1.

[39] *Congressional Record,* September 13, 1989, Vol. 135, No. 116, p. H5641.

[40] *New York Times,* September 14, 1989, p. A1.

[41] *Congressional Record,* September 28, 1989, Vol. 135, No. 128, p. S12110.

[42] *New York Times,* September 30, 1989, p. A1.

[43] *Washington Post,* September 15, 1990, p. A22.

[44] *Report of the Independent Commission to the President of the United States,* September 11, 1990, U.S. Government Printing Office.

[45] *Washington Post,* September 14, 1990, p. D1.

[46] *Washington Post,* October 5, 1990, p. D2.

[47] *Washington Post,* October 6, 1990, p. A1.

[48] Burns (1975).

2

Artistic Freedom, Public Funding, and the Constitution

KATHLEEN M. SULLIVAN

Faces may launch a thousand ships, but art, we now know, may launch a thousand legislative initiatives. The 1989–90 clamor over the photographs of Robert Mapplethorpe and Andres Serrano, and their publicly subsidized display, triggered an extended debate in Congress over the future of the National Endowment for the Arts (NEA). Many kinds of content restrictions on NEA grants were proposed, although few, in the end, were enacted. To those in the arts and civil liberties communities who opposed such restrictions, these bills smacked of censorship, and set off the same alarm as any inhibition of First Amendment liberties. To those who advocated content restrictions, on the other hand, the First Amendment had nothing to do with public funding of the arts.

KATHLEEN M. SULLIVAN is professor of law at Harvard Law School, where she has taught since 1984. Her specialty is constitutional law, and she has published articles on topics ranging from affirmative action to unconstitutional conditions on government benefits. She is currently writing a book, to be published by W.W. Norton & Co., on the NEA crisis and the First Amendment.

Artists, they argued, could do what they wished with their own money, but he who "takes the king's shilling becomes the king's man."

They're both right—in part. Government restrictions on speech do implicate the concerns of the First Amendment, whether they come attached to carrots or to sticks. But, at the same time, placing conditions on what an artist may say in exchange for a grant of public funds is not exactly the same as throwing that artist in jail—one cannot escape the jail cell, but at least in theory one may always reject a restrictive government art grant in favor of a more liberal private patron. The constitutional answer thus lies somewhere between the poles of the popular debate.

Government as Art Patron: Does the First Amendment Apply?

Deciding whether conditions on art funding are constitutional starts with the problem of characterizing the government's role. Is government as patron the equivalent of government as regulator? Or is government more akin to a private patron when it distributes artists' grants? The answer will determine whether or not First Amendment limits apply to the conditions government as patron may impose.

When government regulates private speech, the First Amendment applies with full force. In the absence of some compelling justification, criminal sanctions or other coercive measures may not be applied to expression on the basis of its viewpoint, subject matter, or medium. Artistic expression enjoys these protections as fully as other kinds of speech. Short of work that is found unprotected because libelous or legally obscene, privately produced art cannot constitutionally be constrained on the basis of its content.

Private patrons, on the other hand, can exercise unlimited control over the content of the creations they fund, limited only by artists' freedom to walk away from the arrangement. When a private patron commissions a work of art, the artist is subject to the patron's unfettered taste or whim. The private patron is free to choose the work's subject matter, medium, and even viewpoint. The private patron may withhold payment if a portrait is not flattering or if a mural is too subversive. The private patron may forbid work some would consider sacrilegious, or demand it. The private patron may give good reasons for an exercise of aesthetic discretion, but is free to give bad ones—like the fictionalized emperor in *Amadeus* who tells Mozart that his newly commissioned opera has "uh, too many notes." The private patron is also free to give no reason at all.

Which characterization—sovereign regulator or private art patron—better suits the government when it is funding the production of art? The argument for treating government the same as a private art patron would go as follows: government may but need not fund the arts; if it chooses to fund the arts, it may choose what art it likes. The political majority can exercise its own taste or whim the same as a private patron. Because artists are free to accept or reject the grants, conditions on grants cannot coerce them, and so cannot "abridge" their speech as the First Amendment forbids. Moreover, because private art patronage may flourish free of government constraint, there is no danger that any conditions on the narrow category of publicly funded art will "drown out" nonconforming art throughout the society at large. So long as there is private competition, government may never achieve in its own sector an excessive monopoly over artistic ideas.

The Doctrine of Unconstitutional Conditions

A parallel argument has been made for ignoring the First Amendment in other contexts where the government functions not as overarching sovereign but rather in some narrower, more specialized role—and the Supreme Court has repeatedly rejected it. Take, for example, Justice Holmes's ruling, in an 1897 Massachusetts case, that Boston could forbid speeches on its common unless the mayor approved, reasoning that "for the Legislature . . . to forbid public speaking in a highway or public park is no more an infringement of the rights of a member of the public than for the owner of a private house to forbid it in his house." In other words, if you have something unpopular to say, say it on your own property!

That view, however, has been squarely rejected in decade after decade of cases holding that the First Amendment bars content discrimination against speeches made or literature handed out in public forums such as the streets and parks. In other words, the mere fact that the government acts as proprietor of our public spaces does not mean that the First Amendment does not apply there. Private homeowners may turn away canvassers at their doors because they choose not to save the whales or support a candidate, but in the government's house, all ideas must be equally welcome.

The same sort of argument has been made—and rejected— in the context of government employment. Consider again an example from Justice Holmes, who once wrote epigramatically that a policeman "may have a constitutional right to talk politics but he has no constitutional right to be a policeman." By that he meant that the government as employer should be able to sanction freely the speech of its employees, unlike that of citizens at large. A long line of Supreme Court case law, however, has rejected that suggestion as flatly as Holmes's position on public forums. While the Court has conceded that government may limit speech that would seriously disrupt efficiency and order in public services and facilities, it has held that public employees do not shed their First Amendment freedoms at the workplace gate.

For example, the Court recently reinstated a clerical employee who was dismissed from her job in a constable's office because she was overheard to say, right after the attempted assassination of President Reagan, "If they go for him again, I hope they get him"—a remark the dissenters characterized as "riding with the cops but cheering for the robbers." The Court likewise recently reaffirmed that one may not be dismissed from most public jobs just because one belongs to the losing political party. These cases would have come out the other way if the government had been treated as the equiva-

lent of a private employer, who is constitutionally free to fire
employees for their affiliations or their remarks.

In short, the First Amendment does not evaporate simply
because government is acting as proprietor or employer, even
though in both situations the taxpayers are paying the tab.
Rallies or concerts may not be denied permits in public parks
because the ideas or songs are controversial—even though the
taxpayers pay for the police who keep order there and for the
sanitation workers who clean up the litter left behind. Nor may
public employees be fired for speaking out against the government on matters of public concern—even though the taxpayers pay their salaries. And these same principles apply when
government grants money directly; for example, the Court recently held that public broadcasting stations may not be
barred from running potentially controversial editorials—
even though the taxpayers foot part of their bill. These hold-
ings are sometimes summarized as "the doctrine of unconstitutional conditions": government may not grant benefits such
as money, space, or jobs in exchange for the surrender of constitutionally protected expression, even if the recipient was
free to go elsewhere, and the government was free never to
have offered the benefit at all.

It follows that the First Amendment likewise imposes at least
some limits on government discretion in its role as art patron.
In other words, a public arts endowment is constrained by the
First Amendment in ways that a private artist, patron, or col-
lector is not. What are some reasons why that should be so?

The Supreme Court has sometimes given the answer that a
condition on the grant of government funds is a coercive offer.
It puts one to an unfair choice, this argument goes, between
taking the money and exercising one's constitutional rights.
Just as one should not be subject to blackmail, extortion, or
other "offers" that cannot be refused, one should not be subjected to offers of money in exchange for silence or conform-
ity. The government's threat to withhold money if one speaks
out too freely is little different from the levy of a criminal fine
for that speech. Another argument sometimes made is that
constitutional rights are priceless, and thus should not be trad-

able in exchange for a grant. But neither of these arguments convincingly defeats the point so often made by advocates of content restrictions on art funding—namely, that the artist is free to take or leave a grant, as he or she is not free to take or leave the sheriff.

A better defense of applying the First Amendment to arts funding is that content restrictions in this area will have bad effects on the system of free expression little different from those worked by content-discriminatory criminal or regulatory laws. To take a simple example: it would obviously be unconstitutional to make it a crime to vote Republican. But it would be just as unconstitutional to offer cash bounties to those who agree to vote Democrat. Either way, the world would be skewed impermissibly in favor of the Democrats. A similar skewing effect might follow from restrictions on the content of publicly funded art. For example, bribing a Warhol to paint like a Wyeth works the same result as outlawing pop art: either way, the world is made safe only for landscapes.

The argument that a public art endowment is the equivalent of a private art patron, and therefore equally unconstrained by the First Amendment, accordingly cannot stand up. In the art context as in other areas, the First Amendment has some application even when the government is wielding its checkbook rather than its badge. It is simply a fallacy to say, as content-restrictions advocates so often do, "It's the taxpayers' money and we may do as we like with it!" In a free society, the government may no more purchase orthodoxy by power of the purse than compel it by power of the sword.

But it would be a mistake as well to jump uncritically to the opposite pole, and to conclude that the First Amendment applies identically to government funding and regulation alike. The government cannot fund everything, and so must engage in some selectivity whenever it spends money. Government thus may often discriminate in its expenditures in ways that the First Amendment would bar in the setting of criminal or regulatory law. Art funding is no exception; government may exercise some preferences in funding art that it could not constitutionally exercise in regulating art that is privately produced. Government could not make it a crime to produce "bad art," for example, but surely might decline to fund such work. The question that follows is whether some grounds of selection are more constitutionally problematic than others.

Content Restrictions: A Catalogue

Different grounds for distinction among art projects proposed for public funding would trigger different degrees of scrutiny, under current constitutional law. Following is a series of such possible grounds, in increasing order of constitutional difficulty.

1. *Artistic excellence.* This criterion for art funding is constitutionally unproblematic, even though, as mentioned, bad art could not constitutionally be banned. The reason is that without such a criterion, public arts funding would not exist: promoting good art is the sine qua non of the relevant agencies. The Supreme Court has acknowledged functional limits to the freedom of publicly subsidized speech; just as speech may be curtailed when incompatible with the operation of a public facility or the efficiency of a public job, so art grants may be limited to meritorious art.

It might be objected that artistic excellence is inherently more subjective than, say, scientific merit, and is thus less subject to neutral and nonpartisan determination. But in art as in science, there is a simple solution to keeping government from politicizing this criterion too much: defer to peer review of art by artists, much as in the scientific world.

2. *Obscenity.* The Supreme Court has long denied First Amendment protection to expression it deems obscene. The reigning definition of obscenity since the 1973 decision in *Miller v. California* has been expression that appeals to the "prurient interest" through "patently offensive" depiction of sexual conduct that lacks "serious" artistic or other merit. There are many problems with deciphering this standard even on the regulatory side—for example, how can a work trigger sexual arousal and disgust at the same time? Such difficulties have led to inconsistent patterns of prosecution and disparate

jury results. For example, in 1990 in Florida, two different juries reached opposite results on the question whether works by the rap group 2 Live Crew were criminally obscene, and a federal judge also came down against the group. One person's rap music, it seems, is another's obscenity.

The application of the *Miller* standard to art funding is even more difficult, however, for it would appear self-contradictory to hold lacking in "serious artistic merit" a work that has garnered the artistic approbation embodied in a grant. This is especially so given that artistic merit, unlike prurient interest and patent offensiveness, may not be left to determination under local "community standards." The "serious artistic merit" test raises problems of its own. For one, the distinction between high art and low art has been eroded in many contemporary schools of art. For another, popular and expert views of artistic merit may well diverge. The federal judge who ruled against 2 Live Crew, for example, rejected the testimony of experts who claimed cultural and literary value for rap music. And in a legal first, a Cincinnati prosecutor brought a criminal obscenity case against an art museum director for exhibiting Mapplethorpe photographs that had already graced museum walls in many other cities; the jury, however, ultimately acquitted, deferring to expert witnesses who testified that the homoerotic pictures in question had artistic merit after all.

All these difficulties aside, obscenity is unprotected speech, and so government is at least as free to withhold funding from obscene art as it is to ban it outright. The constitutional problem with obscenity restrictions on art funding is thus likely to arise not on the substantive but rather on the procedural side.

Even if obscenity may be punished after the fact, speech may not be restrained in advance on the ground that it is likely to prove obscene. Antiobscenity funding restrictions that are couched in prospective form—for example, a bar on using funds to produce work that "may be considered obscene"—thus may have the same chilling effect as prior restraints. The problem is not that they discourage unprotected obscenity; the problem is that they also discourage much nonobscene eroticism or sexually suggestive speech for fear that it will come too close to the line. As Justice Marshall once put the point in another context, the problem with "a sword of Damocles is that it hangs—not that it drops."

This problem is compounded if artists themselves are required to certify in advance that the work that they are about to produce will not be obscene. Even where government fears that expression will be unprotected, it is unconstitutional to exact a promise of silence in advance. Analogous reasoning led to the invalidation of loyalty oaths that were required back in the 1950s in exchange for public benefits such as tax exemptions; even though some subversive speech was then considered unprotected, as obscenity is considered now, the Supreme Court held that the state could not place the burden on the taxpayer to disavow all such speech before the fact.

These general points about obscenity restrictions apply as well to restrictions against child pornography, a category of speech that the Supreme Court has more recently held unprotected by the First Amendment, whether obscene under *Miller* or not. The rationale for this decision is that the state has a compelling interest in eliminating the coercion of child models into sexual performances, and their lack of consent to such performances may be presumed. As with obscenity, funding restrictions on such a basis may raise procedural but generally not substantive problems.

3. *Subject Matter Restrictions.* Content restrictions might refer to an entire topic or to a specific point of view on a topic. For example, government might seek to bar "all campaign speeches" or only "Democratic campaign speeches"; "all speech about abortion" or only "speech that encourages abortion"; "all speech near a foreign embassy" or only "speech near a foreign embassy that is hostile to the foreign government in question." Both these forms of content discrimination are constitutionally suspect, though generally subject matter discrimination has been treated as the lesser of the two evils. Viewpoint discrimination is almost always unconstitutional, but subject matter discrimination has also frequently been invalidated.

Some examples of subject matter restrictions in the regulatory context include a ban on nonlabor picketing, a ban on corporate speech in public referendum campaigns except on narrow matters of business affairs, and the exclusion of religious organizations from public campus facilities open to groups focused on other topics—all of which the Supreme Court has strictly scrutinized and swiftly struck down.

In the subsidy context, the Court has also invalidated some subject matter discriminations. The clearest example is a recent decision that struck down a state sales tax law giving exemptions to newspapers and religious, professional, trade, and sports journals, but not to "general-interest" magazines. The Court stated that "the First Amendment's hostility to content-based regulation extends not only to restrictions on particular viewpoints, but also to prohibition of public discussion of an entire topic." The subject matter of a journal thus was an impermissible basis for selective tax treatment.

The difficulty with extending this reasoning wholesale to the funding context is that government must inevitably make some selection among subject matters if it is to fund anything at all. In funding medical research, government may give priority to cancer but not cardiology, and in funding artistic endeavors, it may decide one year to fund music but not visual art. If the government runs a grant program for portrait painting, can a landscape artist complain that his First Amendment rights have been infringed? Some earmarking of funds for subject matter must surely be allowed.

On the other hand, subject matter restrictions may not constitutionally be used as a cover for viewpoint discrimination. For example, a restriction on "plays about homophobia" may amount in practice to the elimination of a gay rights point of view. Government may not eliminate an entire category of expression out of hostility—as Hitler condemned all abstract expressionism on the ground that it was "decadent" art.

4. *Viewpoint Restrictions.* Whether in the regulatory or the funding context, viewpoint discrimination has long been regarded as the cardinal sin against the First Amendment. Government may not exact adherence to one viewpoint over another, even as a condition on granting funds. The government

has an obligation of evenhandedness; it may not use selective distribution of benefits to shift viewpoints in a direction favored by majority will.

The Court has often restated this point. Most recently, Justice (now Chief Justice) William Rehnquist noted it in passing for a unanimous Court, in a case that actually upheld a kind of subject matter restriction: a denial of the benefit of tax deductible contributions to nonprofit organizations that engaged in lobbying. Such a restriction was held not to be a First Amendment infringement but rather a permissible refusal to subsidize lobbying activities. The case would have been quite different, however, Justice Rehnquist suggested, if the antilobbying restriction had been viewpoint based—for example, a denial of tax deductible contributions to nonprofit organizations that engaged in "proabortion" lobbying. As Justice Rehnquist wrote, quoting older cases, "Congress [may not] discriminate invidiously in its subsidies in such a way as to 'aim at the suppression of dangerous ideas.' "

Thus of all the content restrictions outlined, explicit viewpoint discrimination in a funding program is the likeliest to be struck down on its face.

A Final Distinction:
Commissions and Subsidies

It is important to note that the discussion to this point has focused on government allocation of subsidies to private artists who retain ownership of the art they produce, and who retain their private identity while they produce it. Accepting a government grant in this context does not make one ipso facto a government contractor or employee.

The case would be different if the government were commissioning government art—for example, a frieze for a federal office building, a war memorial, or a postage stamp commemorating a late president. Where government is itself producing art, its latitude for discriminating on the basis of subject matter and even viewpoint is necessarily greater than when it is providing private artists with support. For example, it would violate no First Amendment right of the artist accepting a commission if the government vetoed a war memorial carved with the caption "They died in vain," or a postage stamp picturing Harry Truman with the H-bomb mushroom cloud pictured beside his head as an unmistakable symbolic criticism.

Why is the art grantee unlike the artist on a government commission? The answer is perhaps that we value a mixed public-private system—in art as well as in other areas of life. True, a cadre of government artists could be deployed to paint, sculpt, and design art in the government's image. But if one could gain government support only by joining such an army, it would have a totalitarian ring. We do not have national health care and we do not have national art—artists, like doctors, in our system, retain significant private autonomy even when public revenues help support their work.

NEA Reform: What Would the Constitution Permit?

As the National Endowment for the Arts became the focus of heated public controversy, some called for its outright abolition. Even some in the arts community argued for abolition, reasoning that publicly supported art can never truly be free, so it would be better to remove the hand of government from the canvas and keyboard altogether. NEA defenders argued, quite the contrary, that it is an institution vital to American art. I strongly favor the latter position, for I am convinced that public support of art improves its distribution and enhances innovation and diversity. Whether one hears a symphony or sees an exhibition should not depend on accidents of geography or birth; public arts endowments, like public education, help democratize access to art. With art as with public broadcasting, public support can make possible productions too risky or challenging to sell readily on the private market.

But the debate between these two positions is one of policy, not constitutional law. The Constitution neither requires nor forbids public art funding. The government is not constitu-

tionally required to disestablish art, as it is religion. Nor, however, is there any affirmative obligation to fund art, as there
might arguably be, for example, to fund the common defense.
Rather, the Constitution is agnostic on art funding; Congress
may choose to provide it or not.

If Congress chooses to fund art, then the First Amendment
will limit its options, along the lines that have been outlined
above. How would those general observations apply with respect to specific legislative proposals that have been floated at
various times on Capitol Hill? Two categories of restrictions
have occupied by far the most congressional time.

1. *Obscenity restrictions.* This sort of restriction has been more
successful on the floor of Congress than any other. The 1989
NEA appropriations law provided that no NEA funds be used
"to promote, disseminate, or produce materials which in the
judgment of the NEA may be considered obscene, including
but not limited to, depictions of sadomasochism, homoeroticism, the sexual exploitation of children, or individuals engaged in sex acts and which, when taken as a whole, do not
have serious literary, artistic, political, or scientific value."

As discussed above, the category of obscenity as defined in
Miller is not protected by the First Amendment, but this for-
mulation had two constitutional problems nonetheless. First,
it was prospective, barring future art that "may be considered
obscene," and thus had an excessive chilling effect similar to
any prior restraint. This problem was alleviated by the 1990
reauthorization law, which provided sanctions that are solely
retrospective—payback provisions for NEA funded artists who
are adjudged in court to have produced an obscene work. Artists may still feel a chill from such provisions, but they are at
least constitutional on their face.

Second, the 1989 law confusingly intermingles the categories of "obscenity" and child pornography with the categories
of "sadomasochism" and "homoeroticism"—the result of an
eleventh-hour legislative compromise in which the obscenity
standard was introduced as a limitation on Senator Jesse
Helms's originally far broader bill.

But not all depictions of sadomasochism or homoeroticism

are obscene. Some may be, but the Supreme Court has repeatedly struck down restrictions on sexually explicit expression that extend beyond the category of obscenity—especially if they are viewpoint-discriminatory. For example, the Supreme Court has struck down laws banning sexually explicit expression because it depicts adultery too favorably or women too unfavorably, as objects of sexual domination—even though each of these laws restricted speech that overlapped the boundaries of obscenity. Funding restrictions on "homoerotic" or "sadomasochistic" art, standing alone, would suffer from similar constitutional defects, as would a funding restriction on "indecent" art. Because the terms were used in the 1989 bill, however, not to exhaust the category of obscenity but rather to illustrate it, the viewpoint discrimination was not presented in its starkest form. But a strong argument can be made—and was made in court challenges to the law—that at the least this overlapping language makes the law unacceptably vague.

The 1990 reauthorization legislation included no enforceable content restrictions other than the paycheck provisions for adjudicated obscenity, but it did include some hortatory language urging the NEA chair to "take into consideration general standards of decency." An enforceable content restriction barring "indecent" art would be unconstitutional as viewpoint discrimination against a far broader category than obscenity, but this provision is likely to stand up on its face because, although vague and troubling, it is toothless.

2. *Hate-speech restrictions.* Congress has considered, but not enacted, a number of bills that would have flatly proscribed the use of public funds to "denigrate" or "revile" various symbols and members of various groups. To take but two examples, Congress eliminated from a proposed Senate bill in 1989 language that would have prohibited the use of NEA funds to produce or disseminate art that "denigrates, debases, or reviles a person, group or class of citizens on the basis of race, creed, sex, handicap, age or national origin." Language circulated in the House for some months in 1990 would have barred NEA grantees who "deliberately denigrate the cultural

heritage of the United States, its religious traditions, or racial
or ethnic groups."

The constitutional defect of such restrictions would be
straightforward under current law if these were criminal or
regulatory proposals. The Court has required official agnosti-
cism in the regulations of speech, however viscerally offensive
or hateful. As the Court reiterated in the flag-burning decisions, the First Amendment's hostility to viewpoint discrimination prevents government from immunizing any symbol or
idea from symbolic or ideological attack, no matter how sacred
it is in the minds of most Americans. In other words, hateful as
racist, sexist, or sacrilegious speech may be, it is not entitled to
an exemption from the rule against viewpoint discrimination.

But the funding context adds a wrinkle to this problem not
present in the regulation of private speech: when the government funds hate-speech, it may appear to be putting its imprimatur of approval on that speech. Funding thus gives rise to
an arguable government interest in dissociating itself from a
message that symbolically undermines its own commitment to
enforcing equal protection and other laws.

The argument has considerable appeal, but on balance
should be rejected. The risk that government will be associated with hateful messages expressed by publicly funded
artists—if indeed it were even possible for such expression to
survive the gauntlet of peer review—is greatly exaggerated.
We do not associate government with the messages displayed
in public spaces—there is no imprimatur of approval on pro-
life or pro-choice rallies when each takes place on the Washington Mall. Why should it be different for speech subsidized
not by a grant of space but by a grant of funds? Moreover, the
Court has rightly held in other funding contexts that an interest in government dissociation from a publicly subsidized message cannot justify content restrictions on the grantee's
speech: the most recent example is the decision invalidating a
ban on editorializing by public broadcasters, despite the government's claim that it did not want the management's positions confused with its own.

The 1990 reauthorization legislation included no enforceable ban on hate-speech by publicly funded artists, but did include some hortatory language urging the NEA chair to "take into consideration . . . respect for the diverse beliefs and values of the American public." This language is unlikely to be struck down on its face because, although vague, it has no teeth.

Conclusion

The best way to accommodate the public funding of art to the values of the First Amendment would be to continue an NEA that operates the way it did before the crisis of 1989: namely, with a mandate of commitment to artistic excellence, but subject to no content restriction beyond that. The best public art will be that with the least strings attached, for promoting creativity and innovation is one of the NEA's major reasons to be. In a free society, artists do best when they are not the government's puppets, but dance rather each to his or her own tune. The solution is not to abolish the NEA, but to unfetter it.

3

The Artist in an Integrated Society

JOAN JEFFRI

P erhaps the most significant contribution the United States has made to the world of contemporary art is in the very public nature of the relationship between the artist and the consumer. Willingly or not, artists have been drawn into public debate over their work and an accountability to the marketplace—whether that marketplace is manifested in the profit or

---

JOAN JEFFRI is the director and founder of the Research Center for Arts and Culture at Columbia University. She is also professor of arts administration and director of the Graduate Program in Arts Administration at Columbia. Professor Jeffri is the author of *Arts Money: Raising It, Saving It, and Earning It* (1989), *The Emerging Arts: Management, Survival and Growth* (1980), and editor of *Artisthelp: The Artists Guide to Work-Related, Human and Social Services* (1990) and numerous studies on artists, including *Information on Artists* and *The Artist's Training and Career Project.* From 1981–1990 she served as an executive editor of the *Journal of Arts Management and Law.* Her first careers were as a poet, with Louis Untermeyer as her mentor, and an actress, appearing in the national tour of *The Homecoming,* in the Boston company of *The Effect of Gamma Rays on Man-in-the-Moon Marigolds,* and with the Lincoln Center Repertory Company in New York City.

nonprofit sector. James Fenimore Cooper lamented that Americans judged sculpture the same way "they evaluated pork, rum, and cotton," and artists, constantly trying to find a way to integrate themselves into the society in which they lived, kept shuttling between the system of private patronage they forswore when leaving England, the great unwashed public, and the world of arts institutions.

It was the artists who "organized the first institution devoted to art." The Columbianum, organized in Philadelphia by Charles Wilson Peale in 1795, began as a cooperative association for shared communication and instruction.[1]

By the time the famous cooperatives of the 1950s were formed on Tenth Street in New York City, artists were still grappling with issues of how to control their own destinies, benefit from a variety of marketplaces, and retain their artistic integrity. By the 1960s, when most of the state arts councils and the National Endowment for the Arts were formed, artists found themselves once again in a central position of authority through the panel review system in which they judged their peers. Added to this element of empowerment, however, were the imposition of government bureaucracy and, just beyond that, a system of taxpayer dollars in which the "public" was somehow invested (if obliquely) in a vote for (or against) art— that same public that Cooper had accused of the pork-rum-and-cotton mentality.

The Artist and the Government

Skipping wildly through history, one is brought up short at several distinct points in America's brief past, when government became the artist's patron and sometimes his or her audience as well. Until the founding of the National Endowment for the Arts (NEA) in 1965, the most outstanding example of government patronage was the Works Progress Administration (WPA) under Franklin Delano Roosevelt. Clearly a welfare relief program, it nevertheless provided some of our most outstanding American artists with a forum and a paycheck. Legendary artists from Jackson Pollock to Orson Welles live on in the memories of those married to the concept of a better lot for artists through government support.

There is no denying that the WPA provided a special opportunity for artists such as Lee J. Cobb, Lee Strasberg, Alice Neel, José de Rivera, Lee Krasner, Mark Rothko, Canada Lee, John Houseman, and Reginald Marsh. Nevertheless, President Roosevelt summed up a major area of difficulty when he said, "There ain't no sich thing as a masterpiece of permanence in the art of living or the art of government."[2] If the New Deal mixed relief with construction projects and aesthetics, it was riddled with an ambivalence about artists that would recur half a century later in the "hearing" of Richard Serra, the Mapplethorpe controversy, and the Serrano affair.

Serra, Mapplethorpe, and Serrano

In 1981 Richard Serra's 120-foot-long, 12-foot-high corten steel *Tilted Arc* was sited in Federal Plaza in New York City. While his work was chosen through the combined efforts of the General Services Administration's (GSA) Art-in-Architecture Program and the NEA, in 1985 regional GSA administrator William J. Diamond held what many regard as an illegal "hearing" resulting in Diamond's decision that the work could be resited or put in storage—a situation the artist said amounted to destruction of his "site-specific" work. In the late 1980s, *Tilted Arc* was removed from the plaza in the middle of the night.

Soon after, the Corcoran Gallery of Art in Washington, D.C., canceled an exhibit of the photographs of Robert Mapplethorpe in an attempt to forestall congressional anger toward the NEA (which funded part of the exhibit through the Institute of Contemporary Art in Philadelphia) because of the exhibit's subject matter. The exhibition, called "The Perfect Moment," met with continued controversy at the Contemporary Arts Center of Cincinnati, where pornography and obscenity charges were brought against the center and its director. This situation was unique, as the police invaded the institution to "examine" seven photographs that the court felt related to the pornography and obscenity charges.

Almost simultaneously, funds regranted from the NEA through the Southeastern Center of Contemporary Art (SECCA) to artist Andres Serrano became the subject of much dispute. Serrano's work *Piss Christ* depicted a figure of Christ on the cross standing in a pool of the artist's urine, a depiction the artist claimed reflected ambivalent feelings about Christianity and religion. While the NEA did not grant funds directly to Serrano, but rather to SECCA, this situation helped to bring the entire process of regranting and peer panel review under fire in discussions that would continue about the eventual continuation or abolition of the NEA.

The Professional Artist

In 1989 the NEA compiled a report called "Artists." Essentially a state-of-the-artist report, it included concerns and observations about the "field" and NEA responses and issues. Extrapolating information from the Bureau of Labor Statistics, the report said that "1,503,000 persons were employed in artist occupations in 1987—an increase of 4.5 percent (about 64,-000 persons) from 1986." While the 1989 report admitted that these figures underestimate the number of "part-time" artists, a 1987 version stated that "most artists cannot make a living practicing their art and must do other work to survive." This conclusion clearly forms one basis of a commonly accepted view of professional artists, defining them by their ability to make a living at their art.

Artists, however, at least in view of recent findings by the Research Center for Arts and Culture at Columbia University, may have a very different view of professionalism. This may be one clue to help us understand the emotionally charged reactions to issues that emerge from some government funded art activities, such as the WPA's black *Macbeth* or Serrano's *Piss Christ*. In 1989 the Research Center conducted the Information on Artists Project, a survey of 9,870 artists from a variety of artistic disciplines culled from different organizational lists in ten U.S. locations—Boston, Cape Cod, Chicago, Dallas, Los

Angeles, Minneapolis/St. Paul, New York City, Philadelphia, San Francisco, and western Massachusetts.[3] The response rate was 42 percent, or 4,134 respondents. Ninety-two percent of these said they considered themselves "professional artists." When the artists were asked the reasons they felt were the most important in considering themselves or others to be a professional artist, the most frequently cited were "an inner drive to make art," the fact that the artist "considered him/herself an artist," and, less frequent than the other two reasons, that "the person makes his/her living as an artist."

For these artists, at least, "employment" or even "making a living" is not the primary issue, either in relation to other artists or in regard to themselves.

The Artist and Earnings

More than 80 percent of the survey respondents said they earned some money from their art. Half of this group said that money earned from art covered their art related expenses, while the other half indicated it did not.

Fifty-five percent of the survey respondents earned $3,000 or less from their work as artists in 1988; 60 percent earned $20,000 or less in total individual gross income, including artist income, in 1988. Findings from a survey of artists conducted in 1986–1987 by economists David Throsby and David Mills for the Australia Council revealed a startlingly similar figure in the area of artist income. (Australia is one of very few countries conducting similar research on artists.) Fifty percent of the Australian artists had earned less than $3,500 from their creative work, while their individual gross income, including artist income, was less than $13,300. According to the reference librarian at the Australian Consulate in New York City, while the general cost of living in the two countries seems about the same (particularly in major cities such as New York and Sydney), Australians have a lower average wage.

More than a quarter of the Information on Artists respondents earned their primary income as artists, and 69 percent in art or art related occupations. More than a quarter earned their primary income in non–art related occupations, and 13 percent responded in the category of "other." (The total of over 100 percent indicates that some people may have answered in more than one category.)

Grants and Awards

For the small number of artists (680, or 16 percent) who answered a question about the amount of artist income that came from grants or awards in 1988, the median amount was $1,500, and the mode (the figure that appeared most often) was $500.

Two other studies in 1986 and 1988 conducted with the New York Foundation for the Arts (NYFA) indicate a similar percentage receiving grants and awards.[4] The mean, or average, grant amount for respondents was $3,690 in the 1986 NYFA survey, $2,433 in the 1988 NYFA survey, and $3,288 in the 1989 Information on Artists survey. Over a three-year period, these figures represent nearly 5,500 artists, 1,374 of them applicants for NYFA fellowships, with 966 reporting some income from grants or awards.

Preliminary research has also been conducted on the importance of grants and awards at various stages of an artist's career. This research has found that the recognition factor from grants and awards has an importance independent of the income. In the Research Center for Arts and Culture's current research on artists, the Artists Training and Career Project, staff members have been conducting personal narrative interviews with thirty-five craftspeople throughout the United States. While this is not a sample on which to base predictions, these interviews reinforce the perception of government grants, particularly grants from the NEA, as providing an imprimatur and a recognition that artists value.

The Isolated Artist

The issue that emerges in many discussions of the artist in America is the perception of the artist as an isolated, and therefore often threatening, being, living according to his own, not society's rules. This, as well as the myth of the artist starving in a garret, is an image that dies hard in the American mind. In *Romantic Image,* critic Frank Kermode speaks of the artist's "cult of isolated joy" through which the artist "excludes society and its half-baked sensibilities" and is then astonished when "society excludes him." Legal educator Howard Lesnick, in the summer 1986 issue of the *Journal of Arts Management and Law,* describes an "alternative consciousness" of work—for artists and other professionals—where the work one does is validated internally as well as externally (not by whether or how much one is paid).

Part of the threat of the isolated artist comes from that very narrow world the artist has constructed, perhaps for his own protection. Carol Becker, chair of the Graduate Division of the School of the Art Institute of Chicago, describes this situation.

Artists increasingly locate themselves not within a general historical context, but within a privileged dialogue within their own history. Their art refers to art which came before, and the art world has become increasingly hermetic, its discourse incomprehensible to those outside its closed system.[5]

The Artist and the Public

Becker's view is not a view for the 1990s. As Arthur Danto recently explained in "From Pollock to Mapplethorpe: The Media and the Artworld," art has suddenly "gone public." The days when only a select handful of experts dictated art are over.[6] In previous times, writes Danto, "an informal tribunal of persons for whom art matters" decided such questions as "what art is and when art is great and what constitutes a breakthrough." These were matters of continuing discussion and argument. Now, however, a new environment prevails. Museums, which once served to uplift and enlighten the public, even acting as second universities, are the new singles bars; and the government, followed by other funders, has bought into the "numbers game" in which it no longer matters how many angels have danced on the head of a pin, but how many documented pairs of feet we can claim in exhibit attendance. (As controversial as all the newspaper articles on Mapplethorpe were, they frequently mentioned the increase in attendance and memberships at the Cincinnati Contemporary Arts Center.) From the Brooklyn Academy of Music's Next Wave, to the L.A. Festival, and various counterparts in between, what Danto calls "ordinary persons" have "crossed the threshold" into the art experience.

The newly public nature of many of these kinds of art, faced with these eminently countable ordinary persons, has made the artist appear not just isolated or excluded but—in the minds of some people—dangerous. When Danto warns that the art world "faces the rest of life" at "the borderline between art and life," we see a new set of guideposts. This contemporary signage pushes the intensely private up against the intensely public in a way that is difficult for the new ordinary audience to assimilate. The intersection of *Tilted Arc* and Federal Plaza becomes, then, a kind of double rape—first, that of the artist making the people face their own barren environment, and second, the rape of the artist by that very same public. From Serra to Mapplethorpe is merely a change in medium, not method.

In fact, from Serra to Mapplethorpe is a kind of paradigm of abstraction turned concrete. The first question, raised by Serra himself in a Columbia Business School class in 1980, is "what makes public art public?" Is it because it is in a public space; because it is accessible to the public; because it is paid for by the public, usually through taxpayer dollars; because the notion of "public spiritedness" is something we all supposedly share?

In relation to each of these possibilities, we should realize that (1) the nature of public space has changed considerably from the town square or plaza to what Patricia Phillips calls "the socially acceptable euphemism used to describe the area that developers have 'left over,' the only 'negotiable' space after all of their available commercial and residential space has been rented or sold"; (2) access does not simply mean availa-

bility or even proximity of art to the public; (3) civic and private interests have long supported the kinds of public monuments that formed the history but not the model for current
public art; and (4) while many communities have managed to
put in place a process of democratic committees in regard to
the selection of public art, this does not imply sanction by or
even awareness on the part of the "collective citizenry."[7]

Even if we cannot agree on a definition, we realize that public art—like all art—presents certain moral issues. In 1982 two
philosophy professors, Douglas Stalker and Clark Glymour,
branded public art "the malignant object" in the journal *The
Public Interest*. Outraged by the offensiveness, harm, insult, and
humiliation of certain public art, Stalker and Glymour drew an
analogy with pornography that, more than half a decade later,
would help to threaten the very existence of the NEA. They
went so far as to suggest the creation of special zoning regulations for public art—the "red light" district for sculptural activities, so to speak.

Among those who disagreed with Stalker and Glymour was a
professor from the Minneapolis College of Art and Design,
Edward Levine, who touched upon the themes of artistic isola-
tion and public involvement.

There is a sense in which artists are not prepared for working within
the public domain. The work of most artists within this arena is actually art made public, which we can distinguish from public art, in
which the artist's intention was to take into account the restraints of
both the environment and the people who use a particular location.
Artists have, for the most part, been isolated in their studios both as a
result of the nature of their activity and the social situation in which
they find themselves.[8]

Even this situation has changed drastically in the last several
years, so that even primarily mainstream artists are doing artwork

on billboards, subway and bus posters, with public slide and film
projections, in banks, schools, and union halls. Artists are performing
in hospitals near senior citizens' homes as well as in the streets and at
demonstrations. Many of them are learning to adapt their work to

different contexts just as they would make alterations for different mediums.[9]

Supporting this view are many successful projects in the public art arena—from Nancy Holt's revitalization of park areas and a New Jersey landfill to Suzanne Lacy's "Whisper Minnesota Project," a performance piece focused on older women, that garnered the support of organizations throughout Minnesota involved in aging, the arts, education, and feminist theatre.

Public art and artists have not been left only to the public sector. Some of the most successful examples of public art in terms of visibility have been those of corporations. Pepsico's sculpture garden is famous in Westchester, New York, and beyond. Several years ago, the real estate firm of Olympia and York hired Anita Contini away from her own alternative space to run a newly created arts and events department; the public art Contini organizes for Olympia and York's Battery Park development projects in New York City is seen as part of the promotion package for the corporation. The artist Christo formed his own corporation and considers his method of negotiating as well as financing projects such as *Running Fence* along the California coast an integral part of the public nature of his art.

At 59th Street and the Hudson River, New York artist Mierle Laderman Ukeles is constructing a walk-through installation at the city's new Marine Transfer Facility. Ukeles has found an interesting way to deal with garbage. Her unique view of her work, combined with the implementation of her vision in the artistic process, makes this public art with a difference.

For Ukeles, public art is a unique form to examine the relationship of public life, civic action, and the modern systems that shape our collective culture. Ukeles has radically redefined public art, but not simply in order to expand the realm of the esthetic. For her, public art provides a unique position from which to forge connections between the public sphere and the private, and to show that public life is more a matter of routine activities than dramatic events. What her work does best is to challenge the whole notion of public art, to contest our limited conception of art's place in the world.[10]

Connections, such as those made by Ukeles, between public
and private, and between artist and audience, point to a shared
activity that Suzanne Lacy, in her article "Fractured Space,"
calls "meaning-making."[11] This is difficult when the audience
includes the artist's patron, but when that patron is the government, such "meaning-making" smacks of policy. Indeed,
since 1971 the NEA and the General Services Administration's
Art-in-Architecture Program have been developing both policy and programs for public art. In doing so, they have fulfilled
the NEA's original legislative mandates of broad impact and
dissemination—often beyond their wildest dreams. This wide
"reach" is particularly important when it involves audiences
that are traditionally considered nonmainstream, especially
since their populations are increasing rapidly in communities
throughout the United States.

Outreach to such nonmainstream audiences often brings
with it attention to the themes that permeate those audience's
lives. These themes and the ways they are handled by "public"
artists once again create situations that may be inherently political and controversial. In Arlene Raven's 1989 book *Art in the
Public Interest,* art critic Lucy Lippard tells the story of artists
David Avalos, Louis Hock, and Elizabeth Sisco who, in January
1988, took advantage of Super Bowl month in San Diego and
predictions that the tourist population would reach 80,000. In
a project partly funded by public money, they created a
21″ × 72″ poster entitled *Welcome to America's Finest Tourist Plan-
tation,* playing on some signage welcoming tourists to the city.
The poster, which displayed a photomontage including a
handcuffed illegal alien and hands scraping a dirty dish near a
hotel/motel room door, received a special citation from the
Mexican American Business and Professional Association for
raising the community's consciousness about "undocumented
workers." What followed were outrage, explorations of the
appropriateness of "public funding," and a potential censorship case (found legally unsupportable by an appellate court
ruling).

There are numerous issues to explore, even in this brief
overview of the situation, and some have specific implications

for the current funding environment for artists in the United States. First, the artwork was done in a medium that is accessible to the general public and also an instrument of business: the advertising poster. Second, the intersection and resulting confusion of art, politics, advertising, business, and government stirred up many of the same responses that cases such as those focused on Serrano and Mapplethorpe engendered. Third, the combination of theme and medium, as well as distribution on buses around the city, allowed the poster to reach a substantial San Diego public (including a number of the illegal workers who had served as partial subject matter for the work), thereby fulfilling the NEA's mandate to cultivate new audiences. For the artists, "new audiences" also meant people outside the traditional museum/gallery experience. After the initial project, the poster was shown in a number of gallery situations, either framed in gold or crumpled in a garbage can, accompanied by a full spectrum of art world media coverage.

Clearly, Avalos, Hock, and Sisco are dealing with the very public nature of public art that provokes vision as well as thought and attempts to help its audience to see with new eyes. Whether through this example, or Judy Chicago's "Birth Project," which pulled together women from communities across the world to weave their stories into art, or the AIDS Quilt, commemorating our nation's continuing loss through the age-old format of storytelling-through-handwork, it is clear that the artist is only one part of the equation. The "meaning-making" must involve the artist's vision through others.

It is important at this juncture in history that we recognize both the nature of the partnerships that have developed since the creation of a system of government funding that exists at the national, state, and local levels and the responsibility of all the partners—whether public, private, or artistic—to enter into a relationship of mutual accountability. If public art is, as Mierle Ukeles once said, our "possession-in-common," we must engage in its protection together.

The Artist and the Institution

Up to this point, we have been speaking of artists who work in public art as an illustration of new realities for artists in the 1990s. Such an illustration focuses on the independent artist, and we must also consider the position and concerns of the artist working in institutions of art and culture.[12]

While artist-run groups, many of which formed in the 1960s, are only now beginning to mature, more traditional institutions of high art have had a difficult time responding to the demands of living artists. While the Vietnam-era protests at the Museum of Modern Art (MoMA) in New York City resulted in unionization at MoMA and some similar outcomes at other institutions, in the 1990s too many of these institutions view artists as part of their inventory but not their constituency. In music, while many major symphony orchestras have bowed to artists' demands for board or special committee representation, in Seattle the musicians' solution was to form a new union to represent their needs. In theater, as many off-Broadway, off-off-Broadway, university theaters, and a variety of other companies become the somewhat incestuous breeding ground for a handful of Broadway producers, and the regional theater movement meets middle age, we find many artistic directors astonished that they have become part of the Establishment, still bereft of full-time companies, with actors who cannot earn decent livings or be nurtured in ways that the hopes of the 1960s somehow led them to believe they deserved. As these newly Establishment institutions grow more like businesses, increasingly they follow a corporate model, where the boards of directors choose to learn more about marketing and the bottom line and little, if anything, about artistic vision.

Also often missing is a relationship between institutions and their communities, in which artists are seen as an integral part of the development of both. While some community arts activity may be reappearing in the guise of multiculturalism, too many institutions have dropped programs for artists that were community oriented and community based.

Some institutions have formed a relationship with a commu-

nity arts council or a local arts and cultural agency that, often
in return for free office space, deals with living artists. In the
visual arts, a new opportunity has created additional confusion. The growth of the contemporary arts center has posi-
tioned the artist somewhere between the commercial gallery
and the museum. The possible result is that the work will neither sell nor be taken seriously because such organizations
generally are not organized to sell the art, nor are they perceived as carrying the educational mandate of the museum
(though many centers might argue differently). In a sense, we
have ghettoized the living artists into a limbo-like position
where he or she is *of* an institution without being *in* it.

The funding institution is another obstacle for the artist.
Notoriously terrified of living, breathing artists besmirching
their splendid offices, these institutions develop buffer systems
to validate and determine recipients of their money. It is an art
world legend that MacArthur Foundation grantees are picked
by consultants around the country who, if their identities are
revealed, will no longer be consultants. One justification for
the funding agency's fear is the difficulty in choosing between
quality and need in the arts. Franklin Delano Roosevelt saw
this dilemma during the WPA years and chose to throw his
weight behind the work and the administrative structures for
the work, while firmly refusing to institutionalize art as a function of government.

Of course, the good bureaucrat will state that it would be
impossible for an agency such as the NEA, for example, to
fund directly individual artists from all over the country. (Not
since the days of W. McNeil Lowry at the Ford Foundation
have we seen major funding agencies invest significantly in the
quality and the risk of potential artistic leaders.) The National
Endowment for the Humanities funds hundreds of scholars,
teachers, and researchers through the educational systems of
many different levels of school, up to and including the university. School, however, is an institution we all hold in common,
something many in this country are convinced is a societal
necessity. The system of arts institutions, on the other hand, is
no system at all. With all the discipline-specific service organi-

zations, the ad hoc advocacy groups, and the small, medium, and large organizations in each field in every state and city, neither consensus nor common cause exists to indicate a sense of unity the public can perceive as directed, valuable, and whole. Even when artists take matters into their own hands, as they did with faxes, letters, and communication through the National Association of Artist-Run Organizations to protest Senator Jesse Helms's proposed new "obscenity amendment" to the NEA's legislation, they are relatively powerless.

Some agencies do make artists their primary business. In the past, rare private patrons such as Gertrude Vanderbilt Whitney championed the artist's cause. Today, many organizations that do the same are run by former artists. Both public and private, these organizations find a way to take the system in their grasp and act as facilitators between the bureaucracy and the artist—for which they are thanked only part of the time by both sides. Part of this thanklessness results from the basic fact that handling individuals on a one-by-one basis is frustrating, time-consuming, often inefficient, and frequently unproductive, especially when the funding agency's mandates from its own sponsors include increasing the number of clients, the variety of activities, and the reach of services.

The Artist's Rights

Although much recent discussion has focused on the particular funding system that should or should not fund controversial art, a legal system of protection exists that offers both hope and despair to the artist in the United States. Unlike many of their European colleagues, U.S. artists do not have a federal law that protects their moral rights—the rights considered personal to the artists in regard to their work. Sixty-three countries have some variation of moral rights, or *droit moral,* legislation, and a number of international conventions and tribunals deal with issues of literary property.

While a handful of states, including New York through its Artists' Authorship Rights Act and California through its Art Preservation Act, have laws that include provisions similar to the European rights of integrity, paternity, and publication, there is still no protection in the United States against destruction of art. The U.S. view, through both these state laws and federal copyright, is of art as the property of its owner, subject to the care or neglect of that owner.

In addition to *droit moral,* other European legislation that has served as a model for U.S. artists is the *droit de suite.* While the performing arts unions have long provided for American performers to realize royalty and residual payments for repeated use of their work, visual artists have looked to the *droit de suite* as their model for repeated sales of their work. The California Resale Royalty Act was the first U.S. attempt to provide royalty payments to visual artists on sales subsequent to the initial sale of a work of visual art. Since this law was limited to the state of California, there have been substantial monitoring problems. Purchases are often made out of state; there is no respected monitoring agency such as the American Society of Composers, Authors, and Publishers (ASCAP) or Broadcast Music Incorporated (BMI). The provision for the contribution of the artist's royalty to the state arts council if the artist cannot be located within a specified period of time has created certain suspicions, and the complaint has been made that the Resale Royalty Act serves as a disincentive for buyers of the work of emerging artists—the very constituency for which the law was first created.

Another model often cited by American writers is the British Public Lending Right, which charges and redirects authors' royalties back to the authors each time a book is borrowed from a British library. While the concept is supported by the Authors Guild in the United States, the lending right seems important in a symbolic rather than an economic way, especially since the financial returns tend to be modest.

Senator Edward Kennedy proposed a bill several years ago that recommended legislation for artists' resale rights on a national level, but substantial criticism has prevented the bill from moving forward. Nations that have enacted legislation for such rights are: Algeria, Belgium, Brazil, Chile, Congo, Costa Rica, Czechoslovakia, East Germany, Ecuador, France,

Guinea, Hungary, Italy, Ivory Coast, Luxembourg, Madagascar, Mali, Morocco, Peru, Philippines, Portugal, Senegal, Spain, Tunisia, Turkey, Uruguay, West Germany, and Yugoslavia.[13]

Despite the very real protection provided by the copyright law and, particularly, these other emerging types of protection, the legal system cannot force artists either to be aware of or to use such provisions. In the Information on Artists Project, only 44 percent of the respondents said they held copyright on some artistic work of their own creation; 11 percent said they did not know if they held any such copyright. These statistics are sobering, considering that a portion of the respondents were performers who may have no cause to copyright work and that 16 percent felt that copyright was the most important legal area in which advice would be helpful to them in their work as artists.

How the Artist Survives

The figures given in this section illustrate the kinds of grant amounts artists are likely to receive, at least according to the most recent artist surveys. These figures, which range between $2,433 and $3,690 for an *average* grant or award, are noteworthy because they represent artists in New York City's five boroughs, in New York State's counties outside these five boroughs, in cities with a reputation at the time of the survey for being extremely supportive of artists (Minneapolis/St. Paul, San Francisco, and Boston), in rural areas (Cape Cod, western Massachusetts) as well as urban ones, in cities with little artist support (Dallas), and in cities with a reputation for grassroots community development (Chicago) and for making the funding community attend to the needs of artists (Philadelphia). They also represent artists from cities oriented to the commercial as well as the nonprofit marketplace (Los Angeles and New York).

The figures also should be balanced with what we know about artists' incomes from their art. In the responses from the New York surveys and the ten-site Information on Artists Project, we find the following data.

Survey Locale and Year	% of Respondents	Income from Art
New York State 1986	42	$ 0– 2,000
	24	2,001– 6,000
	22	6,001–20,000
	8	over 20,000
New York State outside	52	0– 2,000
five boroughs 1988	18	2,001– 6,000
	20	6,001–20,000
	12	over 20,000

In the Information on Artists survey, income amounts were divided slightly differently and revealed the following.

Survey Locale and Year	% of Respondents	Income from Art
10 U.S. locations 1990	54	$ 0– 3,000
	14	3,001– 7,000
	21	7,001–20,000
	10	20,001–40,000
	4	over 40,000

(Note: in some cases percentages add up to more than 100 because of rounding errors.)

In the ten-site survey, 158, or one in twenty-four, of the 3,892 artists who answered this question earned more than $40,000 from their art in 1988. Forty-eight percent of the respondents earned over $20,000 individual gross income from all sources in 1988, including their work as artists.

Statistics such as these make those who criticize the NEA as a "welfare scheme for artists" rub their hands together in anticipatory glee as they place the contemporary artist (or at least the contemporary *surveyed* artist) squarely in the middle class. Survival, of course, depends on more than income. The Information on Artists Project explored other issues to gain a fuller understanding of artists' survival.

Education

The artists in this survey were highly educated, and 63 percent said they received at least some of their art related training in the city or region of the survey. Sixty-eight percent had a formal degree in the arts; 25 percent had conservatory or professional school training; 42 percent had experience with a mentor or master artist and 41 percent with private teachers. Forty-two percent had a college degree and 38 percent a graduate degree.

Location

Among the most important reasons for artists to stay in their city or region were personal ties (63 percent), cultural activity (51 percent), network of peers (44 percent), and support systems for their art (40 percent).

Workspace

Fifty-one percent of respondents had been forced to move their workspace within the last five years; 51 percent of these said this had happened more than once. Twenty-six percent had to move because that workspace became unaffordable, and 20 percent because it became unavailable.

Health Care

While 82 percent of respondents had some health or medical coverage, 51 percent had been exposed to occupational hazards in their art related work. For 51 percent, this was an "ongoing condition"; 60 percent engaged in preventive medical care in relation to their art work.

Other Benefits

Forty-four percent had life insurance; 43 percent had at least one retirement plan. The median age for survey respondents was 37.

The Future

Just as the federal government has granted exemption from federal income tax to charitable, religious, and other nonprofit organizations, including those in the arts and culture, in exchange for attending to the public welfare in ways in which the government clearly does not wish to attend, so U.S. society has used its artists. Artists, especially in contemporary times, have provided the social glue that has made many cities centers of culture and tourism. They have become the downtown redevelopers, the urban beautifiers, the community organizers, the volunteers for causes from the disabled to AIDS. They have worked in schools, hospitals, prisons, and the streets. They have brought their talents and their work to benefit the illiterate, the homeless, the undocumented, and the poor, as well as the middle and upper classes. They have helped each other through foundations, such as those set up by artists Robert Rauschenberg, Lee Krasner, Adolph Gottlieb, Andy Warhol, and—yes—Robert Mapplethorpe.

These are not only artists who work in the nonprofit sector or who do "arts related" work. These are the actors who do Broadway benefits, the musicians for Live Aid, the movie stars who act as foster parents, the clowns who play for the aged and the infirm, and those involved in prison drama, art therapy, and music instruction.

If the myth of the isolated artist dies hard, it remains equally difficult to accept the artist as an integrated member of society. While this chapter has not dealt with the complex and important issue of the artist's interaction with the marketplace, the government's response to recent controversies could result in what sociologists call "goal displacement"—a strategy to reach goals that are pursued because they are attainable even though they may be inappropriate to the problem. Thus, for example, to disband the NEA or to eliminate public grants to artists and openly throw artists back into the marketplace does not address the goal of a better way to support artists in the United States.[14]

In the recent panic over government and the arts, once again artists themselves have begun to search for answers. In a system that has called on them from the beginning for direction and peer review, they have moved from press releases to advocacy actions to new potential solutions. One suggestion made by recent recipients of performance art grants, who learned that a number of their colleagues had their proposals rejected by the National Council after acceptance by a peer review panel, was to distribute portions of their own NEA grants to those very same colleagues. Another idea was for those "rejected" artists to engage in some broad political theater of their own by taking their acts on the road and billing themselves as "spurned by the NEA."

Conclusion

In sum, artists are the integrators of our society. From their earliest days of self-governance including cooperatives, collaboratives, ensembles, and organizations, they have been both an inspiration and a threat. Illustrating the very principles of democracy, they have depended not only on the kindness of strangers, like Tennessee Williams's Blanche DuBois, but on the kindness—and the fickleness—of patrons, including the government.

It is the very public nature of their work that causes it to be in our interest to recognize their contribution to the fabric of American society—from historical statues to the Lincoln Memorial to *Tilted Arc,* from the Federal Theatre Project to Margo Jones's Dallas '47 theater to a system of regional theaters in communities across the nation, from Henry Higginson's Boston Symphony Orchestra to hundreds of chamber music societies to Lincoln Center Out-of-Doors.

What is the best way to nurture our artists so that they continue to provide the social glue we need to bind us together, to question ourselves in new ways, to find not just leisure but experience, not just knowledge but joy? In Japan, special master artists are designated national treasures and encouraged to take their special talents around the country and pass on their artistic traditions. In Serbia, certain designated artists can receive special pensions. Other countries provide artists with special rights to "social insurance" allowing them access to health coverage for disability and old age as well as reduced taxes. What system or systems should we have to recognize and protect, on a regular, continuing basis, artists' contributions to our collective welfare?

Notes

[1] Harris (1966), pp. 100, 91.

[2] Quoted from Roosevelt to Bruce, October 9, 1941, AAA Reel NDA/TIPI in McKinzie (1973), p. 189.

[3] All information about this study comes from the database and report on Information on Artists of the Research Center for Arts and Culture (1989), Columbia University.

[4] All information about these studies comes from the databases and reports of the Research Center for Arts and Culture (1986 and 1988), Columbia University. More detailed information can be obtained directly from the Center.

[5] Becker (1989), p. 247.

[6] Danto (1990), p. 16.

[7] Phillips (1988), p. 93.

[8] Levine (1982), p. 31.

[9] Lippard (1989), p. 210.

[10] Phillips (1989), p. 51.

[11] Lacy (1989), p. 299.

[12] It should be understood that, due to length limitations for this chapter, a small number of artistic disciplines have been used to illustrate a variety of points. This inclusion should not be taken to mean that disciplines not mentioned here are in any way less important or less relevant to the case being made.

[13] Kernochan (1989), p. 1433.

[14] While it is expected that private sources would continue to fund artists in such a case, it is unclear how important the NEA imprimatur is to some of these sources and how they would behave.

4

More than Minor Disturbances: The Place of the Arts in American Education

DENNIE PALMER WOLF
AND MARY BURGER

Introduction

I n the fall of 1990, in Cincinnati, eight jurors decided—at least until they are challenged—where the border between

DENNIE PALMER WOLF is senior research associate, Harvard Graduate School of Education, and director of the National Center for Diversified Learning and Assessment. Dr. Wolf is principal investigator on Projects in Language Development, a program project for the National Institute of Health aimed at developing expanded and more authentic forms of language assessment in children. She has also been the director of ARTS PROPEL, an innovative, five-year project developing performance assessments in the arts and humanities. Dr. Wolf serves as editor of a College Board series of books on assessing thoughtfulness in high school classrooms, and is the author of numerous scholarly articles, monographs, and books, including *Academic Preparation in the Arts; Reading Reconsidered: Literacy and Literature in High School; Taking Full Measure: Learning and Assessment in the Arts; Practices of Thought: Re-Making Learning, Teaching, and Assessment;* and *Habits of Mind: Performances of Thought.*
MARY BURGER is a research assistant at the Harvard Graduate School of Education who has done graduate work in women's studies,

art and obscenity lies. For many, the questions at stake were the First Amendment rights of artists, the survival of the National Endowment for the Arts, the nature of community standards for pornography, and the question of whether the United States will become a nation that sustains only an orthodox and official art, not a live culture.

The opening days of the trial, particularly the process of jury selection, carried a further lesson:

Eight jurors and one or two alternates are to be selected from among 50 prospective jurors. The questioning so far indicates that few of them know or care much about art, and most are deeply religious and strongly object to pornography and homosexuality. . . . Of the eight men and women questioned so far by the prosecution . . . only three had ever been to an art museum. Others said they had gone to other types of museums, but only on field trips from school. One man in his 50's said he had never been to any kind of museum. The man said he could not relate either to art or its enthusiasts. "They're into that type of stuff," he said during questioning by a defense lawyer, Marc D. Mezibov. "These people are in a different class. Evidently they get some type of satisfaction looking at it. I don't understand art work. That stuff never interested me."[1]

The lesson of this testament is that we are a nation without effective arts education. The major conduit for public arts education, the public schools, do not—at present—educate a population of adults who know or care about art. So much is this the case that the prosecuting attorneys in Cincinnati knew that the forced marches of school field trips to museums do not count. The people they wanted to keep out of the courtroom were adults who draw, collect, or go to museums—anyone who might understand art as invention rather than report, who

studying feminist periodicals in England, the Netherlands, West Germany, and Yugoslavia. The preparation of this chapter was made possible by a grant from the Rockefeller Foundation and conversations with the authors' colleagues willing to share expertise: Nancy Smith, Steve Seidel, Kate Wilson, Connie Wolf, and Tom Wolf. The final recommendations were taken from an earlier task force report prepared in July 1990 for the National Endowment for the Arts.

might argue that the seven offending photographs were part of a larger body of work, or who (along with Goya, Twyla Tharp, or Cynthia Ozick) might understand that to exhibit is not to endorse, but to invite response. But the attorneys can rest assured—at most, only three out of fifty Americans are that dangerous.

Both history and the current practices that are its legacy have a role in the marginal place of the arts in school, and consequently, in public life. Since their first appearance in the curriculum of the comprehensive school in the mid-nineteenth century, the arts have begged and borrowed a place on the ironic condition that they civilize, teach industrially relevant skills, or install the invention and spunk so valued at the patent office. There is, essentially, an unspoken contract—there will be arts in the schools so long as they behave as no more than minor disturbances.

But in the last two decades, across the fields of science, psychology, and the humanities, there has emerged a view of human cognition that values imagery, representation, and a capacity for what might be called possible or multiple worlds. Out of this new view of human capacity have come many insights, not the least of which is the understanding that the arts are not just crafts, or visions, but powerful *ways of knowing and working.* The evidence is everywhere: in the investigatory nature of sketchbooks, the careful experiments with solarized film and crackle glazes, and the rigorous assessments that occur in rehearsals and in the preparation of portfolios. Out of these realizations are emerging new, and radically different, forms of art education. Rather than job training or moral education, these new forms are essentially apprenticeships in the challenging ideas and rigorous practices that adult artists and audience members pursue.

In other words, at the moment there is at least the possibility that art education could become vigorous. But with that vigor comes danger. If students engage in the arts as serious apprentices they will push beyond the safe matters of "balance," "harmony," "design," and "beauty." Questions will erupt about the hegemony of Western art and its canons; gender, body image, and exploitation; race, marginality, and identity. Moreover, if arts education were to become serious, it would be disruptive. It would push for its fair share: full-time arts teachers, studio-length periods rather than parcels of forty minutes, the right to move out of classrooms into concert halls, museums, and the streets, where public art appears. And finally, such arts education would raise questions about the status quo in other areas of education: questions about the need for problem finding rather than problem sets, long-term projects rather than daily assignments, and portfolios and performance assessments rather than standardized tests as indices of learning.

But these kinds of vigor—and danger—are unlikely to be ours unless we understand and undo much that continues to fetter arts education to an older, cramped history: notably its forced alliance with industrial education or its domestication into "appreciation." Moreover, unless we protect arts education from a marginal position in the curriculum and meager funding, it will stay a minor disturbance. And we can look forward to a long, vacant future where only three of fifty citizens think about visual art as anything different from magazine illustration, or exhibitions as distinct from endorsements.

The Emergence of the Arts as Ways of Knowing

We have suggested that arts educators have recently begun to challenge what may have been a too simple, handmaiden role for the arts in education. Educators now argue that the arts are viable, and indispensable, *ways of knowing, contributing to, and participating in a culture.* It is important to explore both how novel and how vulnerable this viewpoint is.

The Arts Enter the Common Curriculum: Values and Skills

[Good music tends] to improve the heart, and thus to be instrumental in promoting the cause of human happiness, virtue, and religion.— Lowell Mason, *Manual of the Boston Academy of Music,* 1843.[2]

In the late nineteenth century, American politicians and tax-payers at last took on large-scale social responsibilities: caring for the sick, attending to the mentally insane, offering services to the poor, and providing public education to all children, not just the well-to-do and willing. Within that framework, public schools were conceived and designed as an organized effort to cope with a pressing social problem: an ethnically and economically diverse population of unemployed and poten-tially unemployable youth all too likely to become a drain on other social institutions, such as hospitals and poorhouses. Together with the order of a scheduled class day, the curricu-lum was envisioned as a way to socialize a heterogeneous pop-ulation and to transform those students into the scribes, clerks, and workers demanded by an increasingly standardized and parceled form of industrial or bureaucratic work. Ulti-mately the curriculum was shaped by several competing rheto-rics. On the one hand, there was the ennobling amalgam of the Jeffersonian ideal of a wise and literate electorate, and the tough Jacksonian myth of access for all (meaning hard-work-ing white boys with the mettle of a Lincoln, an Edison, or a Horatio Alger). This was counterbalanced by a determination to found and run an efficient social institution that would turn out civil, reliable, and skilled workers for offices and factories. It is in this crucible that American public education, and with it, arts education, took its original shape.

What issued forth was a line of argument about the place of the arts: not as culture or knowledge, but as carriers of moral values. Schools, and arts education as a curricular tool, were to be institutions of Americanization; they were to help immi-grant children shed feudal and class-riddled values they brought with them, along with their strange last names. Mass-produced sets of artists' reproductions were sold as sets to the schools, accompanied by manuals instructing teachers how to use the images and their implied narratives to teach the worth of hard work, struggle, perseverance, and the greatness of the emerging American culture. One such card suggests that, using a portrait of a peasant girl, teachers should instruct chil-dren:

... the peasants in Europe are very poor. That is why so many of them like to come to our country. . . . Think how many things you have to be thankful for, to which those peasant children are not born! Do you believe you are grateful enough for having been born in so glorious a country as the United States, where the best in education and art, as well as freedom of life and thought, is the birthright of all her sons and daughters? If you have not begun to express your gratitude and show your love for your country, begin today, and you will grow up to be a better citizen, a credit to your native land, and a help to your fellow-men.

As the American economy went from predominantly agrarian to industrial, educators promoted the vocational side of arts training. As early as the 1840s, Horace Mann argued the practicality of taking up pencil and learning to draw. He stressed the link to elegant and neat handwriting, sharp and objective perception, and especially, industry:

No artisan, in any department of mechanical labor, would fail to reap the advantage of knowing how to draw accurately. Cabinet makers constantly import patterns for new furniture at considerable expense, and even the silver-smith and calico-printer are dependent upon drawings for their improvements in fashions. . . . If the subject of drawing were made an item of public instruction, young people would go forth from the schools partly prepared for entering into the various mechanical trades.[3]

In 1870 Walter Smith, an English art teacher and headmaster, came to Boston to fill the position of state art director. He insisted: "Experience has proved that the surest way of elevating public taste and improving all manufacturing industries is to educate all people in the elements of art and science . . ." and "that the mental habit of scientific accuracy . . . will be of social advantage."[4] The result was a method: practicing isolated elements of design (the curves, symmetrical bursts, and bandings present in fabric, brick ornament, and wallpaper) repetitively until they achieved an utter dependability. In this context, arts educators struggled to emulate manufacturers, by finding basic elements of instruction, routine practices, and modules of activity that resembled the "scientific" and "efficient" work patterns being developed concurrently in factories and municipal bureaucracies.

With the rise of public schools there developed a new market—the production of pupil texts and teachers' materials. Methods and their accompanying materials, like those developed by Smith and Von Rydingsvard, appeared, competed hard with one another, and filled classrooms. In effect, they served to spread a view of learning as the partitioned and highly rationalized acquisition of a series of separable skills. In arts curricula, the hallmarks were the lists of *the* elements of design or *the* components of music, along with the accompanying exercises constructed solely to highlight quarter-note rests or visual balance—as if rests were not a tool in creating an entire rhythmic pattern underscoring a melodic line.

On American soil, the arts were to be reborn as practical and as publicly available. Learning to draw or sing or act was a skill well within the compass of any interested individual who was willing to move through a series of graded exercises persistently: Gladstone's 1847 edition of *The American Drawing Book* opened with the promise that "anyone who can learn to write can learn to draw."[5] Connoisseurship became picture study. Thus at the turn of the century the arts became part of the common curriculum of the public schools. The power of this event was that the arts, as a kind of skills capital, were given a place in the curriculum at all. But the bargain had its Faustian side. The arts became part of common schooling—but with a consequent loss of their distinctiveness as a form of knowledge and as a set of practices. Access and inclusion in the school world meant that the arts, just like arithmetic or history, succumbed to an exercise-driven approach to instruction that gives us, to this day, art and music textbooks with numbered objectives, materials needed, and time required printed at the top and exercises at the close of each lesson, instead of the more authentic, full-scale problems and projects characteristic of artists or composers, dancers, or set designers.[6]

The Faustian bargain between morality or industriousness and the arts is neither quaint nor antique. High on a wall in a high school art studio, more than a hundred years after Walter

Smith's heyday, there hangs this list of the criteria on which student work will be evaluated:

1. Work is turned in complete and on time.
2. Work is neat.
3. Workspace and materials have been taken care of.
4. The student has cooperated with others.
5. The student shows evidence of having tried the techniques and problems that were introduced.
6. Work is original.

With the possible exception of the very last item, these are characteristics that a supervisor could use in an electronics components assembly line or for training candidates in an insurance firm. There is nothing here that argues that artwork demands attention to specific or unique dimensions of process or outcome. There is no call for invention, for the handsomeness of craft, or for resonant meanings.

All the same, it is all too easy to deride the industrial model of arts education and to vilify its originators. Without the bargain they struck and lived by, it is unlikely that the arts would have become even a tentative part of our definition of common schooling. In all probability the arts would have stayed where they were centuries before: in the private preserve of those who had leisure enough for trips to paint watercolors of the Italian ruins and money enough for a spinet in the sitting room.

Arts Education as a School for Creativity

From Romantic artists and philosophers, like Wordsworth, Ruskin, and Hegel, arts educators inherited an image of art quite different from Mason's virtuous psalms or Von Rydingsvard's moral lessons. In the Romantic view, the arts were first and foremost the result of individual acts of imagination—not of literal perception, conventional practice, or the internaliza-

tion of community values. The painting or the poem was virtually the antithesis of industrial craft—it was, in Wordsworth's
phrase, "the spontaneous overflow of strong feeling." Drawing on these ideas and the work of Transcendentalist philosophy, arts education in early twentieth-century America was
slowly transformed from industrious practice to an occasion
for the spiritual experience of beauty and the sublime. Thinkers like Emerson and Thoreau, increasingly repulsed by the
rapidly industrialized landscape, the pursuit of material
wealth, and the rancorous divisions between rich and poor,
urged a return to nature and a refuge in art and craft. In this
context, William Torrey Harris, an American disciple of Ruskin, writing at the turn of the century, argued for the ennobling effects of learning to draw:

The object of art education in the school is to develop in the pupil a
love for beauty and the power to produce beautiful things. Without
this love and power, man is dead to the beauty in his environment. To
speak more specifically, we should teach pictorial representation for
three distinct purposes: First, that we may be able to portray clearly
and intelligently on paper things that can be better presented to the
mind through the eye. . . . Second, we teach drawing that we may be
able to obtain keener perceptions of the beauties of nature, and that
we may preserve what Mr. Ruskin calls true images of beautiful things
that pass away. . . . Third, we teach pictorial representation in order—
and here I am expressing Mr. Ruskin's ideas as nearly as I can recall
his words—that we may understand the minds of great painters and
be able to appreciate their work sincerely.[7]

Just over the cusp of the twentieth century, larger artistic
and intellectual developments contributed to a major shift in
arts education. The invention and rapid spread of photogra-
phy removed the obligation for the visual arts to produce reliable records of faces or of battlefields. Freud and Jung forced
attention toward the recognition of an inner, subjective reality.
Similarly, the emerging work of anthropologists argued that
there might be equally powerful visions and cultures outside
of Vienna, Berlin, Paris, or New York. Scientific work on the
structure of matter and the nature of perception began to hint
at structures in the physical and physiological worlds that were

present and powerful, but imperceptible to ordinary sight or hearing. The arts themselves were marked by the interest in radical invention and self-expression evident in the work of Steiglitz, O'Keefe, and Graham.

Stirred by evolutionary theory and social Darwinism, there was also an interest in origins: ancient cultures, primitive societies, regressed states, and, simultaneously, childhood. G. Stanley Hall, writing in America at the turn of the century, developed a thesis that argued that "ontogeny recapitulates phylogeny"—the life span of the individual repeats the stages through which the species evolved. Insight into the early ages of civilization could be had by studying the development of children. In the world of social reform, leaders like Jane Addams and Lewis Hine drew attention to the plight of the industrial poor of cities, with a poignant emphasis on the waste of children's lives. Their work came back repeatedly to the refrain of how early young lives could be warped by poverty, disease, and alcohol. Concurrent with these developments, an analogy between childhood and artistry appeared with spontaneity and imagination as its terms. Thus between the turn of the century and the 1930s, children went from being "seen and not heard" to being viewed as the great originals. So profoundly was this the case that years later, Picasso (with who knows what degree of irony) could quip that he had "spent many years learning to draw like a child."

In this atmosphere, schooling shifted and changed. Children should not learn small portions of what adults studied; they should, instead, be taught in ways that were meaningful *to them*. In Vienna, in a cabin, in a garden, Erik Erikson taught Anna Freud's patients, throwing away the classical chalkboard and texts in favor of "projects" in which all forms of knowledge were brought together via field trips from which drawings, essays, and questions flowed. In America, Francis Parker and John Dewey developed a child-centered and progressive education borrowing from European educators like Froebel and Pestalozzi. Consequently, and not surprisingly, arts education took on a new shape. No longer a route into citizenship or industry, it became just the opposite: a safeguard against

the routine, the regular, and the predictable. Given their open-
ness to invention, the plasticity of their raw materials, and their
ability to carry multiple message, arts experiences were envisioned as *the* ground for self-discovery, invention, and self-
expression. In this light, the arts were not subjects in themselves, but activities that could enhance the child's
understanding of life and develop a wide curiosity and sense
for good craft. It is a view that takes much from Dewey's definition of art as

an attitude of spirit, a state of mind—one which demands for its satisfaction and fulfilling a shaping of matter to new and more significant
form. To feel the meaning of what one is doing and to rejoice in that
meaning, to unite in one concurrent fact that unfolding of the inner
life and the ordered development of material conditions—that is art.[8]

In this view, the arts were incorporated into other subject
areas as aids to creative learning, such as weaving in the service
of mathematics, the making of dioramas and models as a concomitant of social studies, and the projects of the handicraft
studio. Margaret Naumberg, who founded what was to
become the Walden school, hoped the education there would

go beyond the constriction, the repression, and the misdirection of
the group-minded mass methods of Horace Mann and John Dewey to
a pedagogy that would preserve the vitality of each fresh crop of
children.[9]

The school became the studio and the children, artists, all in
the service of developing "creativity." The crusade for arts
education was to take the children's side in their inevitable
battle to break the stranglehold of convention, commercial-
ism, and pragmatism. Children were to play, discover, and invent, rather than to be taught, to practice, or to copy. As
realms in which it was possible to invent forms and meanings,
educators argued that the arts were healing, confirming, and
even therapeutic. Growth in the arts would occur naturally and
without confining tuition. But chiefly, and centrally, arts
educators promised that the creative spark seeded by the arts
would, with time and permission, become a part of the child's

personality, producing inventive policy makers, patent procurers, and homemakers with a taste for design. In fact, distilling this hope, Viktor Lowenfeld wrote:

In art education art is used only as a means to an end and not as an end in itself. It is the aim of art education to use the creative process to make people more creative regardless of where this creativeness will be applied.[10]

Perhaps nowhere is this impulse to release the natural creativity of children more evident than in the burst of music education methods that came to influence curriculum in American schools by mid-century, particularly those pioneered by Jaques-Dalcroze, Orff, and Kodaly. All these music educators were profoundly at odds with the abstract manner in which musical understanding was taught through exercises in the principles of theory and notation, excluding work in expression and interpretation. These musicians were convinced that these were the primitive forms of musical understanding. For instance, Jaques-Dalcroze spent his entire career exploring the possibility of several aspects of body-emotion-music connections. In his techniques of eurythmics and kinesthesia, he used the body's motions as the fundamental text for learning the essence of rhythm. In solfege, or sight-singing, he used the voice as the entry to teaching pitch and melodic contour. In his work with improvisation, he insisted that children begin their encounters with composition, not with formal patterns, but with playful explorations. His notions of keyboard training provide clear samples of this approach: rather than scales or arpeggios, Jaques-Dalcroze insisted that beginning students play with the piano strings, plucking, striking, stroking, and silencing the sounds in experimental ways. Later, they were to play note clusters on black keys with the entire palm so as to avoid the strain and boredom of early single finger playing. These clusters rapidly turned into compositions in melodrama (improvisations accompanying stories) and improvised dialogue (improvisations built off of conversational patterns). Following in this direction, Orff and his colleagues developed an entire line of simplified instruments, based on African xylo-

phones and Indonesian percussion pieces. Later, when he
added voices to his *Musik für Kinder* it was not the typical adult
lyrics written for children. Instead, he turned to what he saw as
the "natural" sounds of childhood: shouts, chants, and children's rhymes. Both pictured music as fundamentally creative,
rather than re-creative, as expressive rather than technical,
and as a personally fulfilling rather than a conventional activity. The methods they invented assume children's innate musical capacities and their ability to create novel musical patterns
given only their bodies and voices.

From the vantage point of 1990, it has become fashionable
to question our most immediate ancestors. The belief in the
unfolding of the child's innate understanding of rhythm or
images strikes educators as naively unaware of the social conventions and the issues of craft that are an inevitable part of
the making of images, poems, or dances or the ways in which
arts learning requires rigorous, continuous instruction. But a
critique that goes no further misunderstands or caricatures the
seminal contribution of the child study movement and progressive education. This contribution is the widespread conviction that the arts are not merely an occasion for inculcating
values or conveying industrially useful skills. Instead, the arts
require that individuals make use of a quite different sort of
processes than the understanding that underlies either daily
problem solving, or work in science, mathematics, or languages.

Arts Education as an
Instance of Learning

In the last three decades, arts education has been reconcep-
tualized, not as job training, or as a way of protecting spontaneity, but as an occasion for thoughtfulness and an invitation
to participate in reinterpreting the past or inventing a contemporary culture. As in previous periods, this shift in arts education has not occurred *sui generis.* It partakes of a broader network of changes that have given us back a portrait of artists as
thinkers and systematizers—not unlike the one that may have

prevailed in the Renaissance. In the late twentieth century, increasing numbers of artists have claimed the theoretical and historical aspects of artistry. Postmodern architecture is about references to other buildings. Both dance and painting have been invaded by text. Ideas about art have become a medium akin to clay or motion. The intellectual side of the arts, always present, has been claimed and celebrated in work by composers like Babbitt and Glass, choreographers like Cunningham and Tharp, or painters like Albers and Martin.

In this same period, an enormous revolution has also taken place in our understanding of human behavior. Often called the "cognitive revolution," this paradigm shift stresses the human mind's ability to deal in rules, concepts, symbols, and representations. It might also be called a revolution for the place of invention, inference, and imagination. Many scientists have broken with associationist and behaviorist frameworks and taken a new interest in issues like the mind's capacity for entertaining many possible worlds or the uniquely human capacities to think about thinking and to rework earlier impressions and memories. Earlier notions of mind as memory or encyclopedia have expanded to include notions of strategies, expertise, and problem finding. In this light, the arts have been reenvisioned, not as crafts or as occasions for self-expression, but as occasions for meaning-making that depend utterly on fluency in symbol systems. That fluency is many-layered; it includes a feel for the rules and conventions, a rich sense for the history and connotations of forms, and a fierce determination to use those symbols expressively and imaginatively.

Such deep thinking is equal to the efforts required in solving open-ended mathematics problems, designing and executing science experiments, or analyzing primary source documents to make complex and nuanced historical judgments. We can find demonstration of such complex meaning-making in contemporary art in the work of Amalia Mesa-Bains, particularly in an installation titled *Emblems of the Decade: Numbers and Border.*

Emblems, a series of altar constructions, draws on the religious, political, and aesthetic legacies of Mesa-Bains's Hispanic heritage. Mesa-Bains grew up surrounded by the forms of Chicano life: in her family kitchen there was always an *of-frenda*—an altar to household saints that was renewed each year on El Dia de los Muertos, when the souls of dead children and elders return to be honored and cared for. It was in learning the craft of altar making from her teacher, Yolanda Garfias-Woo, a community artist and preserver of ancient practices, that Mesa-Bains began to sense the closeness of art and ritual, altar and installation. In her work she has pursued the question: "how can the ordinary images and materials of Latino heritage be recaptured and rejuvenated to explore the relations between identity and culture?" While the form of the altar in Mesa-Bains's installations has remained constant, the size and shape, the saints invoked, and the messages carried have shifted. Each altar is a new solution.

The course of Mesa-Bains's artwork can be described in a proverb quoted by the poet Anthony Machado, which roughly translates as "traveller, there is no path, the path is made by walking." Two years ago, a scholar-friend, Victor Zamudio-Taylor, introduced Mesa-Bains to the sixteenth- and seventeenth-century Hispanic tradition of emblems: highly symbolic images made by pairing titles, commentary, and vivid images. Mesa-Bains's altars, long the basis of her visual language, evolved into an unforetold new form: large, sculptural arrays of cultural signs, late twentieth-century emblems, portraying both the harshness, and the richness of Latino life. The complexity of this later work derives from the artist's ability to integrate the many vantage points of her cultural identity: the politically active member of the Chicano community, the artist with an absolute eye for the size and color of the forms that will carry her meaning, and the scholar following out the ancient tap-roots of Latino heritage.

The subtitle of *Emblems of the Decade* predicts its meaning. The "numbers" are the harsh statistics that give an account of contemporary American life as lived by people of Mexican and Indian descent: incomes that hover or fall below the border marking off poverty from survival, the increasing slope to the graph of numbers of AIDS patients, the numbers of illegal entrants seeking a new life that they will live covertly. These numbers mix with the dates of an equally harsh political history: dates of conquest, annexation, liberation, and independence. The presence of counting devices and demographic inscriptions suggests the larger quantitative culture that looms behind, collecting, tabulating, and comparing. But cropping up between these dark quantities are also magical and spiritual numbers.

"Border" refers to both the literal and imagined experience of living at the edge. Here the emblems are both those of illegal immigration over what is a political, not a human, border—the underbrush of barbed wire, the ditch and its dark water—and intimate fragments of lives such as photographs and letters. Like some great Mayan calendar, the whole insists on the facets of Latino culture: the overwhelming poverty of many, their marginal and illegal lives, along with evidence of magic, festivals, and spirituality.

Such artwork involves the effort of analysis and synthesis. The numbers and border signs Mesa-Bains uses are laminated; they draw on memory, on the enduring icons of Latino culture, and on her own invented forms. They are plays on ancient themes and current political tensions. To create these emblems, Mesa-Bains has read newspapers, been to political meetings, sketched and made models, visited museums. The eventual result was a set of inscriptions written in the thickest of languages: sensual, symbolic, and deeply cultural.

Although it is vividly American—in its modernity, and its irony—*Emblems of the Decade: Numbers and Border* shares something with other pieces of Hispanic art: Goya's *Horrors of War,* Picasso's *Guernica,* or the murals of Orozco or Riviera. As Ybarra-Frausto writes:

> In ancient times it was the task of the artist to "deify things," to reveal through form, color and line the inherent divinity in all earthly things. Across time and space, the moral dimension of the artist has been maintained. Today, an aesthetic obligation and major duty of the artist continues to be to produce art with a heartfelt intuition—*hacer las cosas con corazon.* While the artistic mind explores and depicts the deep structures of social reality, it is the higher task of the heart to intuit and express the boundless horizons of the imagination.[11]

Emblems confronts, combining the lovely and the unbeara-
ble. *Emblems* documents the diversity of the human present
without bleaching, denying, or condensing it, just as quilts and
pulled-thread coverlets recorded women's lives or field songs
give sound and text to the lives of slaves. Yet in taking up
images and materials from the other side of the border, Mesa-
Bains takes the risk that her audience will not read her emblems accurately or empathetically. After all, she lives in a
larger culture where the images of Latino culture are salsa,
burros, and a figure asleep under an enormous sombrero.

Emblems of the Decade is made from far more than photos,
letters, paint, and wood. It is made—at least as much—from
pauses, from moving an image or object from here to there,
from stepping back to look, from calling in Garfias-Woo or
Zamudo-Taylor to play the critic. The work emerges from research, from painting, and from building—but also from constant, almost ruthless reflection and revision, involving self-
regulation, multiple criteria, and nuanced judgment, as
demanding as any cognitive activity.

Along with recognition of the intellectual aspects of artwork
such as Mesa-Bains's, a major outgrowth of the cognitive revolution has been to rethink childhood and learning as cognitive
development, and so to demonstrate how early and how con-
sistently human beings have the capacity to act as investigators
and thinkers. For example, the Swiss psychologist Jean Piaget
provided careful observations of children counting stones,
pouring water, or playing marbles, and in so doing, described
them as incipient scientists and philosophers chipping away at
the major cognitive issues of life. Thus he describes one of his
own children, early in her second year, playing at going to
sleep, as one of the earliest instances of inventing symbols.

Jacqueline . . . saw a cloth whose fringed edges vaguely recalled those
of her pillow; she seized it, held a fold of it in her right hand, sucked
the thumb of the same hand and lay down at her side, laughing hard.
She kept her eyes open, but blinked from time to time as if she were
alluding to closed eyes.[12]

In a similar spirit, researchers have documented the early, and
stunning, regularities in children's language acquisition. Thus

the commonplace errors of early speech, "I goed" or "where are my pantses," have been recognized as instances of children seeking to apply the rules they have inferred about their language. In this context, the image of children or students either as trainable workers or as free spirits has faded, replaced by a conception of them as active, constructive problem solvers and world makers. And the realms of the arts have followed suit. Thus Jacqueline Goodnow, after watching preschool children draw hundreds of figures, could write:

Perhaps most notable about sequence in drawings is the degree of order and consistency children reveal, even as young as three, four, or five. At a time when in much of their other behavior they appear whimsical, irrational, or easily distracted by the last thing to come along, their drawings reveal a great deal of order. In a sense they proceed according to plan. To me, the discovery of this orderly sequence is as important as the finding that young children's language follows discernable rules. . . . In all these cases children's behavior follows an identifiable principle that can be seen to change with age. So the apparent disorder in children's behavior—its apparent lack of principles or rules—is due to our own ignorance of the principles they work by. . . .[13]

The consequences for the continuing construction of a rationale and theory of curriculum for arts education, though gradual, have been enormous. Slowly, like some great ship turning, many arts educators have moved to a view of the arts as an instance of earned, rather than inculcated or innate, development. We now understand that children gradually construct (rather than just discover) the possibilities of representation in drawing, tonal structures in music, the conventions of theater, and the techniques of dance as those forms are practiced in their culture. As one researcher, N. R. Smith, wrote:

In the past much attention has been paid to understanding the emotions that underlie children's art work. However, (I want to emphasize) the *thinking or cognitive processes* behind children's painting. . . . The effort of children to find means of organizing and making images is the creativity of the child.[14]

Following this impulse, researchers have described stages of visual development with an emphasis on how children *work* their way from stage to stage. Unlike earlier accounts by descriptive researchers such as Luquet and Kellogg, these portraits stressed the mechanisms and sources for children's changing notions of what it is to fashion a symbol: the properties of media, copying, and interactions with peers, as well as the ability to plan and execute sequences of behavior.

Viewing paintings—or dances, films, or sculpture, or even reading—has also come to be understood as involving the understanding and generative application of such complex notions as style. A quote from an elementary school child, pondering Seurat's *La Grande Jatte,* is indicative of how very early children think about and draw inferences concerning what they see. Asked to imagine what else Seurat might have chosen to paint into his park if he had had two more feet of canvas off to the right, the child remarks:

Child: Maybe . . . I think he would have put some more trees like these with the white trunks and the little leaves. And a family coming to have a picnic on the river. Two kids . . . a girl in a blue dress and a boy running after her and then the mother and father with a big basket.
Interviewer: What would the father look like?
Child (pointing to one of the frock-coated gentlemen): Like this one, with a straight-up hat and one of those coats.[15]

Not only does she expect that the trees in the new section of the painting will be the birches of the Paris summer, but that the father in this world will have the look of a frock-coated gentleman, rather than the casual appearance of her own father. Her responses remind us that part of understanding and interpreting the style of a work like *La Grande Jatte* involves being drawn deeply into a particular world characterized by its own time, space, light, and costume.

In the case of music, there has been a similar effort to create a map of the cognitive changes in musical *understanding,* as opposed to the acquisition of the sentiments in songs or the need for exploring sounds. Increasingly, teachers and researchers have sought out the kinds of products and performances that would expose the principles on which children organize their ideas into systems of musical thought. Consequently, we now know something about how children record musical patterns and how they invent new songs. Thus the same nine-year old who has been singing Halloween songs by rote, is capable of struggling with the demands and compromises of a notation system.

He pores over a scrap of paper, marking, then humming to himself, then erasing and remarking. He is trying to notate a tune that he has composed with a small set of percussion instruments. He draws three bursts, "See, here is where the music is supposed to go in three sharp bangs, maybe like car horns. . . ." (He plays these three elements for himself) . . . "no, like crashes." (He outlines the bursts again, heavily.) Then he inscribes three upward arcs "over here where the lines get longer, it's for the slower parts that come after." He sits back and looks at his score. "It's hard to get it right. I don't think I can write everything down."[16]

Emerging Alternatives in the Schools

Yet as recently as fifteen years ago, Arthur Efland, writing in *Studies in Art Education,* described at least the visual arts as mired in an older history—as if drawing had never been seen as any different from practicing handwriting, illustrating a social studies paper, or learning to be diligently observant. Efland described what he called the "school art style": the flat, uniform images hung on bulletin boards in Fort Worth, Litchfield, and Albuquerque. Second, he argued that those images of houses, sunsets, and shoes were different, and discontinuous, from the landscapes and observational sketches that artists, or even children working outside of school, produce. Anticipating much of current critique of curriculum in any number of areas, he pointed out how school art is a domesticated and narrowed version of art as it is practiced by experts, whether those experts are painters, collectors, museumgoers, or art historians. And what he had to say was not unique to visual art. One only has to think of the differences between a band playing through a simplified arrangement of a Sousa march and an ensemble rehearsing a demanding score (raising questions about the composer's intentions, trying different interpretations, playing passages slowly to correct for problems in intonation) to have a sense for how generally Efland's criticisms apply.

However, in the ensuing years, a large and remarkable shift has occurred in arts education. Increasingly, the root image for artistic learning has approached that of an "apprenticeship" in which students learn the full range of practices, perspectives, and ideas that make for expertise in the arts. The National Education Association, for example, calls for the arts to be taught as *disciplines,* to be made available through *creating,* studying, and *experiencing.* The call is for *the development of skills* in and knowledge of the arts. The call is also for school instruction to be combined with the highest quality arts experiences in theaters, concert halls, and museums.

In an effort to connect school arts with serious learning and sophisticated practice, at least two quite different approaches to arts curriculum have emerged: what can be called discipline based and artistry based arts education. Discipline based arts education has been sponsored and nurtured particularly in the visual arts by the Getty Center for Education in the Arts. At the core of discipline based arts education is a commitment to expose even the youngest children to four major modes of artistic knowledge: studio work, art history, art criticism, and aesthetics. The aim is to create widespread artistic literacy, what Eisner referred to as the ability to "recover meaning" from works of art. As a result, skills like the ability to notice the relevant visual characteristics of a work, to recognize how works derive from and build on one another, and to think about the basis for valuing works all play a prominent role in discipline based arts education. The following excerpt from a classroom interaction provides a sample. (The students are eighth graders in an Illinois classroom, observed by Robert Stake.)

The teacher projected a painting by Edward Hopper entitled *Gas* and said, "You probably haven't seen this before."
A student quickly asked, "Is it Rockwell?"
The teacher replied, "No, but from the same period, probably the

early forties. It's an American scene. You recognize the Mobil sign. It's by Hopper."
A student said, "It isn't realistic. It's too clean and perfect."
"Would you say it's *too* perfect?"
"Maybe. Maybe it's something from the Twilight Zone."
"What makes you say that?"
"Well, there's no grease on the station. And the road disappears into the blackness of the trees."
"What is the artist expressing?"
"Distance."[17]

Students confront a strange and puzzling work of art, they build up some understanding of the kinds of images American artists worked with in the 40s, and, perhaps chiefly, they learn to think about art: they encounter the notion that just beyond realism, the world becomes "too perfect." They make connections between cultural icons—*Gas* and "The Twilight Zone." They traffic in the layered meanings of "distance"—that of the highway, and that of the heart. In essence, students learn to think about what they behold. This class, like many other discipline based classes, meets the critique of "school arts," insisting that students push beyond looking on, to looking deeply into. At its richest and best, this approach uses the tools of studio work, art history, criticism, and aesthetics as a means to offer students a range of knowledge and forms of inquiry not unlike those of a connoisseur. Eliot Eisner describes this well:

There is no equivalent of Bach's Mass in B Minor. Words cannot convey what the music has to say. But the messages in these works are not there simply for the taking. They must, so to speak, be recovered. They must be read. The works themselves must be unwrapped to be experienced. . . . I used the term "read" in the previous sentence. I did this intentionally. Visual and musical forms are forms that are patterned. They are forms that reflect a history. They are forms influenced by purpose, shaped by technology, and possess the signature of their authors. To recover the meaning these forms possess requires the ability to read the language they employ.[18]

A different approach, which might be called artistry based arts education, could be represented by any number of exemplars: the work of skilled studio arts teachers, Teachers and

Writers Collaborative, the Lincoln Center Institute, or ARTS
PROPEL (a collaboration of Harvard Project Zero, Educational Testing Service, and the Pittsburgh Public Schools).
Much like discipline based arts education, artistry based education is concerned with widening and deepening the ways
that students come to know the arts. Only its vehicles and the
emphases are different. In artistry based education, students
are challenged to think *in* the arts by becoming involved in
doing the work of artists. The expectation is not that students
will become practicing artists. Rather the conviction is that
direct involvement in the materials, risks, and dangers of the
arts provides a profound basis for understanding. As William
Bolcom, the contemporary composer, remarks:

> How do you get people to pay real attention to music again? A possi-
> ble answer: People become interested in activities in which they have
> participated even reasonably well. . . . Even though a person's partici-
> pation may be far in the past, there will always be an affinity. . . .
> Young people are likely to have fooled around with a guitar or a trap
> set, and that identification affords them an emphatic center in the
> music they hear, a musical locus to identify with.[19]

While artistry based education comes in many forms, several
distinguishing features are common to all: a focus on artistic
problem finding sustained by studio work, constant conversation with art and artists, and a classroom climate informed by
reflection and thoughtful assessment.

In classrooms where artistry based education is pursued,
students do more than learn technique. Instead, they are introduced to the central questions and processes alive in each artistic domain. For instance, in a playwriting class, students
have to learn that writing drama is more than writing out the
turns in chat. This they do by writing, rehearsing, performing,
and revising in the light of performance. In this way, they learn
the language of the unsaid: gesture, silence, and implication.
Moreover, students learn that any script is essentially a score
waiting to be reworked. They do this by casting different actors into their scenes and by letting others direct what they
have written, learning just how much possibility there is in
Blanche or Stanley.

Artistry based education also insists that students engage with works of art and artists. This becomes clear in the following excerpt taken from an interview with a high school senior, who describes a sustained project in which she did a series of portraits of family members. Toward the end of the project, she grew restless, wanting to reach for renditions that would capture something more universal about the nature of family bonds. As a part of pursuing that issue, she visited a museum, where she encountered Giacometti's *Walking Man.* Here she comments on what she learned from the intersection of her own questions and the sculpture.

I was trying for something that I could still keep that family quality and make it universal, so that everybody could see a part of themselves in it. . . . [I remembered seeing] the sculpture of the Walking Man. He didn't have a face really, sort of an indication of a nose . . . it could be any man, anybody struggling. It looked like a very struggling piece. [I wrote in my journal:] "In Walking Man, the figure of the man appeared to be held back as his back foot tried to advance forward." I think the fact that he didn't put in any features in the face—could mean anybody who is trying to get away from something, trying to advance forward in life. But something's holding them back.[20]

Following this encounter with a work that shows her other possibilities for representation, the student turned from portraits to a series of much more abstract works in collage and plaster sculpture that highlight basic forms expressive of the intimacy and differentiation that occur between parents and children. Through such motivated encounters with works—as well as with practicing artists—students learn basic lessons in the social nature of thought and invention. They come to think about the works of other ages and cultures, about exhibitions and performances as vital amplifiers of what their own hands and minds can imagine or accomplish.

Finally, in artistry based education, teachers give considerable place to reflection and assessment—they are eager to have students learn rigorous standards and for them to become insightful critics of their own work. To make this possible, such teachers have adopted the journals, sketchbooks, critiques, and portfolios so common to mature artistic practice. By asking students to keep records of their work and to constantly make and remake a selection of their own best work, teachers have begun to teach students how to be more than passive recipients of grades and scores. They have insisted that students take responsibility for judging their own work and for seeking criticism. Thus in music classes, for example, students make audio tapes of the successive rehearsals of a piece in which they perform. Students, as well as teachers, listen to these musical histories in an effort to understand the student's progress and his or her persistent problems.

In artistry based education, then, the underlying model of artistic cognition is one of a conversation between different aesthetic perspectives or stances, drawn from the methods of practicing artists. Professional composers hardly confine themselves to the work of translating the sounds inside their heads into the notational conventions of their culture. While at work on a composition, they also draw on what they know from the performer's perspective ("can the cellist make these sounds articulately at this tempo?"). They borrow from their own musical heritage and the offerings of other cultures. They apply rigorous standards, and possibly wonder about the changing relationship between music and sound. These stances are not so much formal disciplines as they are ways of approaching and using the resources of mind and culture.

What matters is that *both* discipline and artistry based education argue that the arts *are* a kind of knowledge, just as distinctive, coherent, and powerfully organized as the knowledge of science or history. They insist that work in the arts demands higher-order thinking.

However, if either discipline or artistry based education, or an equally serious approach, were widely adopted and pursued, the arts in schools would become dangerous and demanding. Students who are introduced to the options and demands of the arts are likely to be restless, rather than obedient, citizens and workers. Even as adolescents, they will raise questions about their experience as Americans, as this young writer does in reflecting on the Harlem Renaissance:

World War I was over. Middle-upper and upper class white people were clapping and flapping and trying to forget that past war. On the other side of town in Harlem, New York the greatly gifted Black people were writing, drawing or singing their blues away. Sure they clapped, flapped, and danced carelessly until daybreak, but after, their creative abilities transported to a paperback or on the wall of an art exhibit.

From 1920–1930 there occurred a major outburst of creative activity by Black Americans in the field of art. . . . The "Old Negro" was dying and the "New Negro" was taking its place. The old negro consisted of Uncle Toms and Tiesys that abided by the sickness of Jim Crow laws. The "New Negros" laid down their pain and perspectives on paper and inspired the "Old Negro" to join, and soon to take what was theirs. "The New Negro had long become less a myth than a man. The Old Negro has become more of a formula than a human being," quoted from "The New Negro" by Alain Locke. The New Negro had renewed self-respect and self-dependence and believed and were right that Black is definitely Beautiful.[21]

Such students will want to deal in images that are more than pretty, just as this high school photographer suggests in talking about her work:

I'm not really sure how I thought of using constructed fantasies to illustrate the role of women in society. I suppose it was a combination of witnessing my own family situation, and what I feel society's view is towards women. As I look at my work spread before me, I realize that the project has evolved to deal with three dominant issues—rape, control over women in the home, and advertising. "Altar" (one of the prints about rape) is supposed to represent the "televised" rape—those horrifying and gruesome events that the press makes so much of. "Dead Fish". . . is date rape, or any violation, for that matter. "Her Breasts". . . is a more subtle version of the other two; one almost doesn't notice the black glove creeping down her thigh, just like one doesn't notice the majority of the 87,600 rapes in America annually.[22]

This kind of arts education is exactly as dangerous as the prosecutors in Hamilton County, Ohio, fear. Like the Mapplethorpe photographs, this fuller form of arts education is likely to provoke. In many schools, this student's photographs could not be exhibited. This appearance would jeopardize the existence of the photo class, the public exhibition space for student work, and the teacher's job. But this kind of domestication would be a loss. It would be to train students in a mistakenly bland and bleached craft. Students who have the chance to work long and hard in the arts, whatever their personal preference or politics, will be informed, unlike the jurors in Cincinnati. Consider, for instance, what a high school student who has had the chance to work on her own photographs of nudes has had to say about Mapplethorpe:

I like taking photographs in a way that people get the idea that a photo is not just a snapshot of what happens in everyday life, so that when you show a person it is not just how they always are. So it was Dorothea Lange who really taught me how a portrait could be more than a picture. And Mapplethorpe. Some of his images are hideous, and I despise them. But some of his work transforms the figure like nobody else.[23]

To encounter Mapplethorpe as another photographer is to be able to take a critical stance on his work: to make choices about what is hideous and what is handsome. It is to have the tools to make distinctions.

Towards Collaborative Action

In the past, we have made public schools the major conduit for arts education. But it is clear from the history of arts education that without additional funding, protection, and advocates, the arts have been extremely vulnerable in the context of schooling. They have regularly been used as handmaidens to other purposes ranging from vocational training to Americanization. They have been, and are, taught intermittently and repetitively, rather than constantly and sequentially. Music and art are cut away from school budgets in the first wave of belt tightening, as we have seen in states like California and Massachusetts when Propositions 13 and 2½ were voted in. The result is, in its quiet way, tragic: only those children whose family backgrounds or income permit them private lessons or trips to the museum receive anything like the kind of arts education that would make them avid audience members or wise jurors.

At the same time, it is clear that acting in concert with other organizations, public schools can deliver strong and innovative arts education. For example, both the current initiatives in discipline and artistry based education have emerged from partnerships between foundations, researchers, and public schools. However, if we are serious about a broad based increase in the amount and quality of arts education, private funding alone will be insufficient. It will be essential for city, state, and national governments to enter the equation. What follow are examples of how this might come to be.

Arts Education and City Government

If arts education, fully understood, includes becoming active in cultural life, then it must be designed to teach much more than techniques and art history. Put more pointedly, one of the major goals of arts education has to be to teach students how to care about and use the artistic and cultural resources of their communities. In order to do this, arts education has to come away from chalkboards and books, and move out of schoolrooms, out into the streets, parks, theaters, and galleries. City governments can enable this transformation, if they will. Consider what New York has done recently: in District 2 it turned over unused city buildings to make a middle school for the arts. At present the school is forging relationships with the cultural resources of the city. Children will attend academic classes at the school, but take arts classes in some of the finest conservatory-like settings the city has to offer. Ballet students, for instance, take classes at the Feld Ballet, with skilled teachers and live piano music, mingling with other students and dancers for whom the work that goes on in those studios is central. Or consider what a city could contemplate. As a part of the redevelopment of a city's cultural life, school and city officials could consider moving both middle and high school arts magnet schools into spaces centrally located in the district. Once there, students would have the cultural resources of the district as classroom and text. Qualified students could enroll in dance, theater, and music classes where they would be among working artists and performers.

Music students could take scores and attend several rehearsals of a choral piece, or a new contemporary work, learning first-hand about the decisions and choices that underlie a finished performance.

Any public gallery space under development could, on occasion, be opened to shows that are curated by groups of students. These shows could go far beyond the usual display of student work. For instance, imagine the city's newspaper has an untapped file of photographs of the social life of the city's diverse ethnic community going back several decades. Students working at the intersection of English, American history, and the visual arts could develop an exhibition of these photographs, doing research, arguing out selections, writing a catalogue, and hanging the prints. This approach points out that the arts education possible in such a setting goes far beyond the training of painters and dancers. Students might learn substantial amounts about working as lighting designers, museum curators, or company managers.

But none of this occurs unless a city government takes arts education as the serious preface and underpinning of cultural life. This takes insight and innovation. For instance, how can monies raised for a cultural district be used or extended so that they can fund construction or renovation of educational spaces? What do the resulting partnerships between the city council, the board of education, and the directors of a cultural district look like? If percent-for-art taxes are levied on construction, will council members and city lawyers agree that the resulting monies be used off-site, for instance, to provide public art or arts facilities available to students? How can a city build a public arts program that goes beyond edifices and facilities to arts education programs that make it possible for students to think about the place of art in life? All of this will take considerable adult education. Arts education is a long-term and somewhat invisible investment in the cultural sophistication of citizens too young to vote for mayors or council members.

Arts Education and
State Government

The new appropriation for the National Endowment for the Arts provides 15 percent more money to the states. Cynics predict that states will simply lessen their own appropriations, with the result that there will be no increased funding for the arts. This may well be so, given what looks like difficult times fast approaching. However, if state arts councils were to be richer than they once were, they could collaborate with state departments of education to think about arts education as something other than a tag-along or an afterthought.

If arts education is to be a serious preface to later participation in culture, then it must be sustained and of high quality, just as science education has to be continuous, innovative, and demanding if we are to have informed citizens and skilled scientists. State government can play a vital role in both funding and brokering this possibility. Familiar opportunities abound: a governor's school with scholarships in the arts, or summer stipends for teachers working on arts curricula. But innovation is also in order. The state of Connecticut provides a clear example. The commissioner of education speaks often and articulately about the role of the arts in every student's education. The state department of education is staffed with experts in music, literature, and visual art. 1990–1991 was the "Year of the Arts" with accompanying festivals, exhibitions, and performances. But most significantly, the state, in conjunction with researchers from Harvard Graduate School of Education, is spearheading a national effort to develop more powerful approaches to assessing student learning in the arts. In this effort artists, scholars, and educators are drawing deeply on approaches native to the arts and humanities. They are asking students to perform, to exhibit and discuss their work, and to develop portfolios demonstrating the range and evolution of their work. They will examine what students understand about visual arts, music, theater and dance, writing, and literature by the end of high school. The study will demonstrate just how much learning occurs in those fields, and that artistic work can be rigorously evaluated. In such a climate, the arts are not hangers-on, but equal, and even startling, contributors to a dialogue about educational quality and student learning.

Like cities, states must reconsider some of their most fundamental policies and patterns of funding if they are to support the arts beyond such special initiatives. Students have to have continuous and sequential access to artistic training, just as they do in science or in history. Yet in many states students have to take only a semester or at most a year-long course in the arts. Almost as universally, students can substitute metal shop, typing, or meat cutting—any vocational art—for dance or painting. If states changed these requirements, it would send a powerful message about the place of arts in education. But it would also pledge states to treating their arts education programs on a par with their reading or science programs, hiring staff, developing teaching materials, even buying tickets or hiring buses for concerts and exhibitions.

Arts Education and the National Government

Since the 1960s, the National Endowment for the Arts has provided support in the form of programs like the artists residencies and funding for demonstration projects. However, the agency's resources in the early years were severely limited, and there were many other competing demands for its funds. Further, the early leadership of the Endowment was concerned that its funding of school art and music programs might discourage the U.S. Office of Education from taking an active role. This has led to a very circumscribed role in arts education in the larger program of the Endowment. However, in its five-year planning process, mandated by Congress during the 1980s, every panel was asked to rate its priorities for the 1990s, and virtually every one put arts education high on its list. Perhaps this is due to the reported decline in audiences for arts events in the 1980s, the first such decline since the 1950s. Perhaps it is because of the dramatic demographic changes and the growing concern that Americans must be able to appreciate each other's culture. The Endowment's 1988 publication, *Toward Civilization,* certainly highlighted its much widened mandate: particularly the importance of pluralism, attention to folk and popular arts, as well as the fast-emerging place of technology in artistry. Given the events in Congress in the summer and fall of 1990, there was also an increased concern that we do not have a population that can accept the challenges of contemporary art. Taken together, all these forces have produced a receptivity to the view that the National Endowment for the Arts should make a place for arts education at the very center of its mission.

But there is a challenge. The Endowment must break step with business as usual and formulate a clear and coherent vision for arts education. Given its limited resources, the Endowment must turn in its history of responding to a diverse and often divided field, adopting a sharp leadership role in education. There are both organizational and funding implications that flow from taking on this role. In terms of organization, every department at the Endowment should be asked to develop a program of support for arts education. These programs might range from appreciation activities to professional development programs, but each should be designed to have a maximum impact on the lives of young people. Each panel should be asked to develop guidelines that include review criteria relating to arts education. Every panel at the Endowment should have at least one member who is a practicing arts educator or is knowledgeable about the field of arts education as it relates to the discipline. Specifically, the Endowment should acknowledge the central role that teachers play in exemplary practice in the field of arts education and recognize their importance as agents of change. It should include teachers in high-level discussions about arts education, encourage training opportunities, and find other ways to support their work.

In terms of funding, it would be wise if the Endowment chose a few critical foci for its work in the coming years. The Endowment should find ways to develop long-term support for these chosen areas. It can take a decade or more to institutionalize arts education programs. A year or two of funding may not be an effective use of resources if there is no way to follow it up. Several candidate areas seem clear. The first is programs that emphasize the multicultural nature of art and culture. The second is research on the effects of sustained arts education, along the lines of the studies of the effects of the Headstart program. Such studies would have to select districts where the arts are valued and taught and follow their children longitudinally. A third initiative would be the recognition of the life span aspects of arts education, supporting learning opportunities for adults as well as children. In particular, building on the experience of science and history museums, the Endowment would be wise to encourage arts education programs that recognize families as contexts in which children learn to value the arts and to see them as a vital and interesting part of adulthood. In all of this, the imprimatur of the Endowment is crucial. While it cannot fully fund longitudinal studies of the contributions of sustained arts education, it could provide planning and seed money, using its considerable influence to put together diverse partnerships of support that might well include corporations and state arts councils.

At the close of the Cincinnati trial, the museum and its director were acquitted for displaying the Mapplethorpe photographs. It was a victory for First Amendment rights. Even so, the workings of the trial contain curious messages for arts education.

To keep its case uncluttered, the prosecution called only four witnesses. Three of them were police officers who merely confirmed that the exhibition had taken place; the other was a communications specialist who has worked with anti-pornography groups. . . .

The defense, by contrast, paraded expert after expert, from directors of leading museums to the original curator of the exhibition, each of whom testified to the brilliance and seriousness of the late Mr. Mapplethorpe's work.

While the prosecution tried to play to the artistic naivete and seeming parochialism of the jurors . . . it was the jurors' admitted lack of exposure to art that worked for the defense in the end: the jurors deferred to the experts.

"All of them, to a person, were so certain it was art," said James Jones, a thirty-six-year-old manager of a warehouse. "We had to go with what we were told. It's like Picasso. Picasso from what everybody tells me was an artist. It's not my cup of tea. I don't understand it. But if people say it's art then I have to go along with it."

The jurors decided that the photographs appealed to prurient interests and depicted sex in a patently offensive way. But the weight of the defense testimony forced them to concede that the works were art. . . .

"It shows that human beings, even if drawn from a vacuum, who had never seen the exhibit, who hadn't been to a museum in years and were about as homogenized as a jury can get, that they can learn something," said Edward Marks, a Cincinnati lawyer. "They learned what art is."[24]

The lessons are many: most American adults do not have opinions about art. Art is so inconsequential in their lives that its worth and nature are a matter for expert testimony, just like scientific tests to establish patrimony or determine time of death. At the same time, given only two short weeks of deliberation, eight individuals who found Mapplethorpe's homoerotic portraits and naked children prurient came to understand the difference between pornography and art. So, the most complex issues in contemporary art, the ones that threaten to savage the lives of artists, are apprehendable—with education.

As a nation we have often squandered the place given to arts education, domesticating drawing and music, theater and dance, into vocational training or civilizing hobbies. But we could claim other aspects of our history as arts educators: the determination to make the arts available to all, the recognition of the inventive and expressive face of art, and the growing realization that to do art is to think. But to make these claims, we will have to make schools, not courts, the crucible for understanding the reasons why the dangerous work of art might matter.

Notes

[1] *New York Times,* September 24, 1990.
[2] Lowell Mason, *Manual of the Boston Academy of Music,* 1843. In Choksy et al. (1986), p. 6.
[3] Efland (1990), pp. 209–210.
[4] Wygant (1983), pp. 226–227.
[5] Efland (1990).
[6] Webster (in press a) and Webster (in press b).
[7] Efland (1990), pp. 270–271.
[8] Mayhew and Edwards (1966), p. 348.
[9] Cremin (1969), p. 212.
[10] Lowenfeld (1957), pp. 4–5.
[11] Ybarra-Frausto (1986), p. 13.
[12] Piaget (1962), p. 96.
[13] Goodnow (1977), p. 51.
[14] Smith (1982), p. xiv.
[15] Wolf (1989), pp. 26–27.
[16] Wolf (1989), p. 22.
[17] Getty Center (1985), p. 35.
[18] Eisner (1972), p. 65.
[19] Bolcom (1988), p. 545.
[20] 1988 interview with Ella Macklin.
[21] Woodard (1990), p. 1.
[22] 1990 interview with Lee Fernside.
[23] 1990 interview with Brett Lally.
[24] *New York Times,* October 10, 1990.

5

Tax Policy and Private Giving

STEPHEN E. WEIL

Introduction

The chapter that follows is bottomed on the premise that the arts in all their breadth constitute an important public "good" and that, to the extent they cannot be fully supported through the marketplace, the federal government should furnish some form of supplementary support.[1] The question it addresses, thus, is not "whether," but "how." While it touches as well on direct federal funding for the arts, it does so chiefly to provide a better perspective on what remains its central focus—the use of the federal tax code as an incentive for private giving.

STEPHEN E. WEIL is deputy director of the Hirshhorn Museum and Sculpture Garden of the Smithsonian Institution in Washington, DC. Prior to assuming his present position in 1974, he was administrator of the Whitney Museum of American Art in New York City. He is the author of *Beauty and the Beasts: On Museums, Art, the Law, and the Market*, published in 1983, and of *Rethinking the Museum*, published in 1990 by the Smithsonian Institution Press.

In the early 1980s, there were many who urged that federal support for the arts, if such support was to be provided at all, should be channeled entirely through some centrally administered agency where funding decisions could be made in the full light of public scrutiny. "Specifically," asked Feld, O'Hare, and Schuster, "why should aid to the arts be shielded from the legislative review to which the food stamp program or national defense are subjected?"[2] To be curtailed, in this view, was the then (and still) current system of tax incentives through which the cumulative and decentralized decisions of a myriad of taxpayers ultimately determined how a substantial number of forgone tax dollars (the tax savings generated by charitable deductions) would be distributed in support of the arts.

As will be argued in the pages that follow, the arts in the United States would have been dealt a serious blow had that view prevailed. If the arts in all their breadth are to be stimulated and made available in this country—not merely the polite and gentle arts, but also those that may be fierce or impudent—then the continued encouragement of private giving would appear essential for their support. To provide that encouragement, a system of tax incentives was first introduced into the Internal Revenue Code during World War I. Unhappily for the arts, changes made to the code during the past decade would now appear to be eroding those incentives, and further such changes may lie in store. It is critically important to the arts community that it understand what is at stake, that it be in a position to resist what may be avoided, and, to the extent possible, that it be able to take the initiative to recapture what might be restored.

The first four sections of this chapter discuss the arts generally and address the current plight and prospects of direct federal funding. The fifth section briefly considers the location for tax purposes of cultural organizations within the larger nonprofit sector. The sixth and seventh sections examine the theory and recent history of tax policy as a stimulus to private giving, and the final section sets forth some summary conclusions. The opinions expressed throughout are those of the author and do not represent the views of any organization with which he is or has been affiliated.

Art of Two Kinds

We tend for the most part to discuss the issue of public funding as if the arts constituted a single domain, separated certainly into a number of disciplines (poetry, dance, painting and sculpture, music, theater, and so on) but nonetheless reasonably homogeneous throughout. For the purposes of this analysis, however, works of art will be roughly divided into two distinct and polar categories based upon two sharply contrasting ways in which they might from time to time be perceived to function: either (a) as agents of social cohesion and continuity, or (b) as agents of social disruption and change.

While cutting across all disciplinary boundaries, such a division is not intended to have aesthetic implications. Works of art of equal merit may be found in either category. Neither would such a division be intended as fixed. With respect to any given work of art, its categorization would depend upon a perception of how that particular work was principally functioning in a specific setting and at a specific time.

As scarcely need be added, works of art can function in manifold ways, and any such categorization must necessarily be oversimplified and to a degree arbitrary. Moreover, in grouping works of art around just these two opposing functions, a number of overlapping paradoxes must be taken into account:

- Works of art themselves combine elements of continuity and change. ("Good music," Martin Gardner has written, "like a person's life or the pageant of history, is a wondrous mixture of expectation and unanticipated turns.") It is not the predominance of one or the other of these elements, however, that will determine how a given work might be categorized at a given time, but rather how the surrounding society is using that work at that time.
- At any particular time, a given work of art may simultaneously be functioning as an agent of social cohesion and continuity in one milieu but as an agent of social disruption and change in another. In one setting, Boris Pasternak's *Dr. Zhivago* could make its way as a romantic fiction and com-

mercial film. In another, it was suppressed for many years as posing a threat to the established authorities.

• The principal function that a particular work of art performs may change (and change more than once) over time. It may ultimately function in a way far removed from the artist's original intention or achievement. Consider Beaumarchais's *Marriage of Figaro* and its transformation over two centuries (with some help by Mozart) from a revolutionary statement into an opera house standard.

Art as an Agent of Social Cohesion and Continuity

Like language, the arts are one of the principal means by which a society binds itself together and transmits its beliefs and standards from one generation to another. The arts perform this function when they embody, reinforce, and celebrate the values of their society, when they confirm and exemplify the lessons simultaneously taught by the family, by the formal structures of education, and by the various mass media in all their variety. In this function, the arts play a critically important role. Not only do they provide a kind of social "glue," but they also furnish a means by which a society can identify and distinguish itself from others.

Important to note here is that the use of the arts today, and especially the visual arts, is not wholly continuous with the past. The critic Robert Hughes has pointed out the enormous extent to which the mass media have taken over the celebratory function once performed by art, particularly the officially patronized art once employed to glorify the reigning authority.[3] No longer do those who govern require, as did Napoleon, a Jacques-Louis David to serve as first painter and popularize the ruler's image to the very corners of France. That function today has been all but completely usurped by the evening newscast and the morning paper. So too has the official presidential photograph replaced the sculpted portrait busts that once served to decorate the public buildings of Rome and its successor empires. Without an ongoing stream of such officially patronized art, much of the art that functions today to give a society its cohesion and continuity is older art.

By no means was all the older art that now plays such a binding role originally intended to perform that function. Some was specifically created to question or provoke. Nonetheless, as a work of art is preserved over time and folded into a society's accumulated heritage, it tends to take on the function of providing that society with an element of stability. In the 1990s, the audience for *Faust* (the opera, anyway) is more likely to be focused on its own social solidarity than on the question of whether or not one should make deals with the devil.

To some extent, the arts in this first category are able to support themselves through market demand. Because of widely varying production costs, though, the situation may vary greatly from one artistic discipline to another. A novel for which 10,000 readers are prepared to pay $19.95 can be a commercial success. A Broadway musical for which no more than 10,000 theater-goers will pay $50 for a ticket would be an economic disaster. Nonetheless, a substantial segment of the art in this category continues to be successfully organized on a commercial for-profit basis. Publishing, the recording industry, much of film, network television, and the Broadway theater would all be examples. To be noted is the extent to which these arts are contiguous with (or may even overlap) what we might also categorize as "entertainment."

Where the market demand for these arts has not been adequate to sustain them, we have still considered their maintenance as sufficiently important to justify providing them with supplementary federal support. Initially such support was provided indirectly through the system of tax incentives first introduced during World War I and described in the sixth section of this chapter. Since 1965 those incentives have been supplemented by direct assistance in the form of grants from the National Endowment for the Arts (NEA) and, to a lesser degree, the National Endowment for the Humanities (NEH). These grants have been intended not only to stimulate the creation of new works of art, but also to provide greater access

to and understanding of the older works of art that have
achieved the status of heritage.

Art as an Agent of
Social Disruption and Change

Just as the arts, in some instances, may be used to embody,
reinforce, and celebrate the values of their society, in other
instances they may come to function as the vehicle by which
those values are confronted and questioned. It is in this second
and more "romantic" function that the creative individual is
sometimes seen as the rebel, outsider, or *artiste provocateur* who
employs his or her art to wage guerrilla warfare against established forms, authorities, values, institutions, and truths.

Functioning as agents of social disruption and change, the
arts in this use may intrude rudely upon our everyday sensibil-
ity, force us to consider the most extreme possibilities of the
human condition, and prod us to think more profoundly than
is comfortable about ultimate matters of life, death, and our
own contingency. Just as the evening newscast may have
usurped some of the once celebratory function of the arts, so
in turn may the arts—especially as they seek to address moral
and ethical issues—have usurped some of the traditional roles
of religion and philosophy.

The arts in this category use an enormous variety of strategies to challenge the dominant culture and the prevailing
ideologies in virtually every area of human activity. Sometimes
they approach this task through gentle persuasion. At other
times, they will be strident and harsh. Sometimes, instead of
probing for truths, posing questions, or seeking to undermine
deeply held assumptions, they may instead provide us with—
the phrase comes from the Swiss writer Martin R. Dean—"uto-
pian correctives" by which we can compare what is with what
might be.

Moreover, the arts here may function to agitate, to aggra-
vate, to provoke. When they address matters of immediate
public concern, they may give every appearance of being political. In modes that can range from the bawdy humor of an

Aristophanes to the Spartan minimalism of a Samuel Beckett, they may summon us to resist or even revolt against inherited attitudes and the complacent acceptance of things as they are. The arts in this function may even question the validity or meaning of art itself.

The arts that function in this manner are no less vital to the well-being of our society than those that function as agents of social cohesion and continuity. Whereas the one provides us with stability, the other provides us with the stimulus to grow. Thus, for example, Secretary Robert McCormick Adams of the Smithsonian Institution, addressing the issue of controversial art, wrote as follows in the August 1990 *Smithsonian* magazine:

Surely art has always—and perhaps cumulatively—extended the boundaries of insight and perception, providing much of the ambience of individual liberty and cultural diversity toward which, to our pride and pleasure, the whole world now strives. From this viewpoint, I am even tempted to suggest that some part of art may belong precisely along the shifting boundaries that successive ages assign to the morally abhorrent or legally impermissible. By evoking the extremes, it helps us all to find a context for the prism of changing norms through which we view the human condition.

Terser, but to the same effect, is another observation by Robert Hughes. "Art," he wrote, "is the mole. It works below the surface of social structures. Its effects come up long after it has been seen. . . . It is done for us, not to us."[4]

In this same vein are the words of the American playwright Terence McNally. Writing in the July 19, 1990 *New York Times*, he said:

It's not easy to be an authentic grown-up. Our national divorce rate and romance with alcohol and drugs attest to that. But if we are to mature fully, we need to be told the truth about ourselves and the society we live in. Wise men have always depended on artists to tell us those truths, however painful or unpopular they may be. Society needs artists, even if it doesn't realize at the time how much it does.

Society needs artists, and it needs art. The art that it needs, though, is not merely yea-saying art. It does need that, but it also needs an art that is free to say "no," to be taken to whatever lengths or whatever new places it must go in order to do its job—to tell society the truths, sometimes painful, that it needs to know if it is ever to grow and become mature.

How is such art supported? To some extent, the arts in this second category are also able to support themselves through market demand, albeit not always as successfully as art that functions in a more affirmative mode and may provide greater entertainment. There is not, however, universal agreement that the arts in this category ought be supported in this way. Some commentators, in fact, have expressed concern that the search for such market support might actually be self-defeating by putting into jeopardy the very integrity that makes this art important. Paul J. DiMaggio of Yale, for example, has suggested two reasons why this might be so. "First," he says,

> the logic of the marketplace is in many ways inimical to the efforts of nonprofit arts organizations to present innovative productions and exhibitions of the sort favored by many artists, curators, and critics. Second, the marketplace is unsupportive of policies that expand the social range of the audience for the arts, serve the poor, or pursue the goal of public education.[5]

Where market demand has not been adequate to support art in this second category, then federal subsidies have been provided—indirectly through tax incentives and, more recently, by programs of direct grants. (It should not, incidentally, be assumed that the quest for these subsidies is any less competitive than the search for support in the marketplace; the competition is simply for a different source of approval—from patrons in the case of indirect funding, or from peer-group panel reviewers in the case of direct funding.) It was just at this point, however, in connection with such direct grants to support art that was perceived by the public to be "confrontational," that the support system began to show severe signs of strain in the late 1980s.

Strains on the System

In a more ideal world, the American public and its political representatives might accept a concept of artistic freedom that in some measure paralleled the tradition of academic freedom that has, by long effort, been established in this country's institutions of higher learning. Implied by such a concept is that funding agencies ought to maintain a stance of neutrality toward the content of the work produced by the arts organizations and artists chosen to receive their grants. Central to such a concept would be a more clearly drawn distinction between sponsorship and endorsement. That the NEA, for example, had sponsored an activity need no more imply any federal endorsement of that activity than a university's sponsorship of a lecture need imply that it necessarily approved the content of that lecture. Art works would be sponsored for what was judged to be their aesthetic excellence or interest, not on the basis that they functioned either to affirm or to question some element of the status quo.

That ideal is still far off. Repeatedly, first in the late 1930s when the several fledgling art programs launched by Franklin D. Roosevelt's New Deal were either terminated or eviscerated, and again in the late 1980s when the NEA first came under fire in connection with the work of Robert Mapplethorpe and Andres Serrano, critical politicians and members of the public alike have by-passed questions of aesthetic value (or even of procedural regularity) to concentrate their hostility on works of art that (in some combination of their style and content) were perceived as subversive, blasphemous, pornographic, or otherwise in conflict with mainstream values.

As might be expected, this response has been triggered most frequently by art that was intended from the outset to function as an agent of social disruption and change. In both its manner and matter, i.e., its language and content, such art is far more apt to provoke such hostility than the art of cohesion and continuity. Whether as a strategy to attract attention or as a symbol of its breaking away from established norms, its language (verbal, musical, pictorial) may be unfamiliar and novel—at the extreme, even crude, abrupt, or vulgar—and genuinely offensive to many. Most often provocative in content, it may pose a direct threat to those whose authority it questions.

To the extent that the direct federal funding of such art is involved, the hostility it provokes generally finds expression in a pair of linked questions:

- Why should taxpayers have to pay for art that the majority of them find repugnant?
- Why should this or any country support art that seeks to undermine its values?

Those are scarcely new questions; they go back half a century and more.[6] Their very familiarity notwithstanding, to this day the American arts community seems to have a difficult time providing a compelling set of responses.

One response, of course, and perhaps one of the best, is that in a democracy public monies may eventually wind up being spent on many things that one or another taxpayer might find repugnant or at least of no interest—Star Wars, tobacco subsidies, electric chairs, and baseball stadia all come to mind—if the majority so wishes. Art perceived as repugnant may differ only in its profound ability to seize the public's (or at least the media's) attention.

Another answer might be procedural. A grant-making process, like any other process, will tend to produce a bell curve of results in terms of public acceptability or even of freedom from error. In that, it resembles our system of democratic elections that occasionally produces a genuine aberration, or our system of military procurement that from time to time will produce a remarkably expensive wrench. That is simply a condition endemic to systems. Unless and until a system begins to produce more than a tolerable number of what might be considered aberrant results, then that system ought not to be lightly discarded or set aside. The point to be stressed to the public, rather, is that any system can be made to appear preposterous by concentrating on the few examples that lie at its extremes and by ignoring the far more numerous ones that can be found under the heart of the bell curve.

Not so compelling (and even, to a degree, dangerous to the future of direct federal funding) are some other answers that those within the arts establishment have occasionally offered. One of these involves the so-called Van Gogh fallacy, i.e., that the greater the initial rejection of a work of art, the more wholehearted will be its eventual acceptance. While it is true that many works of art that the public initially found baffling or repugnant have since become cherished parts of our cultural heritage, it is equally true that many more of such works have either remained to this day baffling or repugnant or, not infrequently, have been forgotten entirely.

Related perhaps is the response that the recipients of federally subsidized arts grants have been selected by panels of disciplinary experts. Since those experts understand their subjects more profoundly than does a lay public, their choices ought therefore to be respected. That this too is true may be beside the point. Authority no longer carries the weight it may once have borne, and those who most strongly advocate an art that functions as an agent of social disruption or change can scarcely complain when the public, itself to a degree rebellious, refuses to bow before the opinions of "experts."

In this same line is the "castor oil" response—that even though the public hates the taste of something, it should nevertheless swallow it for its own long-term good. Once more, that may be both true and beside the point. Taxpayers are mostly adults, and simply will not tolerate being put in such a childish position. That such an answer might also (and rightfully) be perceived by them as arrogant does not help the argument.

Finally, there is a response that argues for a sort of "proportional representation" in grant making. The public, so this argument goes, has a wide range of preferences. Even though a majority may find something repugnant, a minority may favor it. This minority has its rights too. A form of this argument has been advanced, for example, by Tim Miller, one of the four performance artists (Karen Finley, Holly Hughes, and John Fleck were the others) whose panel-recommended grants were vetoed by the NEA's chair in June 1990.

Responding angrily in *Theater Week* (July 16, 1990), Miller said that he ought to have:

the full power to create art about my identity as a gay person, art that confronts my society, art that criticizes our government and elected officials, and maybe even some art that deserves a few tax dollars from the 20 million lesbians and gay men who pay the IRS. . . .

Notwithstanding how just that may appear to some, the fact is that our democratic system, for better or worse, simply does not work that way. The majority is not entitled to merely a majority of the spoils. Within constitutional limits, the majority gets all the spoils. It is for precisely that reason that the decentralized system of subsidy through the charitable deduction is so vital to maintain. It provides an important counterbalance to what some may (rightly or not) perceive as majoritarian repression.

Unless and until there is a better public understanding of the distinction between government sponsorship of the arts and government endorsement, we may no longer be able to protect the federal grant-making process against what threatens to become an annual round of political sniping. Given the nature of the arts in this century, and given also that thousands of such grants are made each year, there will always be some number at the extremes of the process that can be used as targets.

In the case of funding by the NEA, for example, it may be irrelevant for potentially controversial art (a) whether that sniping ultimately destroys the agency entirely; (b) whether it eventually results in the inclusion in NEA grants of specific restrictions on content; (c) whether the imposition of a floor on the size of NEA grants operates to exclude support for individual artists and for the smaller groups that tend to be more experimental; (d) whether such incessant sniping simply frightens the staff, peer review panels, chair, and National Council into a state of chronic timidity; or (e) whether it induces such a state of self-censorship in artists and arts organizations who might otherwise apply for grants that their work will in any case be drained of provocation. In any one or more of those events, such sniping will have succeeded in cutting off such potentially controversial art from a major source of support (not just financial support, but also the opportunity to receive the nationally recognized imprimatur that NEA approval confers).

Paradoxically, the threat to such funding may not come only from those who reject provocative or controversial art because they see it as an attack on the status quo. Such funding may also be threatened, albeit in a different way, by those who themselves most strongly believe that the status quo is in need of change. This second threat involves the debate over whether "quality" and "aesthetic excellence" exist as discernible qualities in works of art, or whether these have become code words that conceal what Brenson described as "artistic and cultural repression."[7] (For a second and contrary opinion as to this, also see Kramer.[8]) Unless "quality" or "excellence" or some similar term of comparison is acknowledged as an appropriate basis for judgment, however, on what other grounds may NEA or state council peer review panels recommend which grants are to be awarded? Moreover, unless works of art (by definition, it is what keeps them from being spoons or mousetraps) include an identifiable aesthetic dimension, not even "aesthetic interest" would be available as a criterion on which to base such decisions. Certainly, grant panels could scarcely give awards on the basis of content. In the case of both federal and state grant programs, that would most likely raise such a host of First Amendment questions as to bring down such programs entirely.

The fight to keep programs of direct federal support in place and open to art of every kind—both art that affirms and art that questions—must be conducted with all the vigor that the arts community can command. At the same time, however, it must be understood that this fight may not be won or wholly won— it was entirely lost at least once before—and that attention must be given to maintaining and strengthening the other principal means by which the federal government can provide or stimulate support for the arts. That brings us, finally, to the nonprofit tax status of most arts organizations and to the use of tax policy as a stimulus to private giving.

The Nonprofit Sector

Notwithstanding that some part of the arts activity in the United States can be supported through market demand, the overwhelming preponderance of such activity (beyond, again, what may be classified as "entertainment") is carried on through thousands upon thousands of privately governed, privately supported, and wholly unrelated nonprofit organizations, some formed as charitable trusts but most as not-for-profit corporations. These organizations include more than half of the country's museums and virtually all of its symphony orchestras, dance companies, experimental theaters, chamber music societies, opera troupes, and literary magazines. To suggest the magnitude of this activity, the aggregate annual operating expenses of these organizations was estimated in the mid-1980s to be $10 billion. It has surely grown since.

This constellation of cultural organizations is, in turn, just a part of the larger nonprofit sector, a category of so-called tax exempt organizations that includes major parts of this nation's systems of higher education and health care, its recreation and human service organizations, as well as religious congregations of every description. So vast and sprawling is this nonprofit sector that efforts to map it with any accuracy are still at an early stage. A "Statistical Portrait" that appeared in the January 9, 1990 issue of *The Chronicle of Philanthropy* estimated that as of the end of 1989, it included some 907,000 active nonprofit organizations with an aggregate operating expense of over $325 billion and more than 7 million paid employees.

In relation to this nonprofit field, cultural organizations play a relatively small role. Whether measured by the number of entities, by annual expenditure, or by paid employment, they constitute something less than 5 percent of the total universe. In terms of the private contributions they receive, they are only slightly more weighty at 6 to 7 percent. Thus while cultural organizations have played a critical role in shaping such programs of direct federal aid as the NEA's, they have been a relatively minor factor in shaping the tax provisions of the Internal Revenue Code relevant to charitable contributions generally. Historically, their fortunes have ebbed and flowed with those of the greater charitable community.

Whether and to what extent cultural organizations might ever obtain separate tax treatment focused specifically on their own particular problems and needs is by no means certain. Art museums, for example, have fought unsuccessfully for two decades to reverse a provision of the 1969 Tax Reform Act that deprived artists of a full fair market value charitable deduction for gifts of their own art works. They have been equally unsuccessful to date in reversing a 1986 change (discussed in the next section) in the tax treatment accorded to gifts of works of art from donors other than artists.

The Charitable Deduction in Theory

Notwithstanding its name, the principal benefit of federal tax exemption to a nonprofit cultural organization is not exemption from federal tax. That is mostly an incidental benefit. In general, the operating results of these organizations are not such that they would generate any substantial income to tax even if they were not exempt. The real significance of tax exemption is in the fact the contributors to tax exempt organizations are entitled to deduct the value of their contributions in computing the amount of their income that will be subject to federal income tax.

The effect of this charitable deduction is to make the federal government, in essence, a cocontributor. If $1,000 is contributed to a nonprofit cultural organization by a taxpayer whose marginal tax rate—the rate, that is, at which his topmost dollar of taxable income would otherwise be taxed—is 31 percent, then the after-tax cost of such a gift to the donor is only $690. The remaining $310 represents revenue that will be forgone by the federal government. It is that $310 (multiplied many times over) that will hereafter be referred to as an indirect federal subsidy. It is also sometimes referred to as a "tax expenditure," a designation coined by the late Professor Stanley Surrey of the Harvard Law School in an effort to emphasize that it was actually a tax related forgone revenue and, in his view, came just as surely out of the federal government's coffers as if it had been spent directly.

Income tax deductions generally serve one of two purposes. They may either be compensatory for a taxpayer's diminished (and usually involuntary) ability to pay the tax that would otherwise be due at a particular level of income (for example, the deduction for substantial medical expenses or for casualty losses) or may serve as a stimulus toward some activity that those who formulate tax policy consider to be socially desirable. First introduced in 1917, the deduction for charitable contributions to educational, health, and cultural organizations was clearly intended to fall under this second heading, i.e., to serve as a stimulus.

How *strong* a stimulus it might be at any given time depends upon the tax rates then in effect. Since giving to cultural organizations tends to come principally from the most affluent taxpayers, the most critical of these tax rates would be the maximum marginal one. Over the past three decades, that rate (except for the 3 percent upward blip in the 1990 budget settlement) has moved steadily downward. As recently as the 1960s, this rate still stood at 77 percent. That meant that a $1,000 contribution from the most affluent taxpayer might have an after-tax cost of only $230 with the remaining $770 to be provided as a federal subsidy or tax expenditure. Since then, the maximum marginal rate has fallen to 70 percent, then to 50 percent, under the Tax Reform Act of 1986 (TRA '86) to 38.5 percent in 1987, and 28 percent for the three years subsequent and then come back to 31 percent. To recapitulate: the $1,000 charitable contribution that in the 1960s carried an after-tax cost to the taxpayer of $230 (and triggered a tax expenditure of $770) will, beginning in 1991, have an after-tax cost to the taxpayer of $690 (and trigger a tax expenditure of only $310).

Given the breadth of its impact and its persistence through every administration since John F. Kennedy's, there is little reason to believe that this downward movement in the maximum marginal tax rate has been particularly motivated by animosity toward the nonprofit sector (although the periodic discovery of questionable practices in foundations and other charitable organizations has not warmed public feeling toward that sector). Impelling it, rather, has been a new two-pronged strategy toward tax writing that has sought:

• To simplify and lower tax rates, while simultaneously
• Eliminating or constricting the deductions that might otherwise be available to reduce the income base to which those lowered rates would apply.

Thus far spared from the second prong of this strategy has been the itemized charitable deduction for contributions of cash (but not contributions of appreciated property or contributions by nonitemizers, both of which are discussed below). It would nonetheless appear, in theory at least, that the value of the charitable deduction as an incentive for private giving has been substantially eroded simply by the ongoing reduction in the maximum marginal tax rate. (The actual outcome will be considered in the next section).

Moreover, as both the administration and the Congress began a more earnest search for additional tax revenues in 1990, one of the earliest trial balloons to be floated was the notion that a further shrinkage of deductions, possibly including the charitable deduction, might be a more politically palatable way of proceeding than an increase in the existing tax rates. One model of this balloon involved a tighter percentage cap on deductions. Another would have imposed a floor similar to the one that has eliminated most job related and miscellaneous deductions in recent years. In the end, just such a floor was adopted. While its impact is expected to be modest, it does represent a further erosion of the system of deductions previously in place.

Concerning the charitable contribution of appreciated property—stocks, bonds, and, most importantly for museums, works of fine art—TRA '86 substantially dampened the considerable incentive that had existed previously. Prior to 1987, the donor was entitled to deduct the full fair market value of such property at the time of its gift. TRA '86 changed that radically. It required that the portion of any such contribution representing the appreciation over the donated property's original cost basis be included as a so-called tax preference item in the computation of an alternative minimum tax (AMT). (The AMT is a complicated device intended to ensure that no one can use tax shelters or extensive deductions to escape payment of income taxes entirely.) In a worst case scenario, that might reduce the federal tax benefit that the donor could derive from any such contribution to just 21 percent (24 percent after 1990) of his or her original cost basis. That such a change occurred just as the art market was experiencing an enormous upward surge meant that potential gifts of works of art might be affected with particular severity. While the application of this rule is to be suspended for 1991 for gifts of works of fine art (but not stocks or bonds), it is scheduled to reverse in 1992.

To illustrate how dramatically this change could affect the incentive for such gifts, consider the case of a painting originally purchased for $10,000, with a fair market value of $100,-000 at the time its gift to a museum might be contemplated. Immediately prior to TRA '86, the after-tax cost to the taxpayer of such a gift would have been $50,000 with the remaining $50,000 serving as a subsidy or tax expenditure. The reduction in the maximum marginal tax rate effected by TRA '86 would, in itself, have increased the after-tax cost to the taxpayer (for 1988 to 1990) to $72,000. If the taxpayer was already liable for the AMT, however, then his after-tax cost would be further increased to $97,900. At that point, little or no tax incentive to give would be left. The situation will be only minimally better for future years. After the one-year respite for 1991, from 1992 on the donor's after-tax cost will be $97,600.

That, of course, is a worst case example. The impact of the AMT would not be as harsh on a potential donor not already in its grip (although such a gift could, in itself, push him into that status). Nonetheless, the complexities involved in computing the potential after-tax cost of a gift of appreciated property—a computation that may require an extensive and intimate knowledge of all of the donor's other tax-relevant financial transactions—are so formidable that in all likelihood many such gifts simply fail to be offered out of confusion, discouragement, or uncertainty as to their ultimate tax consequences.

For a brief period, from 1982 through 1986, a charitable deduction was also permitted to taxpayers who did not otherwise itemize any other deductions. While initially subject to modest limitations (the maximum deduction permitted for each of the first two years of its gradual phase-in was $25), its only limitations by 1986 were the same percentage caps that applied to taxpayers who did itemize. It is unclear, however, whether this deduction for nonitemizers ever provided any important incentive for contributions to cultural organizations.

Studies of charitable contribution patterns conducted in the 1970s[9] strongly suggested that the overwhelming share of such contributions by lower and even middle income taxpayers was directed to religious organizations and to community funds. Given the fact that this pattern was already in place before 1982, there is considerable doubt as to whether the charitable deduction for nonitemizers actually served as an incentive, or whether such a pattern of giving would not have continued in any event. That cultural organizations nonetheless continue to lobby actively for the restoration of this nonitemizer deduction may be principally a matter of politics. It reflects more clearly their need to maintain good relationships within the larger charitable community than any substantial benefit they might hope to receive.

One federal tax provision that does still provide a substantial incentive for gifts to cultural organizations is the charitable deduction that has been available under the federal estate tax since 1918. Unlike the income tax, the estate tax's marginal rates are still sufficiently high to provide a substantial reduction in the after-tax cost of charitable gifts that take effect at death. First cutting in at a 37 percent level on an estate (other than one left to a surviving spouse) with total net assets above $600,000, the rate rises rapidly to 55 percent for estates of more than $3 million (with an extra surcharge of 5 percent for estates between $10 million and $20 million). At those levels, more than 50 percent of the full fair market value of a charitable bequest could still be recouped in the form of a tax subsidy or expenditure. In the case of a gift of appreciated property, treated identically to a gift of cash, that contrasts sharply with a gift made during the donor's lifetime for which the total subsidy might be as little as 21 percent (24 percent after 1990) of his or her original cost basis.

Too complex for extended consideration here is the cluster of sophisticated tax devices generally gathered together under the term "planned giving." Included under this heading are a variety of split-interest trusts, various life insurance packages, and a number of pooled-income or annuity arrangements. Common to all of these is a (two plus two makes five) combination of tax savings to the donor and benefits (sometimes deferred) to the charitable donee. The extensive paperwork required for some of these devices often limits their utility to substantial gifts of, for example, $25,000 or more.

Many of these devices first came into being under the Tax Reform Act of 1969. In general, colleges and universities were well ahead of cultural organizations in exploring their use. More recently, particularly because TRA '86 cut off so many other paths to tax minimization, independent financial advisers have begun aggressively promoting these devices as being among the last remaining forms of tax shelters still available. Fears have been expressed by a number of experts in this area (university development officers in particular) that the zealousness of such efforts may eventually attract negative congressional attention, and in time trigger reconsideration of the very substantial tax incentives that these devices can currently provide.

Also beyond the scope of this presentation are the tax incentives for private giving offered by the great majority of states and many localities that impose income taxes. Suffice it to say that, in both their application and in the policy considerations shaping them, these vary considerably both from the federal tax incentive and from one another. Common to all, however, is the intention to serve as a stimulus to charitable giving (sometimes local giving in particular), not to achieve tax equity.

What are the objections raised by those who would either eliminate or substantially modify this system of providing indirect federal support to the arts? For one thing, they point to the fact that the bulk of giving to cultural organizations comes from a relatively small handful of affluent taxpayers. Through their control of what may be more than $2 billion of tax expenditures annually (a fair estimate for 1989, and some ten times as much as the federal government provided to the arts that same year in the form of direct funding), this handful of taxpayers is in essence able to spend the public's money without any of the administrative safeguards or democratic participation that would normally accompany such a public expenditure.

If procedural regularity were the most important desideratum in providing support for the arts, this criticism might carry considerable weight. Most observers, however, would probably agree that what is more important still is to assure that support can be provided for the arts in all their breadth, whether functioning as agents of social continuity or as agents of social change. That seems far more likely to occur when funding decisions are decentralized to a myriad of taxpayers and not monopolized by a central bureaucratic agency that by its very nature must be guided by majoritarian prejudices and a tropism away from controversy. In the same vein, these observers might also argue that such decentralization gives the best possible assurance that this important source of funding will remain free from government interference.

If tax incentives for charitable giving are nonetheless to be retained in some form, then critics of the present system have urged that at the very least, they should be modified to produce greater tax equity. Because the charitable deduction reduces the amount of income that is to be taxed rather than the tax that is to be paid, and because the progressive rate structure of the federal tax system (though greatly flattened today from what it was previously) makes such a deduction more valuable to a high-income taxpayer than to one in a lower bracket, these critics argue that the incentive offered for individual giving to organizations should at least be in the form of a credit against tax rather than as a deduction from income. As such, it would provide the same dollar benefit to every taxpayer, regardless of his or her tax bracket. "A fair tax code," says Teresa Odendahl, writing in *The Chronicle of Philanthropy* (April 17, 1990), "would provide such a deduction for all citizens or none."

If the genesis of the charitable deduction was an effort to produce "fairness," this might be a convincing argument for such a change. As noted earlier, however, the charitable deduction's origin was a public policy determination to stimulate financial support for a category of organizations thought to be important to the society at large. That this stimulus should be aimed at those most able to provide that support is in furtherance of that policy. An alternate system might be more fair, but it would also be self-defeating unless, in the aggregate, it stimulated the same dollar amount of contributions as does the present system. Tax incentives, to be effective, should be targeted to where the money is.

Less theoretical is a third criticism that concerns the tax treatment of gifts of appreciated property, particularly works of fine art. In such cases, the work's fair market value at the time of the gift must be determined through an appraisal process that may necessarily involve a considerable degree of subjective judgment. Appraisal is also a process that may be (and, beyond question, on occasion has been) abused.[10] In fact, concerns about abusive valuation practices were voiced as early as the middle 1960s and, among other things, resulted in the establishment of the Internal Revenue Service's Art Advisory Panel in 1968.

To meet these concerns, the Congress amended the Internal Revenue Code in 1984 to introduce a rigorous new substantiation requirement in the case of any such gift for which a value in excess of $5,000 was claimed by the donor. Under that law, substantial penalties may be levied against the taxpayer whenever such a valuation is proved to be excessive by 50 percent or more. In such an instance, disciplinary action may also be taken against the appraiser. (A fuller explanation of these safeguards can be found in the booklet *Gifts of Property: A Guide for Museums and Donors* published jointly by the American Association of Museums [AAM] and the Association of Art Museum Directors [AAMD] in 1985.) This valuation problem may have been (or may ultimately be) rendered moot by the change introduced by TRA '86 requiring that the appreciated portion of the fair market value of such a gift be included as a tax preference item in the calculation of the donor's AMT. Over the long term (and notwithstanding the suspension of this rule for 1991), that is expected to reduce substantially the number and aggregate value of these gifts of appreciated property.

A final criticism of the system of charitable deductions as a conduit for indirect federal support is that the system's incentives are directed at stimulating the support of arts *organizations*, not artists themselves or art activities directly. (The system of direct federal support through the NEA, by contrast, can channel grant funds either to arts organizations for programmatic support or directly to writers, painters, musicians, and other creative individuals. Not incidentally, it is these latter grants that have most often attracted the sharpest criticism.) The consequences of such exclusively organizational support may differ from discipline to discipline.

In the visual arts, for example, the introduction of another level of decision making (such as the museum or art center) may work beneficially to dilute the public's sense that a particular activity or event has been funded in part by forgone tax revenues. The controversy over the Robert Mapplethorpe exhibition organized by the University of Pennsylvania's Institute of Contemporary Art swirled entirely around the direct support that the institute received from the NEA specifically for that exhibition. The fact that the institute (both directly and through the university) was also the recipient of indirect federal support for its general operating expenses (and undoubtedly in a far larger amount than was received directly from NEA) did not occasion the same adverse response.

On the other hand, in disciplines not traditionally institutionalized—modern dance is sometimes cited as an example[11]—the fact that the system of indirect federal aid requires an organizational channel through which the funds must flow may have had a more negative impact. Is it the best use of a dancer's talents to have to create a corporate framework through which to work? Once assembled, do the institutional imperatives of that framework (a truly representative board of trustees, charitable registration, an increased emphasis on fund raising) stand in uneasy balance with the ongoing creative interests of the artist? To the extent that the current system of charitable deductions adds weight to the organizational side of that balance, then this last criticism might deserve some closer consideration.

The Charitable Deduction
in Current Practice

When TRA '86 was enacted, there was considerable speculation as to its impact on the level of charitable contributions. On the one hand, there were those who believed that the increase in the after-tax cost of giving would lead to an overall reduction in such contributions. On the other hand, it was argued that affluent taxpayers would be left with considerably more disposable after-tax income than they had previously enjoyed and, accordingly, would be well inclined to increase their contributions over what they had given in prior years.

What, in fact, has actually happened? The evidence to date is sparse. What it suggests, however, is that while no enormously dramatic change has yet occurred with respect to gifts of cash, and that such charitable giving (both in nominal and inflation-adjusted terms) has continued to grow, the rate of that growth has slowed somewhat. It is not clear whether and, if so, how deeply that reduction in growth is connected to any change in incentive. On the other hand, gifts of appreciated property appear to have declined substantially. This evidence comes from scattered sources.

• The most widely used figures in the field are those compiled annually by the American Association of Fund-Raising Counsel (AAFRC) based in New York. TRA '86 took effect at the beginning of 1987. For the three years before and the three years after, AAFRC estimated total charitable giving as follows:

Year	(In *Billions*)
1984	$ 70.55
1985	80.07
1986	90.90
1987	95.15
1988	103.87
1989	114.70

• AAFRC has also broken out separate figures for contributions to arts and culture. While these have also continued to increase, as in the figures above, this increase appears to have been more vigorous in the years 1984–1986 than in the years 1987–1989. AAFRC's figures are:

Year	(In *Billions*)
1984	$4.50
1985	5.08
1986	5.83
1987	6.31
1988	6.79
1989	7.49

• Independent Sector (IS), a Washington based nonprofit coalition of 700 corporate, foundation, and voluntary organizations with national interests in philanthropy, has studied the contribution patterns of taxpayers with incomes of $1 million or more. It found that the average contribution per donor in this group had dropped from $200,000 in 1986 to $93,000 in 1987, the first year that TRA '86 was in effect. It is not clear to what degree both those figures may have been skewed by donors accelerating planned 1987 contributions into 1986, as many tax advisers were then recommending that they do. In general, IS appears to believe that the impact of the lowered tax incentive on donors of cash is not so much to reduce the number of donors as to reduce the size of their individual gifts.

• More conclusive, perhaps, are figures compiled by the AAM concerning the value of objects and other appreciated property donated to American museums during the two years before and the two years after TRA '86 took effect. These suggest that the change in the tax treatment of such contributions (i.e., the classification of appreciation as a tax preference item in calculating the donor's AMT) may thus far have had a stronger negative impact on this kind of gift than the reduction in the maximum marginal tax rate has had on gifts of cash. Of particular interest in the following figures is the comparison between 1985 and 1988 that should be relatively free of whatever skew might have been caused by gifts being accelerated from 1987 into 1986:

Year	Objects (In *Millions*)	Other Appreciated Property (In *Millions*)
1985	$ 79.125	$12.815
1986	103.825	17.414
1987	72.363	9.701
1988	40.251	8.622

• A survey covering those same four years by AAMD found a comparable decline in gifts of appreciated property following 1986. Notwithstanding a rising art market, the value of gifts received by art museums in 1988 was reported as 28.8 percent below the value of those received in 1987 and 63 percent below the value of those received in 1986.

At least one ghost, however, may haunt those figures. The extent to which fluctuations in overall charitable giving may be affected not simply by tax incentives alone but also by general economic conditions is unknown. For example, during the eleven-year period ending in 1985—a period in which there were also significant changes in the federal income tax, including a sharp reduction in the maximum marginal tax rate—the annual total of charitable contributions, as a percentage of the gross national product, never varied by more than plus or minus 5 percent from an average of 1.93 percent. The range was from a low of 1.84 percent in 1979 to a high of 2.0 percent in both 1984 and 1985.

While the relative constancy of those figures in the face of declining tax rates might be attributable to a concomitant increase in the sophistication of fund-raising techniques, it also suggests what a complex set of variables may be involved. Full deductibility, maximum marginal tax rates, and the treatment of appreciated property would all appear to be factors, but these may only be some of the dimensions of tax policy that impact on charitable giving. With respect to appreciated property, the treatment of capital gains must certainly play some role as well. Beyond that, most important of all may be the Internal Revenue Code's general impact on the national economy. In that respect, American cultural organizations might in the future do well to address themselves to tax policy in broader terms than they have sometimes done in the past. To concentrate simply on maintenance of the charitable deduction in its present form might be too parochial a focus.

Some Conclusions

How might the present situation concerning federal support for the arts be summarized?

• Direct federal funding—while the less significant component in terms of dollars, still vitally important as a model and an imprimatur—may be severely threatened in its ability to support the whole spectrum of the arts. That is particularly so with respect to those vitally needed arts that function as agents of social disruption or change. Even if the life of the

NEA is indefinitely extended (and extended without restrictions), the danger seems very real that the agency may have a period of real timidity in prospect. It could well become what its then-Acting Chair Hugh Southern referred to at the American Association of Museums' 1989 annual meeting in New Orleans as the "National Endowment for Nice Art." (More recently, National Council on the Arts member Lloyd Richards expressed a similar fear that NEA might come in time to stand for "National Endowment for the Agreeable.") In view of such a possibility, the maintenance of a strong system of indirect federal funding must be considered all the more essential.

- The system of indirect federal funding through tax incentives may have been weakened to a degree over recent decades. Nevertheless, it still appears to work, albeit more so for gifts of cash than gifts of contributed property. Some of the most useful of its remaining incentives may involve "planned giving," an area that cultural organizations might productively explore further than they thus far have done.

- Such indirect funding may nevertheless face a further diminution, not because the arts are in any particular disfavor, but because the entire system of tax deductions may be slowly eroding as the Congress reshapes the tax laws toward something more politically palatable and/or administratively simple. While the arts community will resist this erosion, it can only do so effectively by making common cause with the larger charitable world.

- Proactive strategies through which the arts community could work to strengthen the tax incentive might include (a) finding allies to join in seeking permanent restoration of the pre-TRA '86 treatment of gifts of appreciated property in the same manner as it was restored for 1991; and (b) reviving an idea originally advanced in the 1970s, the calculation of the charitable deduction for cash gifts, at least for lower and middle income taxpayers, at some multiple (double or less) of the amount actually contributed.[12] In all likelihood, however, neither of these initiatives can advance very far unless and until the tax climate has changed greatly from what it is at this writing. A combination of domestic and international events has put the federal budget process under enormous strain. Until this can be eased, it is no more realistic to expect that programs of indirect aid (not merely to the arts, but across the entire spectrum of federal assistance) will be enhanced by the relinquishment of tax revenues than that programs of direct aid will be the recipients of substantially increased appropriations.

Finally, it ought not be concluded that direct funding through the NEA and tax code incentives to private giving exhaust all the possible ways in which the arts are or might be publicly supported at a national level. There still appears to be widespread agreement that the arts, at least as an abstract concept, constitute an important public "good" and that they contribute in unique and vital ways to the quality of our national life. We need to explore further how best to translate that good will into active programs of federal assistance that can help stimulate and provide access to the arts in all their many manifestations: pleasing and nice, outrageous and nasty, gaudy or grand, and everything that is neither or both or in-between or none of the above, just as the arts have always been and still can be.

Notes

[1] For many of the principal arguments for and against this premise, see Netzer (1978). For a distinctly negative view, see Banfield (1984).

[2] Feld, O'Hare, and Schuster (1983).

[3] Hughes (1986).

[4] Hughes (1986).

[5] DiMaggio (1984).

[6] Larson (1983).

[7] M. Brenson. "Is Quality an Idea Whose Time Has Gone?" *New York Times.* July 22, 1990, section 2, p. 1.

[8] Kramer (1990).

[9] Weil (1983).

[10] For a chronicle of actual abuses, as well as a summary of other criticisms directed at the fairness of the full fair market value deduction, see Speiller (1980).

[11] Erb et al. (1984).

[12] Weil (1983).

6

Cultural Equity

*Part 1: Cultural Diversity
and the Arts in America*

ROBERT GARFIAS

Introduction

With each day we note steady changes in the demographic pattern of the United States. Increasingly, the nature of these changes gives cause for concern and reflection on what actions now might help us adjust to the changing configuration that is the certain future of our country. The magnitude of the changing demographic pattern has meant that practically no aspect of our lives can remain untouched by it. In this picture, the arts also stand at a critical juncture. This chapter will sketch out some of the major implications of de-

ROBERT GARFIAS is professor of anthropology at the University of California at Irvine. He is also a member of the National Council on the Arts, the Smithsonian Institution Council, the advisory committee to the president on the awarding of the National Medals of Art, and the Arts in Education Advisory Board of the National Endowment for the Arts. A musician and the author of numerous books and articles on ethnomusicology, Professor Garfias has recently spent several months in Turkey doing research on Ottoman classical music under a grant from the Turkish Ministry of Culture.

mographic change for the arts community and the barriers to constructive action that must be understood before we can hope to respond constructively to the new conditions.

No More the "Melting Pot"

The old adage about America as the "melting pot" seemed to work for quite a while. In the minds of many, it is still the only viable solution to our condition and the one that rings truest to our concept of the American Dream. Close scrutiny of the cultural nooks and crannies of our nation reveals a cultural diversity of immense proportions lying just below the surface of the uniform facade of Holiday Inns and Burger Kings. The melting pot concept, while not openly contested, has been quietly subverted all along. Today the pace at which new cultural communities are experiencing growth is such that the idea that we can still melt them into a single cohesive, yet American, entity seems impossible, given our understanding of the process as it has worked until now.

America is, at its core, a nation rich, complex, and diverse, and in essence something quite different from the Western European framework that our cultural and educational institutions have imposed on it. Searching beyond the obvious Caribbean enclaves of the East Coast, the Mexican and Central American substructure of the West, and the Vietnamese and Korean cities within cities of the West, one now finds a myriad of small communities also growing in the East, each proudly practicing and maintaining a strong sense of cultural identity. There are communities of Spanish Menorcans living in northern Florida and old Spanish cultures in northern Louisiana still practicing sixteenth century forms of Spanish poetry. Thousands of Ukrainians in New York, as well as Los Angeles, still maintain their own language schools for their youth. Basques are scattered in great numbers throughout rural Oregon, Idaho, Montana, Utah, and California. They still regularly send their children back to Spain in order to touch again upon their roots. Then there is a vast network of proud Native Americans holding on to their traditions as tenaciously as ever in spite of our nation's long history of attempting to "civilize" them by destroying what it is they have been trying valiantly to preserve.

The list is truly endless. There are Portuguese in New England, the Irish and Italians in Boston and New York; and then there is Hawaii, with Puerto Ricans, Okinawans, Native Hawaiians, Samoans, Portuguese, Mexicans, Japanese, Filipinos, and Chinese, each maintaining their own traditions and mixing them with others. The whole is a living example of the refusal of Americans to submerge their identity into one mass culture. The reality of America is a land covered with diverse cultural enclaves of all sizes throughout the country.

By and large, these are not people who have chosen to defy the American Dream. Instead, out of a deep sense of conviction, they are people who have decided they can be as American as anyone else, at the same time proudly transmitting to the next generation the best of what they remember. This is really what everyone agrees that civilization is about. The difficulty is in agreeing on who decides to civilize whom and how.

Community vs. Absorption

On the surface at least, the smaller cultural communities quickly recognize that they must absorb and be absorbed if they are to survive in the new environment. What is difficult for many Americans to comprehend is that with the larger and, in particular, the new waves of Latinos and Asians, it is not unwillingness to accept this principle that is the obstacle. The immense and rapid response to the amnesty programs for undocumented workers was a demonstration of their desire to cooperate and to join. But it is the sheer numbers that mitigate against smooth absorption. Their own communities offer a bedrock of support to newcomers, a comfortable alternative to striking out on their own, an option so attractive and easy that it becomes virtually impossible for most ever to break out. Yet we blame these new Americans for what is perfectly natural. Americans attached to the military in Asia and in Europe rarely venture beyond the base and rarely make friends with local people unless this has been structured for them. Mainland tourists flood Hawaii all year long and yet few ever venture beyond the beaches and tourist sites, and would be hard pressed to find a way of striking lasting friendships with the locals.

The need to establish community is indeed very strong. When the Hmong refugees, as well as the Cambodians and the Laotians, were first admitted into the United States, they were systematically scattered by the authorities throughout the country from Hawaii to Maine. Gradually networks of communication were established and subsequently a steady migration and resettlement in southern California began. However, what has occurred is that the Vietnamese, Korean, Iranian, and Latino communities in southern California, to take one example, have become so large as to be virtually impermeable to entry by outsiders, and it is just as difficult for insiders to find a way out. Even when the arts in America do decide to roll out the welcome mat to these other Americans, they are not likely to respond to the invitation.

The reasons for the reluctance to participate are complex. In essence, the environment has initially appeared to be hostile to these new immigrants. At almost every furtive foray into the larger unknown territory, their initial perception has been reinforced. Everything they see around them appears to reject who they are. The contrast between the comfortable support of their community and the hostility and lack of acceptance on the outside makes excursions into the exterior uninviting for all but the very few. For many Americans, our concert halls, museums, and libraries represent an aspect of their lives they deeply cherish and need. But they also represent, even more pointedly, for these communities of newcomers, the same hostility and unwelcomeness they experience when they venture out. Even more than in other realms, our cultural institutions seem to say, "You must belong here to enter," and, "You must know what you are doing here." For these immigrants and a good number of other diverse ethnic groups in America, there is little or no incentive to respond to the challenge. To them, our open doors appear as tightly shut as ever. The hostility of our cultural institutions to the noninitiated is vividly clear to those on the outside looking in, but difficult to comprehend by those who are working within mainstream structures.

For the most part, an impression of exclusivity and elitism is no longer intended by our arts organizations, but they continue to be viewed in that light by the "outsiders." Our educational system has taught us to believe that the cultural values we hold are innately correct. Those other traditions, newly arrived, are quaint, exotic, or political. You must appreciate our stuff if you really want to understand "art." One need only look at the manner in which the newly arrived cultures are regarded in the hierarchy of national, state, and local arts funding and in our arts education endeavors.

All of this is not to imply that evil work is afoot. The efforts toward wider dissemination and recognition of our diversity of cultures have been genuine. It is all the more frustrating then that after years of telling these heretofore neglected audiences that what they like does not quite fit with the accepted view of art, there is no inclination to participate now that the invitation has been tendered.

Even for those who are vigorously committed to seeing change come about, the potential for blunders and pitfalls must often seem daunting. But many are content to blunder on and to insist that their particular Western European cultural solution must be required of everyone. This kind of cultural myopia lies at the base of much institutional thinking in America, and it is in these areas of miscommunication that the greatest danger to our future lies. The only effective way to eliminate it is to be certain that individuals who can serve as spokespersons for the different cultures are seated around the table when plans are being discussed and decisions made. This means seeking out not only those who have already adopted mainstream cultural values, but also those who have not, and a willingness to hear and genuinely try to understand what they are saying.

Many in the arts have labored long and hard to find means of reaching out to these previously overlooked audiences. Many have done so out of a genuine sense of good will and a conviction that this is, indeed, the right thing to do. But the efforts made to date have had little positive effect. Solutions are needed right now, and yet no viable ones seem available.

A Place to Start:
the Board and the Staff

It is often pointed out that the governing boards and staffs of the major arts institutions do not reflect the diversity of the population. Recent surveys in San Francisco have demonstrated that the dominant arts organizations in the city have virtually no diversity on their boards, and little on their senior administrative staffs. There is every evidence that San Francisco is not unique in this regard and that the same criticism could be leveled at every major city in the country.

Seeking diversity in support staffing is one area in which more can be accomplished. Some will assert that only a few qualified people are available, but there are many more than most realize, and it is important that this imbalance be corrected. Obtaining diversity on boards of directors is quite another thing. Mainstream organizations have very specific expectations for their board members. In most organizations, their primary function is to give or raise money. While this may seem obvious, it is not necessarily self-evident for people coming from minority communities. Most have not been exposed to this ethic, and it will be difficult to find those who are willing and capable of adapting to it. The private club atmosphere of many boards can also be an alienating factor.

When well-meaning organizations assert that it is virtually impossible to identify minority group members who are willing to serve on their boards, funding agencies tell them there are many wealthy blacks, Asians, and Latinos in their community, and they simply have not worked hard enough to recruit them. But the idea that there are many such people out there waiting to be invited is patently absurd. There are probably a few who would fill the bill nicely, but being a prominent member of a minority community makes one highly visible when there are few others to share the burden of responsibility. As a result, these few are asked to do everything for their own community, as well as to represent it to groups on the outside. Thus it is very seldom that a person who is already serving organizations dealing with poverty, drug abuse, education, voter registration, and medical services is in a position to join a mainstream arts board. To expect or to demand it ignores the reality.

Attracting the Audience

Even supposing that greater minority participation on boards and staffs can be achieved, this alone does not solve the fundamental problem of finding ways to assure that the audience reflects the diversity of the population. More and more projects are proposed and funded that are intended to reach out to new audiences. Unfortunately, too many of these consist of expedient and inexpensive modifications of traditional programing. This rarely succeeds. It does little good to target new cultures if there has been little or no thought given to providing radically new incentives to cross over into new and seemingly hostile territory.

Yet funding agencies continue to fund outreach programs on the basis of plans and expectations, when there is little attention to evaluating their end results. A museum is given support for an exhibition of works by a minority artist who was most likely selected by experts outside his or her community. Not surprisingly, very few people from his or her community attend. It is not the artist who has failed, but the museum board and director who entered into the project with the wrong expectations.

Given the present structure of our arts institutions, it is difficult to see how this could be otherwise. All the best attempts to achieve diversity have seemed doomed to fail. The inability to look squarely at the problem is locked into the structure of the organizations themselves. Diversity is regularly and routinely sought on panels for government, state, and local agencies. It is also sought on the boards and committees of arts organizations, but more to satisfy the formal requirements for minority representation than to seek diverse opinions. As a result, minorities are often chosen because their backgrounds match the expectations of those already in the structure rather than because they represent another point of view. Such individuals may be valuable, but they alone cannot be expected to change the status quo.

A Corporate Solution?

Corporate philanthropy has not been successful in solving the problems of inequitable access to the arts. Minority organizations are constantly chided to seek corporate support in order to decrease dependency on public funds. But to expect this is naive. Recently, in Orange County, California, the struggling Black Actor's Theatre, in attempting to seek private support, was criticized for stating in a flyer that its request for support had received such responses as "We are already committed to the South Coast Repertory Theatre and the Orange County Performing Arts Center, and we feel this support serves the Black community." Can it really be that these corporations have not noted the almost total absence of blacks, or any other minorities, at the performances of the theatre or the center?

As it stands now, there is little chance that minority organizations can expect help from corporations while these institutions support the mainstream groups regardless of their track record in addressing diversity in their audiences. By the same token, if minority organizations are expected to find philanthropic support within their own communities, this reflects a fantastic view of the distribution of wealth in America. What little wealth there is in these communities is being tapped by acute social needs of which the arts are not perceived to be a significant part.

Is Education the Answer?

It is frequently said that education is the only answer. Some outreach efforts are, in fact, being aimed precisely where they might, in the long run, do the most good, that is, in the public schools. Yet here also, well-intended efforts often meet with only a minimum of cooperation from the schools themselves. Furthermore, minimal financial support for these efforts limits them to far too few students to change cultural patterns or foster a sense of ownership in the programs. To be effective in changing the pattern of attitudes about the dominant culture and developing a long-term interest in the arts, young people must be saturated by exposure. Upon becoming adults, they might then someday venture of their own volition into our palaces of culture. Short of sustained exposure to the arts, they will grow up knowing only that these things exist, but will have no direct sense that these are any different from the abstract political institutions they learned about in school.

In addition, it is still too often true that the artists on stage in the schools attended by minority children do not reflect the diversity of the students for whom the performances are held. Once again the message is clear—"Look but don't touch—this is really not for the likes of you."

Politics and Public Funding

There are serious political implications in the situation that take the matter beyond the realm of simply "doing the right thing." Arts organizations, like institutions of higher education, are coming under increasing scrutiny for their failure to represent the communities they serve. The use of public monies, without which few arts institutions can survive today, means that fair application of funds to all parts of the community becomes a matter of law. Increasingly these groups and funding agencies alike are being questioned about how well they are serving their constituencies. While larger and larger amounts of public support are necessary, audiences are not growing commensurately, especially the audience of "other Americans" who have been excluded in the past.

In California, to take an example where the problem is acute, a recent Department of Finance report indicates that within thirty years, the population will consist of 16 million Anglos, 14.9 million Latinos, 2 million blacks, and 5 million Asians and other. It is also important to note that a large proportion of the Anglo population will be retired.

It does not take a lot of imagination to visualize the volatility of the situation. If minorities, soon the largest segment of the population, continue to feel that the arts are not theirs as well, the pressure to change the pattern of public support for the arts will only grow. Private support, including corporate philanthropy, will similarly be affected as the complexion of the public changes.

Responding to the Challenge

As this profound shift in the nature of the population takes place, the established arts organizations may fail to see that the light at the end of the tunnel is a train coming their way. They tend to be so enmeshed in the struggle to keep afloat that the line of least resistance is to fall back upon their own established values. They still tend to behave as if everything would be all right if they could only reach these "other people" and make them part of the mainstream audience. Once in the door they, too, will be convinced of the superiority of the European tradition. What seems impossible for the Eurocentric arts establishment in America to accept is that one set of values may be as valid—and as arbitrary—as another.

This is *not* to say that it does not matter to which set of values we subscribe. The set of values agreed upon by consensus becomes a unifying culture and a basis for communication and cooperation. What has occurred, however, is that the arts establishment behaves as though their values are inviolable, almost resembling religious doctrine. But their missionary efforts have yielded few converts outside the walls of the citadel.

Europe Has Not Prevailed

There are many indications that the condition described above is nothing new. Apart from the European immigrants, mainstream arts traditions have been adopted by few other newcomers. One notes this in particular among long-established third and fourth generation immigrant communities in America, such as the Japanese and Chinese. While many individuals from these groups have achieved the social and economic stability that other minorities in America might wish to emulate, only a small number attends performances of mainstream arts organizations or serves on their boards. There is no reason to believe that, achieving similar status, other groups would behave differently. From all the evidence of the way the Japanese and Chinese have adjusted to the opportunities of life in America, a positive and participatory role by the most recent minority groups to reach our shores is highly unlikely.

The Barriers to Change

The foregoing would seem to suggest that only those who came to this country with a European cultural background will ever participate fully in the Western European arts. But clearly this cannot be so. Otherwise it would be impossible to explain why some of the most important interpreters of European music are Japanese, Korean, Indian, and Chinese. No, it is something we are doing—or not doing—right here.

Everyone, left to his or her own resources, tends naturally to reject the foreign and cling to the familiar. Through the process of education and experience, what we accept and seek out is gradually expanded. The very size of our country is no doubt a factor, as are the long-recognized isolationist attitudes of many Americans. Combine these factors with the diversity of cultures that constitutes our population and we see a society that is increasingly fragmented. As long as the mainstream

hangs on to its system of absolute values, the cultural heritage
of the "other" Americans will be seen as being of less stature
and importance. It relegates the cultures of the other Americans to a lesser category. In higher education, the situation is
worst of all. Cultural traditions other than the European tend
to exist only as an afterthought, not even marginal to the established curriculum.

The same attitudes are reflected in the country's arts institutions. As the diversity of the population increases, the message
is clear: you can only enter if you leave your own culture behind.

Arts organizations continue to hammer away at the same set
of values while, at the same time, talking more and more about
cultural pluralism. It is difficult to see how Eurocentric values
will ever accommodate any other cultural perspective by talk
alone. The crosscultural perspective needs to be introduced in
the funding and programing of all aspects of the arts in America. Funding agencies need to look beyond the good intentions
expressed in multicultural proposals, and begin looking with
close scrutiny at whether the goals can be achieved. There is
no point in funding multicultural outreach projects of any
kind, be they small museum exhibits or city festivals on the
scale of the Olympics, if they do not successfully reach significant numbers of the target populations.

It is also not enough to provide funding in the name of
cultural diversity for an ethnic community organization if that
organization does not have the capacity to reach its own community on a broad scale. This is not to say that such organizations should not be supported, but only that expectations
should be more realistic. We need to look past our expectations and into the communities themselves to see how well
they are being served, and then proceed accordingly with
plans and proposals that are commensurate with the need.
Prejudices and preconceptions must be left behind.

We must become far more aware and concerned about how
our cultural resources are applied. Unless we substantially
modify the manner in which we think about the arts in this

country, and how and to whom we provide support, we can only continue down the road of propping up organizations that are serving dwindling audiences. The end result will be that the majority is paying for the cultural enrichment of a small elite.

Re-education offers the only solution to all of these dilemmas. How else can we begin to change and expand the concept of what is good and beautiful? But even before the slow process of education can have its effect, we need to reassess our own past. Rick Simpson and Scott Walker have said, "As the world becomes more of a single economic entity, there is a corresponding need for all citizens to have not only a fundamental understanding of their own culture (in part to conserve it), but also a knowledge of the cultures of the rest of the world." The systematic destruction and devaluation of the cultures of non-Europeans must stop. Rather than blend us all into the melting pot, it has only driven a wedge between the various segments of our population. Now that the non-European segment is growing ever larger, the utter folly of well-intentioned thinkers like William Bennett and E.D. Hirsch seems clear. The emphasis on Western civilization as the universal culture has not succeeded in any large measure, and there is little indication the future will be any different.

Years of denial and ignorance about the traditional cultures of the other Americans have resulted only in indifference on the part of those we have been attempting to reach. They have also left us unprepared to meet the challenge. As a professor of humanities at the University of Virginia said recently, "We know how to put things in the Western tradition in context, but most of us don't have the slightest idea what the contexts of Indian music, Japanese poetry, and Indian philosophy are."

Faced with the clear reality of cultural and demographic change, the "cultural literacy" movement seems little more than a backlash, a death rattle that offers no help to the problem that faces us. It is time to recognize, in James Baldwin's phrase from *Notes of a Native Son,* that America is white no longer, and it will never be white again.

Part 2: *Cultural Democracy*

GERALD D. YOSHITOMI

Other writers in this volume have documented the role played by the National Endowment for the Arts in the development of the philosophical and structural framework for federal, state, and local government support of the arts. Implementation of this support system over the past thirty years combined with the commitment at the local level to build symphony halls, museums, theaters, and other infrastructure have, combined with increased audiences and growing contributed support, resulted in tremendous growth of the nonprofit arts sector over those three decades.

However, as we enter this last decade of the twentieth century, we must ask ourselves whether these same philosophical and structural frameworks provide for the most appropriate support to the arts of today and the twenty-first century or whether it is the time to develop new approaches for support of the arts.

A Changing America

Each of us is aware of the dynamic demographic and cultural changes that have always been a part of the American experience. Yet those continuing demographic and cultural changes,

---

GERALD D. YOSHITOMI is executive director of the Japanese American Culture and Community Center in Los Angeles. He is also chair of the National Task Force on Presenting and Touring the Performing Arts and has served as a member of the California Arts Council, the Los Angeles Culture Heritage Commission, and chair of Performing Arts Subcommittee of the U.S.–Japan Culture Exchange Conference. Previous positions include the Western States Arts Foundation, the Arizona Commission on the Arts, and the Office of Economic Opportunity.

combined with the economic, political, and social changes of the past decade, as well as those predicted for the current decade, describe a markedly different America than the one in which the NEA was created.

The American educational system is in crisis, no longer able to afford the teaching of the arts, and not able to effectively teach the subjects still within the required curriculum. Our economy has shifted from industrial to service, and mergers and foreign ownership have placed corporate headquarters thousands of miles from their employees and customers. Audiences for the arts are aging, and newly arrived immigrants and younger people are not taking their places. Technology continues to have great impact on the art we produce, as well as the ways in which we each participate in it. The number of different languages and cultures from which our world views are derived are now so many that the permutations of the different kinds of relationships are too numerous to count, let alone to define and participate in. It is a veritable Richter scale as one moves from six to seven to eight, let alone over one hundred cultures.

Robert Garfias ends his remarks in this volume with the quote from James Baldwin that America is white no longer and will never be white again. That pointed statement written only forty years ago couldn't predict the complexity of the America of the current decade. We are not merely shifting from one paradigm to another. Rather, we are shifting from one to many. If that is the case, what can we say about the public arts support system and its capacity to support this broader society. At one time one could say that the Baldwin quotation referred to a white vs. black society, but now we have over one hundred ethnic groups that make up the mix of what it is to be American.

The great experiment of the democracy of America has survived throughout its history by incorporating each of us and the cultures of which we are a part into that great fabric. We have not always been able to do it with grace or compassion, and we have made tragic mistakes of which we must be constantly reminded and continue to diligently redress. Yet we have been able to maintain the resilience to accept the next dilemma and welcome the next immigrant. We omitted slaves from the Declaration of Independence, but less than one hundred years later endured a Civil War to guarantee (we thought) freedom. And we joined freedom rides one hundred years after that to fight for freedom once again.

We know as Americans that we will always have to give of ourselves to guarantee our own rights and the rights of others. When a woman's right to choose is taken away from her and a person's sexual preference results in discrimination, we know as Americans that we must speak out. We know that we must accommodate the views that are different from ours, or else the right to express our own views and cultures may be taken away from us. As a society, beginning with the first killing of Native Americans by the "immigrant" explorers, we haven't been able to address the issues within sufficient time to prevent the tragedies of violence, death, and great human suffering. Yet possibly we have had the benefit of learning from our hundreds of years of history to understand our cultural differences and the need to incorporate those differences into our communities, our broader American culture, and into our laws and civic leadership. We have always believed in the potential of this country to address its issues and to solve them, incorporating the broadest spectrum of the American public into that process.

A Country of Cultural Diversity

But now our confidence has been shaken. We have more cultures in this country than we can possibly understand, and although the process of incorporation can occur quickly, we do not know if we have the resources, public and individual, to incorporate all of these cultures into what we hope will be the America of the twenty-first century. We don't know if so many cultures can be amalgamated so quickly into the fabric of America. We are faced with this great American dilemma of the twenty-first century: will the country depicted in the Emma Lazarus poem at the base of the Statue of Liberty ("Give me your tired . . .") succumb to the quick and easy answer of requiring everyone to accept American mass culture and to leave behind the culture that serves as the basis of their humanity, or are we willing to deal with the complexity of each of our cultures, and to work to incorporate those cultural perspectives into the broad fabric of what it is to be an American as well as to assist in the search for cultural background for those whose rush to jump into the American melting pot seared away their cultural roots.

We've been told that the arts will provide a perspective from which we can redefine what it is to be an American. Yet this process of redefinition, or at least refinement, creates a great dilemma for each of us. In this time of great demographic and social change how do we encourage the new without losing the old? How do we encourage diversity without being unfocused as a culture? How do we fully accept each other without losing some of ourselves?

The Language for Discussion

These questions may not have answers today, nor may we be able to fully answer them in the future. Furthermore, we may not even have the language to address the issues that now confront us. As represented in *An American Dialogue,* the statement of the National Task Force on Presenting and Touring the Performing Arts, words used to discuss the issues of cultural equity, diversity, multiculturalism, etc. were defined differently by many of the participants. The task force sometimes found that two people talking about the same matters—using outdated language or language that carried conflicting meanings and personal associations—scarcely understood one another. Terms like "multicultural," "ethnic," and "minority" are often euphemisms for African American, Asian, Latino, and Native American. Excellence is viewed by some to be the most important concept in the NEA's enabling legislation, while others see it as a codeword for racism. Such language blurs discussions of race and culture, making agreement difficult. Culture does not equal race and the "minority" population in some places in the United States is white.[1]

In order to encourage dialogue, however, we each must be encouraged to utilize the words and language with which we are most comfortable. We must accept each other's words and language as we begin our discussions just as we hope to accept each other's cultures at the end. I will utilize words such as "mainstream," "ethnic," and "culturally specific" as a means to address areas of concern, rather than to fully define our various fields. They are the best words to describe the issues I can identify and the indulgence of the reader is requested in order that the understanding of the concepts can get beyond the limitations of current vocabulary. It is also requested that the reader not jump to conclusions about the viability of the public policies and/or funding programs that may come from this presentation. Once we carefully consider whether we must establish new goals for public arts policy, we can then examine whether we can develop the mechanisms to reach those goals. This is a time of learning, to listen and think about what we've heard rather than to jump to conclusions. The issues of this decade require acceptance of the ambiguity of our circumstances.

No Longer the Melting Pot

Rather than the melting pot, some have suggested that the current analogy is that of a stew, bouillabaisse, or mixed salad, in which each culture stays intact, but mixes with the influences of everyone else to develop a culture that is greater than the sum of its parts.

Others suggest that the concept of multiple paradigms would envision not just one bowl or pot cooking on the stove, but a number of diverse pots, both large and small, that would reflect the diverse cultures of America. There might be big containers, to accommodate the stews, bouillabaisse, and salads, but also smaller containers, in which specific cultures and tastes would choose to be nurtured, preserved, and modified, prior to (and possibly instead of) joining the larger kettles. This model would reflect both an integration of cultures and a process of selective, focused separation. There would, of course, be many cooks, and each culture would be integral to several of the pots.

A foreign dignitary visiting the United States recently remarked that the America of the 1990s is in fact the world in microcosm. He said, "If America is successful in bringing its people together, maybe the world has a chance."

The American Public
Arts Support System

The public arts support system as it exists in the 1990s represents a system created in the 1960s to address the needs and structures of the organizations that existed at that time. Today we must question whether those institutions will be able to address the arts needs of the current decade, let alone the next century.

As conceptualized and developed in the early to mid-1960s, public arts was designed to help preserve and stabilize institutions that were producing important bodies of work within their own communities. Many of these had begun to face significant deficits and were actively seeking government aid for the first time. The government, through the National Endowment for the Arts, did begin to provide some assistance, and later developed a challenge grant program whose principal purpose was to generate more private funding for the large institutions. There was much encouragement to broaden the private support base from individuals, corporations, and foundations, but very little emphasis on reaching new audiences and underserved communities. The funding "model" of the large organization was assumed to be the one that all other nonprofit groups, of whatever size, should follow and according to which they should be judged.

Expanded popularization of the arts, increased time for leisure activities, and the geographic decentralization of the population encouraged the creation of new arts organizations and facilities in cities throughout the United States. Size of budget, matching grants, payments to professional artists, and corpo-

rate leadership on boards of directors were all utilized as requirements by which the "less meritorious" could be differen-
tiated from those to be funded. Regional opera companies
were established under the same basic form as the Lyric Opera
of Chicago, and the local museums adopted the same practices
as the Metropolitan Museum of Art. The assumption was that
these "standard" ways of operating should be replicated
throughout the country, and that large sums of contributed
public and private support would be available to offset the gap
between earned income and expense. It was also predicated
on the assumption that levels of public support should increase as an organization's budget increased and equated support for arts institutions with support for the arts. Rather than
decreasing public support as an organization's audience and
contributed income increased (as, for example, in the sliding
scale of social security benefits), it was assumed that public
support would increase as private became more available. It
was also assumed that the public treasury, as well as the American corporate community, could afford to provide increasingly
large sums of support to relatively small numbers of selected
institutions within each locality. In other words, sufficient
funds were available to support one museum, one opera company, one ballet company, one theater, etc., and these institutions would be able to accommodate the cultural needs of cities.

It should also be noted that the system was created not to
support art directly, but to support nonprofit arts organizations that in turn were expected to produce and present the
arts. It was a support structure designed to assure the permanence of arts organizations, with the assumption that those
organizations would assure the permanence of the arts within
our society and their availability to the broadest numbers of
the American public. The allocation of large amounts of public
and private funds to support the construction of the various
performing arts centers and museums throughout the country
in the last three decades continued under the rationale that the
facilities required by these institutions should be built as public (rather than private) resources and maintained as annual

public expenses. The performing arts centers were built under the assumption there could be one "center" that would house all of the arts events important to a city, much as a central library could house all the books needed in a city collection.

"Peer review systems" and standardly accepted practices were developed over a fairly short period of time for this new field of nonprofit arts organizations, and graduate programs were developed to train the future leadership of this new profession. Guidelines were developed that focused on developing the most effective systems of supporting already existing organizations, often with direct consultation with the key leadership of their various disciplines. Over the course of time, guidelines and procedures were rationalized, sometimes to the point of a bureaucratization of the system. Models were "institutionalized," with the assumption that large earned income vs. expense deficits could be made up with annually increased contributed income, rather than focusing on expanding public participation and earned income. Decisions were often made to provide the largest grants, facilities support, and tax subsidies to the largest organizations, rather than seeding newly developing art forms and groups with substantial support in their early years.

Toward Integration

The majority of funds to support music went to those organizations whose repertoire and personnel reflected European classical music traditions, and similar patterns were followed in the support of opera, museum, and theater organizations. As it became clear, however, that the arts in the United States should not be limited to those aforementioned traditions, attempts were made to "democratize" the public support systems. Concern was also expressed that the focus of support was not broad enough for the expanded public purposes espoused within the enabling legislation of most public arts agencies. Audiences, musicians, administrators, artistic directors, and board members were still primarily of European ancestry and did not seem to be impacted by the civil rights movement and the integration of other publicly supported institutions. Even though the student bodies of the public universities were much more integrated, the audiences of the public concert halls were not.

Many important steps were made in the 1980s to encourage the process of democratization of the American arts support structure, the institutions they supported, and in some cases even the art that was being presented on the stages of the performing arts centers and on the walls of the museums. This was and is still being advocated in varying degrees by the NEA, state and local arts agencies, and some foundation and corporate funding sources. Yet still we have major discrepancies between the ethnic composition of our cities and that of our arts audiences in their major public institutions. In fact, as one public art agency official in North Carolina recently observed:

Over my lifetime almost all the public institutions have been integrated. People from all cultural groups join together to study in our public universities, swim in our parks, read books from their cultures in publicly built facilities. But unfortunately that is not the case in the arts. I often wonder whether the arts are the last bastion of publicly supported segregation in North Carolina.

Culturally Specific Arts

Throughout history, each of America's cultural and ethnic communities has persevered to maintain its own cultural tradition, often attempting to counteract the actions of the government or other public systems. Public policies have encouraged and at times even mandated the attempted genocide of various Native American nations, the separation of the African American family through the slavery system, prohibitions against speaking our native tongues in the public school system, and the destruction of Japanese American cultural materials in the relocation to the concentration camps of World War II. Yet communities have established their own internal structures without public assistance to support cultural preservation through churches, social centers, and fraternal organizations.

During the 1970s and 1980s these cultural communities, almost all of which had long-established informal systems of cultural preservation, developed cultural and arts organizations that received "seed money" support from public arts agencies. Social service, educational, religious, and fraternal groups also developed arts projects as central elements in their cultural, community, and political mission. Cultural survival was at the core of many of these projects and organizations. In the area of the dramatic arts, African American, Latino, and Asian American theater companies were developed in the 1970s with the hope that by the 1990s they would be able to be as strong as "mainstream" theaters. But these companies, quite understandably, were unable to reach the critical mass of private funding according to the larger mainstream "model." Consequently, their grant support from both public and private sources remained minimal and their growth disappointing. Media coverage did not help, because it was limited and often written by critics who were unfamiliar with the work being presented. In addition, access to the "mainstages" of the large public performing arts centers was generally impossible, reserved, as they were, by the mainstream organizations that had frequently been part of the case made to the public and private donors responsible for building the centers.

At the beginning of the 1990s, all but a few of the African American, Asian American, and Latino theater companies established in the 1970s are still in existence, and it is a time in which it appears there may be more support than ever to support culturally specific theater. Finally the concerns of cultural diversity, coupled with the persistent pressure by key public policy activists and national foundation leaders and the simultaneous development of outstanding writers, directors, and actors, have resulted in many recent productions. Most of these plays have been produced in the "laboratories" of the large mainstream theaters, supported with grants of significant size; yet some have reached the mainstage.

Access vs. Control

Some might say that these centralized mainstages are where all the best work should be produced. Yet there is concern expressed by many cultural groups regarding the issue of access vs. control. Twenty years ago, most would have been pleased with the mere access to the facility, no matter who produced the work. Now, after a history of unfortunate past experiences, people are asking for control of their own cultures and cultural symbols. They've seen the work of the best Latino playwrights "reworked" by directors who don't possess an understanding of Latino cultural traditions, and they've seen centuries old Asian traditions trivialized by unknowing producers. In the visual arts, they are demanding that African American curators and institutions be involved in the selection of work for exhibitions and have central roles in the interpretation of those materials for their own and broader communities. The concern is stated in *An American Dialogue:*

. . . when the content of one culture is left solely to another to express, without any consultation with that culture's community, then the result is usually distorted, unintentionally or by design. This outcome is even more likely—and more threatening—if the two cultures are at odds: haves and have-nots, majority and minority, victor and vanquished. . . . In short, no culture can survive intact if its interpretation and transmission are controlled by people outside the culture.[2]

People are asking that this process toward access (or integration) continue but only with the inclusion of culturally specific communities to assure them the control of their cultural symbolism. Access only is no longer sufficient. One method of assuring control and self-determination is to provide direct grants to the culturally specific organization to mount the production on the mainstage of the larger institutions. Yet often the culturally specific organization receives far less support to produce the work on its own stage than is received by larger organizations to produce the same work. When collaborations are discussed, control by the larger organization often becomes a condition of acceptance.

Democratization

To assure the plurality of control systems that would be suggested by these issues one could simultaneously "integrate" or "democratize" the mainstage museums, certain within each that culturally specific communities are included on the ground floor in the planning and selection of the art to be produced and presented, as well as in strong culturally specific theater companies, dance ensembles, etc., to produce and nurture the work. These organizations would be as much community based as the mainstream institutions and would have significantly different operating systems.

It is possible to democratize the nation's largest cultural resources. Although this process will require much energy and effort, it is imperative if we are to have resources and create a "common ground of American cultural experience," as someone has described it, in which all citizens can participate. It is important to all of us as Americans that we each experience the works of George Balanchine, Paul Taylor, and Bill T. Jones. All of our children must hear the music of the world's great composers played by outstanding symphony orchestras; yet we must also broaden our standard definitions of who is to be included in that "great composers" list. We all must make every effort to work to that end. The future success of this country as a true democracy and the incorporation of our various cultural traditions requires this "democratization" of our largest cultural resources.

The Development of Culturally Specific Arts Resources

The development of strong culturally specific artistic resources, on the other hand, is more problematic within our current system. Toward that end, during the democratization efforts of the 1970s and 1980s, many culturally specific organizations found that they were supported, through expansion arts and other "multicultural" programs intended to provide "access" to start-up funds. In most cases, it was the intention to provide significantly increased sums of money over time to "institutionalize" these culturally specific organizations. Unfortunately, in the latter half of the 1980s these organizations found that they were in fact on a "dead end road." They had met pilot criteria and "advancement" criteria, but as they attempted to move into larger funding levels comparable to other institutions, they found that the doors were closed due to limitations in the public funding projected to be available during the 1990s, combined with the large institutions' ever-increased needs for public support, as indicated above. A system that allocates public resources based on the amount of private contributions will by definition always provide the greatest amounts of support to the wealthiest organizations. Democratization has assured that culturally specific organizations are not denied entry, but they often face situations in which funding is limited because of specific guidelines. Access to funds at the highest levels of support have been denied by the system. Some have described this systematic denial as being allowed entry into the club, with access to the main dining room, but not being allowed to eat in the private lounge upstairs. They feel that they might have reached the "glass ceiling" often experienced by minorities and women as they attempt to make their way up the corporate ladder. These difficulties are even more pronounced for the individuals and cultural groups who are newly arrived in this country, attempting to hold onto their cultural traditions, while also attempting to participate in the American cultural system.

Some would act to merely change the guidelines, but the problems with the current American public arts policy are much more systemic in nature. Established public arts policy (or at least that which we have accepted over the past thirty years), augmented by civil rights legislation and political advocacy, is able at best to support the establishment and democratization of centralized cultural institutions. Yet in order to create and present the culturally specific art to be produced within those centralized institutions to be shared with others, we must have culturally specific organizations that preserve, educate, train, and produce that work within an ongoing community context. More importantly, for each culture to survive in this country, and for each citizen to have a cultural framework upon which he or she can base his or her participation in the broader American society, each must have access to one's own cultural symbols, activities, and traditions. American public arts policy has not succeeded in supporting culturally specific organizations nor the cultures in which they are rooted.

The failure of American public arts policy to effectively support the arts of our broad range of cultural communities is due to the inappropriateness and ineffectiveness of previously developed support systems for the arts. These systems were created in the 1960s on an old institutional model. The model, however, has demonstrated its ability to support certain kinds of institutions and should be continued to do that work. On the other hand, to support culturally specific work, new systems must be developed that are more appropriate to the cultural systems of the communities they are attempting to serve. The fundamental problem presently is that our arts policies are not in congruence with the needs of cultural development and support. Once established, these systems will bring our cultural policies into congruence with our democratic goals of inclusion and pluralism.

The Development of Cultural Policy

Arts administrator and philosopher Hope Tschopik posits that America has an arts policy, not a cultural policy.

As developed, our arts policy concerns itself with artist, the art, and the audience in a narrow social context, rather than with the community from which art emerges, or the values and traditions which establish the context or art. We have an arts policy based on an idea of a "superior culture," a European definition of art, that which hangs in the museum or is performed in the concert hall or theatre; that which is secular or derived from court tradition; that which is contemporary and professional. We place little value in art that is based in other cultural traditions or one that is subordinate to a social, communal, occupational, religious or familial context. Our arts policy, in theory, is supposed to serve our pluralistic society. In practice, it is dysfunctional by design.[3]

We appear to be operating under the assumption that the most important music is that which is played by large ensembles in 3,000-seat concert halls, because that is where most of our public funds to support music are allocated. The gospel music sung by millions of people every Sunday morning cannot be supported within our current system of support unless it is taken out of its natural support mechanism, the church. Because it cannot be supported directly, by connotation we are saying to each other that one type of music is more important than the other. Or to put it another way, we may be saying that one of the only live cultural experiences an African American child encounters on a weekly basis is not art. These issues are particularly compelling to me, because when I was a child in school and learned about art and music (when those subjects were still taught in schools), I learned that Japanese prints that my grandmother hung on the walls in our home were not the "real" art that was described in the books. I learned that ikebana and bonsai were hobbies, not art. I learned that the barrio mural painted by my classmate's uncle wasn't art either. I also learned that the jazz played by our neighbor down the street wasn't music. As a child, I mourned the loss of my culture, and of myself as my own cultural symbols, and those of my friends, were being systematically eliminated from my experience.

Others have suggested that culturally specific communities should create their own institutions to support their cultures. However, these institutions need to be created in forms different from the present norm. The question has been asked within cultural communities, do we want to be like the institutions that:

- treat the remains and sacred objects of our ancestors as novelties on display?
- say that they are broad based, but don't allow our music into their concert halls?

• say that they reach diverse audiences, but will not allow theater in our languages onto their stages?

Tschopik continues:

With our current arts policy we are inhibited by the inability to see
beyond what we are already doing. We have developed round holes
that work well to accommodate round pegs, but are inadequate to
accommodate the pluralistic challenge of square, octagonal or trian-
gular pegs. We have created a strategy based on the assumption that
the challenge of pluralism can be met by structural rather than systemic solutions. In our pursuit of excellence first and accessibility
second we have designed tactics that resolve the issue of professionalization and dissemination of the arts but have not really, practically or
substantively, strengthened participation in arts and culture, broadened the definition of art or embraced other cultural contributions.[4]

Different Systems of Support

Culturally specific communities support their cultures in
ways that are markedly different from the commonly viewed
broader American arts support system and also differ from
culture to culture. Culturally specific support structures are
often nonhierarchical, yet at other times are extremely hierar-
chical. Many cultures focus on the preservation of the cultural
form, not on the support to a particular artist. Some cultures
support their forms through "regular" arts support organizations, while others do so in churches, for-profit clubs, and fraternal organizations. Some forms have been impacted greatly
by the commercial and popular entertainment industry, while
others have been protected from commercial influences. Over
the past thirty years, many of these systems of support have
been excluded by guidelines and eligibility criteria as they
have attempted to seek funds from public arts support structures. The arts guidelines have continually excluded culturally
specific organizations because the arts support structures
often have the wrong focus. What is needed are not revised
guidelines, but the development of new systems and mechanisms to support culturally specific organizations.

Fellowships are generally considered to be the best way to support individual artists, but in certain nonhierarchical arts structures, the awarding of a fellowship to one person could create divisiveness and destroy the fragile cooperative relationship that exists between artists. Potential turmoil could be avoided by strategies that would seek to support the continuation of the cultural form rather than to recognize a specific artist. Recognition both from within and without the culture is an issue of great potential conflict.

In other communities, spiritual and religious observances are central to the music of the culture. To remove the religious context would remove the meaning of the music. Yet guidelines often require the separation of church and state.

The distinction of amateur vs. professional is distorted when the ongoing cultural and economic system compels cultural workers to have other livelihoods in order to exist. Is the gardener who plays the shakuhachi less important to the Japanese American community because he is also a gardener? Even the concept of the word artist is not a part of every language and culture. How do we differentiate the concept of the amateur vs. the professional from community to community?

In economic development and social service organizations, the arts receive their importance from the value to their societies in addressing specific societal issues rather than in narrow definitions of the word quality. In that case, how does one define (and support) excellence?

How do we understand "process" oriented forms such as the Japanese forms of calligraphy, ikebana (flower arrangement), and tea ceremony, when the process of creation may be just as important as the product that resulted?

There was a time when many of these issues could be relegated to folklorists and anthropologists, but the examples are too many to be relegated to a list of exceptions and small programs. The issues have also crossed the boundaries from folk to contemporary, and the concerns of cultural system differences impact on both the contemporary painter and the woodcarver, the traditional dancer and the modern dancer. What this suggests is the reworking of arts support systems from the bottom up, not dealing with culturally specific issues as the exception, but rather with the expectation that the core of the activity to be supported will be culturally specific. It would be a process that would look more toward support of culture than to art or particular artist. It should establish parallel support systems for culturally specific artists and arts organizations.

This would also suggest the support of multiple "centers" that are culturally specific in perspective and that support the arts created from and within their cultures. These "centers," whether they be theater companies or museums, or even social and community service centers or churches, serve to support the cultural development of their particular communities. These culturally specific organizations serve to preserve and protect the cultural resources of their communities through programs of training, education, creation of new work, public presentation, and tours to other locales. These are in fact protected environments or homes where artists can "reside" in a haven between the efforts to perform in larger, more democratized places. Culturally specific organizations also serve as the "home" into which members from outside cultures can be invited to share a community's cultural resources. Support systems can be established that would support these organizations as "centers" and "homes" rather than as producing organizations that are product based.

Cultural Democracy

While the support for the "integration" of large cultural facilities might be called the "democratization of culture," providing support for these many culturally specific centers might be called following a strategy of cultural democracy.

Cultural democracy requires the acceptance of the concept that the various cultures that make up American culture have their own methods of defining support to their arts and artists, and that support systems need to be developed that are very different than those that have been established to support "art" through centralized institutions. It suggests that the public policies that best support cultural democracy must be different from those that accept the democratization of cultural institutions.

It is very difficult, however, for people to accept the concept of parallel systems of support, particularly those who have worked for years toward "integrating" all the cultures together. The premise, however, is that it is necessary for culturally specific organizations to be "separated" for a certain portion of time in order to most effectively support them in their work toward cultural preservation and survival.

These concepts challenge one's fundamental beliefs about American culture, and in so doing become very difficult to understand, let alone accept, when one first encounters them. It is hoped that the reader will consider these typologies not so much as answers but to seek, as Judy Baca calls it, a higher level of questioning.

It also may require one to cross the threshold of acceptance that there may be cultural systems and methods of support that we do not understand. The democratization of culture requires only that we each understand the common support system. Cultural democracy requires each of us to try to understand each other's systems of cultural support. It also requires the trust to believe that cultural groups developing their own cultures under the protection of a separated subsystem will also choose to share their cultures with others.

These issues come to the forefront at a time when other issues of cultural integration and separation are being debated throughout our society. It is essential, however, that our views of specific legal and economic issues not color our views of this fundamentally important American issue of cultural democracy, for in the end, cultural democracy can bring us together as a society in a way that is much more successful than other integration strategies.

It is also important to note that these models are not absolutes. No one actually lives only in one culture, and as Guillermo Gomez-Pena says, all of us live on the borders. Most people travel back and forth from culturally specific to "centralized" environments within the course of each day and week. We each live in worlds that contain multiple cultures, and most of us work to make certain that these cultures can be shared with others. It is hoped that these typologies might assist in the analysis, rather than be seen as absolutes.

As expressed in *An American Dialogue:*

This profound shift in the way we define American culture and American art has tremendous implications for public and private funding agencies and nonprofit presenting organizations. Demographic change is already rewriting the story of community dynamics and institutional responsibility. As power shifts (and it will, despite tremendous resistance), the present economic, political, and cultural stories must be written to reflect new realities.

The art we sustain and how we sustain it, the artists on our stages, and the audiences in our halls must attest to the equity amid diversity that is our goal. This comes at a time when all arts organizations, including many presenting organizations, are struggling to survive. The support structures for many organizations are stretched to capacity, making it nearly impossible to do what they have always been doing, let alone more. But this is our challenge: to keep all of our arts and cultural organizations strong while expanding the art, artists and cultural expressions they present and the audiences they reach. This includes recognizing, helping to establish, and supporting organizations dedicated to culturally specific work and artists of color.[5]

The discussion on these subjects is often made difficult by the urgency for change felt by culturally specific groups contrasted with a reluctance to change by those in policy-making positions. The urgency of these matters is not created by the calendar of arts politics, but rather by the imperative of cultural survival. Cultural equity becomes a matter of utmost urgency when, as one national task force member lamented, "the sands of our cultures are slipping through our fingers."

Yet we must develop this "common agenda" with all people. Whether we "live on the hyphen" or not, we are all Americans, no matter what our national origins. We each live in communities and neighborhoods, and we each have a part to play in the cultural future of this country. We must find that "common ground" of working together. Racism is not a white man's disease, and sexism is not the exclusive domain of males. We all have misperceptions about each other, and we need to dispel them as best we can to develop a truly multicultural society.

Our previous perceptions have often come from "old stories." Today, however, we must create and listen to the new stories. To take the final statement from *An American Dialogue:*

Our job then, is to make certain that the new stories that represent our common experiences are developed as creatively as we know how, and that they touch as many people as possible. If we succeed, our lasting legacy will be the work of those most creative among us—the artists who are best able to see beneath the surface of our actions and make order of our infinite complexity.[6]

Notes

[1] Keens and Rhodes (1989), p. 58.
[2] Keens and Rhodes (1989), p. 61.
[3] Tschopik (1991), pp. 5–6.
[4] Tschopik (1991), p. 8.
[5] Keens and Rhodes (1989), p. 58.
[6] Keens and Rhodes (1989), p. 61.

7

Decentralization of Arts Funding from the Federal Government to the States

PAUL J. DIMAGGIO

O f all the threats to the National Endowment for the Arts (NEA) during the congressional reauthorization hearings of 1990, one of the most menacing to the agency's supporters was the specter of dramatic decentralization. Since the

PAUL J. DIMAGGIO is associate professor at Yale University in the Sociology Department, the School of Organization and Management, and the Institution for Social and Policy Studies. A former executive director of Yale's Program on Non-Profit Organizations and a former member of the Connecticut Commission on the Arts, he is author or editor of numerous articles and books, including *Managers of the Arts, Nonprofit Enterprise in the Arts, Structure of Capital: The Social Organization of Economic Life* (with Sharon Zukin), and the forthcoming *The New Institutionalism in Organizational Analysis* (with Walter W. Powell). He was the recipient of a John Simon Guggenheim Memorial Foundation Fellowship for 1990. Professor DiMaggio gratefully acknowledges helpful substantive and editorial suggestions by Stephen Benedict, Eva Jacob, Ruth Mayleas, and Mark Schuster and generous assistance in interpreting the National Standard data from Geoffrey Love, as well as grants from the Ford Foundation, the Rockefeller Foundation, and the John Simon Guggenheim Memorial Foundation.

early 1970s, the Endowment has passed a minimum of 20 percent of its program funds on to state and regional arts agencies, 15 percent in the form of block grants (basic state grants or BSGs), allocated by a formula that includes a $200,000 base and an additional per capita portion.

On May 16, 1990, two members of the House subcommittee responsible for reauthorization, Representatives Tom Coleman (R-Mo.) and Steve Gunderson (R-Wis.) announced a plan to mandate a 60 percent pass-through of Endowment program appropriations. Half of the new funds (20 percent of program monies) would be part of the BSG. According to a summary of the proposal distributed by Representative Gunderson, the states would be required to use this increment for "arts education programs and arts activities which were formerly funded in full by the NEA." (Because the NEA funds no organizations "in full," it was not clear what they had in mind.) The other half would be reserved for the states "through a discretionary grant program" administered by the NEA "for expanded access to arts through rural and inner-city arts programs."

The chaotic atmosphere of the reauthorization process, due to an uproar over NEA grants to several artists whose work critics deemed "pornographic" or "blasphemous," made decentralization of funds attractive to legislators who would just as soon have put the Endowment and its problems behind them. When the dust had cleared, House and Senate conferees had passed legislation, to be phased in by 1993, that increased basic state grants from 20 to 27.5 percent of Endowment program appropriations and reserved an additional 7.5 percent for competitive grants to states and local arts agencies for rural and inner-city programs.

Although the issue is resolved for now, questions about the extent to which federal support for the arts should be managed centrally or delegated to the states will not go away, for they are as old as the Endowment itself. The Endowment's framers had in mind a strong role for the states, though they varied as to its specifics. In 1962 Senator Joseph Clark proposed legislation to establish a federal arts agency that, aside from research and demonstration projects, would serve

largely to nurture and support state and local entities. Senator
Claiborne Pell's National Arts and Cultural Development Act
of 1963 incorporated Clark's ideas into a plan for a more dynamic federal agency. According to Gary Larson, author of *The
Reluctant Patron,* a history of federal support for the arts, Pell
explained to first lady Jacqueline Kennedy that "this matching
fund provision to each state has great political appeal" to
legislators and their supporters back home.[1]

The legislation establishing the National Foundation for the
Arts and Humanities authorized block grants to the states.
During the early years, the Endowment devoted approximately one-third of its limited program funds to that purpose.
As the agency's budget soared in the early 1970s, this proportion sank toward the 20 percent of program funds at which it
was set legislatively in 1973. Actually, a smaller percentage of
NEA grant funds—about 17 percent during most of the
1980s—was guaranteed to the states. The reason for this is
that two parts of the Endowment appropriation, challenge
funds and treasury funds, which together accounted for close
to one-fifth of the agency's nonadministrative budget during
the late 1980s, are excluded from the base from which state
grants are calculated. Moreover, a portion of the set-aside is
granted to regional organizations created by state arts agencies to oversee touring and other multistate programs. But
NEA's discipline programs (those devoted to particular art
forms like dance, theater, or music) also make grants to state
arts agencies, raising the total. In 1987, for example, approximately 22 percent of the agency's grant dollars were received
by state and regional arts agencies.

The relationship between the NEA and the states has been
complex. Except for the New York State Council on the Arts
(NYSCA), which Governor Nelson Rockefeller created in 1960
and on which the NEA was modeled, the California agency,
and a few less active commissions, the states established arts
agencies between 1965 and 1967 to take advantage of federal
funds. At first state appropriations (aside from NYSCA budget, which exceeded the Endowment's during the 1960s and
most of the early 1970s) were low, and the state arts councils,

as they were called, were creatures of the NEA.

During the 1970s, however, the state agencies grew in size, experience, and managerial capacity, a trend that accelerated during the Reagan era. By 1975 the states challenged the Endowment vigorously, demanding more flexible guidelines for the funds they regranted, more influence in developing guidelines, and symbolic acceptance as partners, rather than subordinates, in the policy process. Despite NEA efforts to represent state leadership more fully on panels and in policy discussions, relations remained tense during the Carter years, and some in the states advocated wholesale decentralization of federal arts funds.

Livingston Biddle's upgrading of the "Federal/State Partnership" office, which he placed under a deputy chair in 1978, and more routine consultation between the Endowment and the states on many matters helped to heal the rift. The Reagan administration's efforts to eliminate federal arts support in 1981 and subsequent battles to avoid deep cuts in the NEA's budget quieted dissension within the arts community. Under Frank Hodsoll's leadership, the NEA also created its first major program for local arts agencies, whose ranks and activity had expanded dramatically along with the rise of the states. (Congress authorized such support in 1980, and many states were decentralizing portions of their own grant making to community and regional bodies.) Yet tensions continued to simmer below the surface.

Despite the passions that proposals for further decentralization arouse, however, all parties have shared some basic assumptions. Each of the NEA's chairs has recognized the importance of vital state and local agencies to the U.S. system of arts support. And few, if any, in the states question the significance of the NEA as the symbolic flagship of public art support or deny the legitimacy and distinctiveness of the federal role. Given this common commitment to pluralism and to the federal/state/local division of labor, the problem lies in finding an allocation of funding, authority, and responsibility that satisfies both sides' understandings of these principles.

Decentralization in Context

"Decentralization" is a general term that refers to the redistribution of resources or authority from a single agency or level of government to one or more others. Because different things may be decentralized in different ways, we must equip ourselves with a more precise vocabulary if we are to get very far in understanding the policy alternatives. Two distinctions will help.

First, funds may be redistributed from the federal government to the states with or without the authority to determine their use. Let us reserve the term *delegation* to refer to decentralization of funding to the states for the implementation of federally designed programs; and *devolution* for the redistribution of both funds *and* the authority to determine their use. (As I use the term, devolution may be *de facto,* when it results from separate budgetary processes at the federal and state levels, or *de jure,* when it represents a legislatively mandated transfer of federal tax revenues to the states.) The distinction between delegation and devolution is not entirely clear cut: implementation invariably involves discretion, and devolution usually is governed by general guidelines. But it is useful, nonetheless. The arts endowment's artists-in-education and dance touring programs have represented *delegation* of federal resources to states to implement programs the NEA designed. The basic state grants constitute *de jure devolution* of funding and authority.

Second, policies and programs may be decentralized either *vertically* via delegation or devolution to more local levels of government, or *horizontally,* among agencies at the same level. Let us call functional decentralization within one level of government *fragmentation,* a term that wide usage recommends despite its unwarranted pejorative connotations. The division of labor in grant making to museums among the NEA, the National Endowment for the Humanities, and the National Institute of Museum Services is an example of fragmentation in this sense.

One part of the context for considering decentralization of support for the arts includes more general trends within

American federalism, which have expanded the role of the states and substituted devolution for delegation in many policy areas. Compared to such fields as housing and education, federal arts funding has retained substantial central authority with respect to the monies that Congress appropriates.

A second part of the context has to do with developments of the 1980s that were specific to the arts. First, without explicit change in the allocation of federally appropriated arts funds between federal and state agencies, steady real-dollar decline in the NEA budget, along with sharp gains in state appropriations for the arts, led to what was, in effect, a wholesale *de facto* devolution of funds and authority from the federal level to the states. At the same time, the Reagan administration's elimination of federal social programs that supported the arts as part of a more general mission (from the Appalachian Regional Commission to the Comprehensive Employment and Training Act) reduced the fragmentation (and the volume) of federal support for artists and arts organizations. In other words, as a by-product of broader policy changes, *de*centralization, through *de facto* devolution from federal to state government, was accompanied by *de facto* centralization of control over arts funds *within* the federal government.

American Federalism in the 1980s

Throughout the western industrialized world, public arts funding is relatively decentralized. The most comprehensive study of the topic, Mark Schuster's *Supporting the Arts: An International Comparative Study,* reports that local and regional governments provide 45 percent or more of public arts dollars in each of the eight nations he studied. In the U.S., grant-making arts agencies exist at the federal, state, and local levels. If anything, the absence of a European-style Ministry of Culture makes the state and local role even more significant in the U.S. than abroad.

If the federal/state division of labor is a fixed characteristic of U.S. government, the terms of the federal-state relationship have changed markedly at several historic junctures, most recently during the Reagan administration. (Richard Nathan and

Fred Doolittle provide the most thorough overview in *Reagan and the States,*[2] and I draw on their work here.) The Arts Endowment was created during the 1960s, an era of federal dominance, in which a wide array of "categorical" grants made funds available to state or local agencies to implement programs designed in Washington. During the 1970s, the Nixon administration instituted revenue sharing and Congress replaced categorical programs in several areas with block grants that states could put to flexible use. The Reagan administration accelerated the shift from categorical to block grant strategies (i.e., from delegation to devolution): where federal social programs could not be eliminated outright, funds and responsibility devolved from the federal government to the states.

The Arts: Devolution by Default

In formal terms, the NEA was untouched by these changes, as the state pass-through requirements remained the same. But not all, perhaps not even most, of the devolution of funds and responsibilities from the federal government to the states during the Reagan years was a direct result of legislative action. In many areas, *de facto* devolution occurred more or less behind the back of explicit public policy, as the result of concurrent reductions in federal resources and increases in appropriations by the states.

This was true of the arts. Between 1972 and 1983 the federal government played the dominant role in the public arts–support network constituted by the NEA, the state agencies, and their local counterparts. Figure 1 depicts congressional appropriations to the NEA and state appropriations to state arts agencies between 1966 and 1989.[3] The Arts Endowment budget peaked, both in real dollars and in comparison to state appropriations, in 1979. Between 1979 and 1989 the NEA budget declined approximately 40 percent in purchasing power after inflation. Most of the decline occurred between 1979 and 1982 as the result of inflation and federal budgetary policies. In 1989 state legislatures appropriated $268 million and Congress appropriated $169 million for the NEA, of which approximately 20 percent of program funds (roughly $25 million) was granted to the states. (The 1990 reauthorization legislation increased NEA appropriations to $175 million, of which 27.5 percent is set-aside for state agencies.)

The result was a virtual reversal of the federal and state budgetary shares. Whereas in 1979 NEA funds were approximately 80 percent greater than state legislative appropriations for the arts, by 1989 state appropriations totaled approximately 60 percent more than the NEA grant budget. Between 1979 and 1983 the change reflected a marked decline in appropriations for NEA, accompanied by incremental growth at the state level. Between 1983 and 1987, as economic revival boosted state tax revenues, the reversal reflected dramatic increases in state appropriations and static funding of NEA. The outcome was a dramatic, if unplanned, *de facto* devolution of arts funds from the federal government to the states.

FIGURE 1

Appropriations to NEA and State Arts Agencies

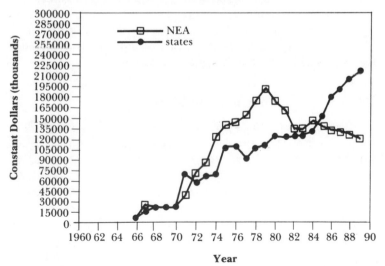

Note: Dollars adjusted using Consumer Price Index (1982–84=100)
NEA=Appropriations exclusive of administration (NEA Annual Reports)
State Arts Agencies=State Legislative appropriations (NASAA)

Actually, these figures understate the shift in responsibility from federal to state levels because they do not take account of substantial support for the arts from federal agencies other than NEA. Although the small Institute of Museum Services (IMS) gained about 33 percent in purchasing power during the 1980s, The National Endowment for the Humanities (NEH), like NEA, faced real-dollar declines during the Reagan years. Moreover, the Reagan administration cut sharply or eliminated many programs that were not designed to assist the arts, but did so as part of larger missions—the Labor Department's Comprehensive Employment and Training Act (CETA), the block grants of the Department of Housing and Urban Development, even the Law Enforcement Assistance Administration.

Thus at the same time devolution from the federal government to the states was "decentralizing" arts support, the federal government's arts programs were becoming more centralized. Although few hard data bear on the matter, it is likely that fragmented federal programs both reinforced NEA grants (because many Endowment grantees had the staff and experience to capitalize upon the availability of funds from other sources) and (because such programs had very different goals than NEA) provided support to many artists and organizations that were not eligible for Endowment assistance.

Does Devolution Matter?

The fact that by 1990 much *de facto* devolution had already occurred and that Congress had mandated more *de jure,* did not necessarily mean that the *results* of government spending on the arts had been altered or will be in the future. If federal and state agencies do exactly the same things, reallocation of arts resources between them may make a big difference to the morale of federal and state officials, but little difference to the public, artists, or arts organizations.

The question, then, is to what extent does devolution affect which goals, out of the many that cultural policy might entail, are addressed effectively by public spending? For example, does devolution influence the fortunes of large, established organizations that produce and exhibit Euro-American art to a wide middle class public? Does it help or hurt small organizations working in non-European traditions, or organizations (in any tradition) pushing the boundaries of innovation? How does it affect the generosity, scope, and political neutrality of grants to artists? How does it influence efforts to increase the number of Americans participating in the arts, either as audiences or producers?

What We Need to Know

Answers to such questions are vital if we are to make informed decisions about the instrumentalities of government support for the arts. Unfortunately, this section must begin with the disclaimer that the observations that follow are necessarily speculative. The problem is that we have not invested in the information necessary to provide the answers we need. It would be easier to do so now than in the past, however. During the 1980s, under contract to the NEA, the National Assembly of State Arts Agencies (NASAA) developed a grant accounting system, the National Standard, that makes it possible to characterize patterns of state arts grant making flexibly and with some precision. Although NASAA has been open to sharing the data with independent researchers, few have taken advantage of it. And although the NEA in its 1986–1990 Five Year Plan stated as a priority "full Endowment compliance with the Standard," it has yet to implement this intention. Thus close comparison of NEA and state grant making remains impossible without costly reclassification of Endowment grants.

If NEA grants were classified and tabulated according to the National Standard format, we *would* learn a lot about whether and how artists and organizations supported by state arts agencies differ from those assisted by federal funds. This would be an essential start; but it would not enable us to predict the results of devolution for several reasons. For one thing, if the NEA had less money and the states more, each might do different things than they do now. At some expense in data preparation, we could gain some purchase on this by comparing systematically how Endowment and state grant making changed during the 1980s era of *de facto* devolution. We could also analyze the grants of particular state agencies that experienced sharp increases or declines in funding to see how they changed, in order to predict short-term effects of federal/state fund redistribution.

Such research would be helpful indeed in anticipating the impact of specific devolutionary actions like the 1990 increase in the states' share of program appropriations. It would not allow us to make precise predictions about devolution per se, however, because the effects of devolution depend on at least three things.

First, what is the overall level of public arts funding? During the 1980s, the real-dollar amount of combined NEA and state arts agency appropriations (from Congress and the state legislatures) remained roughly constant. If *de facto* devolution had been accompanied by dramatic declines or increases in total state and federal funds devoted to the arts—if it resulted from even deeper cuts to the NEA without increases in the states, or occurred in the context of massive increases in arts appropriations at all levels—its effects would have been different. The fiscal woes of many states during the early 1990s ensure a different context today than in the prosperous second half of the 1980s. Without sharp increases in state appropriations, further declines in NEA grant-making ability might generate pressures on state arts agencies, for example, to spend more of their funds on large institutions that have relied on ongoing support from the Endowment and less on small and mid-sized organizations.

Second, the effects of congressional action to increase the share of the NEA's appropriation that goes to basic state grants depend upon the formula used to allocate BSGs among the states. To mention only the two polar alternatives, an equal-share formula or a per capita formula might have quite different consequences. (Through 1990 the formula, which the 1990 legislation did not address, represented a compromise between the two.) Its effects also depend on the strings attached to it. Insofar as Congress attempts to control not just how money is allocated, but also how it is used (i.e., pursuing a policy of delegation rather than devolution), the past is a poor guide to the future.

Third, the effects of devolution will depend on the state arts agencies' own relationships with local arts agencies, which, according to NASAA figures, received about 13 percent of state agencies' grant dollars in 1987. According to informed estimates, the United States has more than 2,000 local arts agencies, many small and volunteer-run but more than 600 of them professionally staffed. During the late 1970s and 1980s, many states devolved some of their own grant making onto such agencies or other local or regional bodies, and more federal-state devolution would increase pressures for decentralization at the state level. We have virtually no hard data on what local arts agencies do with their funds, but we know that they do many things, including providing information services and management assistance to local arts groups, engaging in cultural planning, making grants, and running arts festivals. Anecdotal accounts suggest that their programs, objectives, and orientations are diverse and often different from those of the Endowment and the state arts agencies. Given the increasing share of the public arts dollar that local agencies control, compiling reliable information about them should be a high priority for researchers.

NEA and the States:
Stereotypes and Political Imperatives

Given these caveats, it would be rash to jump to firm conclusions. But it may be useful to inspect some of the arguments used to characterize the NEA and state roles in the U.S. system of arts support, if only to caution against sweeping generalization and to suggest hypotheses that might guide systematic research.

Government agencies have stereotypes, just as people and

groups do. Over the years, there has emerged a conventional view of the differences between the NEA and the state arts agencies that, while seldom publicly articulated, has shaped discussions of their respective roles.

The Endowment, so the story goes, supports "excellence" or "quality," by which is meant the major Euro-American cultural institutions—art museums, orchestras, theaters, dance, and opera companies—and the leading artists. The NEA also supports artistic creativity at the cutting edge and such scholarly or professional concerns as the preservation of art and the development of means to maintain records of choreographic work.

By contrast, state programs are believed to support smaller organizations, younger artists, and programs advancing the goals of access, diversity, and equity. In some quarters, state programs are viewed as more politically accountable (for better or worse) than the NEA, and less accountable to arts professionals.

Although stereotypes may contain germs of truth—the NEA has long taken a special interest in the welfare of major arts organizations, and the states during the 1980s directed attention to cultural diversity—they are based largely on anecdotes. They are taken seriously, however. People who believe that supporting major institutions and leading artists is the most important function of public policy tend to favor a stronger Endowment. People who place a higher value on support for diversity and access (however these are defined) tend to advocate a larger role for the states.

Such stereotypes ignore the similar political contexts of public arts support at the federal and state levels. All public arts agencies, the Arts Endowment as much as its state counterparts, depend on legislative appropriations. Whatever else they do, they must keep legislators happy in order to survive. Legislators like programs that are popular with the voters who elect them, avoid controversy, and are backed by organized constituencies with numbers and clout.

These political realities establish two survival imperatives for arts agencies. First, they must spread their funds around. The NEA must make grants in Alaska, Montana, and Mississippi even though most artists and large arts organizations are in New York, California, and a few other states. State agencies must support the arts in rural and suburban counties, even when most arts organizations are in cities. (Legislatures in some states, including New York, mandate per capita funding formulas, and informal pressures are substantial almost everywhere.) The solution is usually a compromise: states and cities in which artists and arts organizations are concentrated get more funding than one would expect on the basis of their population and less than one would anticipate on the basis of their proportion of artists and arts activities.

Second, arts agencies must develop coalitions of supporters that include both the major Euro-American institutions and smaller organizations reflecting the cultural traditions or interests of other Americans. (Because artists and highly experimental organizations are rarely well organized, they are usually less important parts of these coalitions. This is one reason they are easy targets for opponents of public arts support.) Although the relative power of "the majors" and the "emerging organizations," as the two groups are called, varies from state to state, agency budgets almost always represent a compromise capable of keeping both parts of the coalition in harness.

References to these political realities are sometimes invoked by arts agency critics to question the legitimacy of public arts programs. That is not the intention here. Geographic decentralization has made the arts more accessible to more people. Support for artists and organizations outside the major European fine arts traditions has aided creativity and enriched our stock of cultural resources. An agency pursuing many combinations of legitimate policy goals might allocate its funds in much the same way as existing arts agencies, even without political pressures.

The point is that federal and state arts agencies have no choice: they must support large institutions in the Euro-American mainstream (codeword: "excellence") *and* small, emerging organizations outside it (codewords: "access" and "diversity"). Consequently, whatever the stereotypes of the NEA and the state agencies, their actual program allocations are likely to diverge far less than the stereotypes suggest. Thus the Arts Endowment established its "expansion arts" program in 1973 to support racial and ethnic minority and rural arts organizations, and an NEA analysis reports that minority artists, institutions, and projects received 13 percent of the agency's grant funds in FY 1987. Conversely, Edward Arian reported (in *The Unfulfilled Promise*) that almost all the state arts agencies he studied in the early 1980s had settled on a quid pro quo that gave major institutions between 40 and 60 percent of their grant dollars.[4] The proposal of the Arts Unity Group that Representative Pat Williams (D-Mt.) convened in summer 1990 to negotiate a united front in support of NEA reauthorization, which called for a higher Endowment appropriation, struck a balance between support for major institutions and for "access" and "education." So did the Coleman-Gunderson plan, which would have slashed the Endowment's resources.

NEA and the States: Preliminary Conclusions from Sketchy Evidence

What evidence, if any, is there that the Arts Endowment and the state agencies are more similar in their patterns of funding than the stereotypes imply? In the absence of fine-grained data on specific grants, we can only compare state and federal funding in terms of gross categories. Because the categories by which the states and the NEA report their grants differ, the comparison is necessarily imprecise. Nonetheless, it may be illuminating.

Excellence vs. Access?

The opposition of "access" to "excellence" is patently false because many arts institutions and projects provide both. But much discourse about arts policy employs these terms in a special way: "excellence" as a codeword for large organizations in the Euro-American mainstream and "access" as a codeword for almost everything else. Even if we reject the categories and their labels, as I believe we should, it is worth seeing if grant making by the NEA and the states fits the stereotypes.

If one assumes that the rate at which applicants are turned down is a measure of "excellence," then NEA has the edge, because it funds just a little more than one in four applications. By contrast, the forty-five states and territories that provided NASAA with information on this topic in 1987 gave grants to 59 percent of the artists and organizations that applied for them. (Proportions ranged from 23 percent in Oregon to 90 percent in Maine.)

Funding rates are poor measures of "quality," however. First, state agencies have the resources to work with applicants more closely in developing proposals and to cool out would-be grantees whose chances are slim. Second, the high state funding rates reflect the policy of many states to make many small grants, often for administrative support or program development, to promising organizations too young or too small for the NEA to assist. Therefore, the difference in rates may reflect differences in policy and the division of labor between NEA and the states rather than differences in the emphasis on quality in agency decision making.

The states collectively make many more grants than the Endowment and fund many more organizations. According to NASAA's *Summary of State Arts Agencies Grantmaking Activities for Fiscal Year 1987* (which includes reports on approximately 90 percent of state grant making in that year), state agencies made 24,430 grants. According to my own count of program subtotals in the Endowment's 1987 Annual Report, the NEA made 4,654. There are at least three reasons for this. First, collectively, the states have more money than the Endowment. Second, the proximity of staff and panelists to applicants enables them to evaluate the work of organizations that would be unfamiliar to many federal staff and panelists. Third, most states, for reasons of policy, politics, or both, prefer making many small grants to fewer large ones: that is, the average state grant is substantially smaller than the average federal grant. Thus the states fund more small and "emerging" organizations than the NEA. (Whether they would continue to do so if the larger NEA grants were not there to provide steady funding for their largest constituents is another question.)

It does not follow from this, however, that the states give a much smaller *proportion* of their money to the "majors" than does the Endowment. According to NASAA, as of 1989 "42 state arts agencies had a program of general operating support for major institutions representing almost half of the grant amounts awarded by states in support of the arts." Twenty others operated challenge grant programs that, presumably, also focused upon "core" or "major" institutions. Not all of the states' "major" organizations are large, mainstream institutions presenting or exhibiting Euro-American art. But if we make the heroic, but not unwarranted, assumption that roughly 80 percent of "major organization" operating and challenge funds go to such institutions, and that they may pick up another 5 percent or so from other categories of support, then a ballpark estimate of state grants to organizations that are both large *and* predominantly devoted to nonexperimental work in Euro-American art forms would be roughly 50 percent.

Conducting the same operation for the NEA requires even more heroic assumptions. The 1988 annual report "financial summary" records $80,306,000 in categorical and challenge commitments for the dance, museum, music, opera–musical theater, and theater programs, which includes most of the NEA's grants to "major institutions." In addition, let us assume that roughly half ($13.63 million) of the state and local funds found their way to large organizations. By contrast, assume that grants in the design arts, expansion arts, folk arts, inter-arts, literature, media arts, visual arts, arts-in-education, policy, planning and research, and advancement programs were made to artists or small and emerging organizations. (All the NEA programs depart from these stereotypes to some degree, but let us assume that departures balance one another out.) This procedure yields a ballpark estimate that 55 percent of the Endowment's funds go to the "majors"—close to the total for the states.

The reader should not take these percentage estimates very seriously. The purpose has been to demonstrate that the conventional stereotype—the notion that the NEA funds large mainstream institutions presenting art in European styles whereas the states assist small emerging organizations in a wide range of cultural traditions—is too simplistic.

Differences in Disciplinary Emphasis

Both the Arts Endowment and the state arts agencies claim to base their grants on "excellence" or "quality," and, insofar as reasonable men and women can agree on those criteria, within grant categories they usually do. On the other hand, unless one is prepared to claim that certain art forms (as opposed to artists or organizations working within a given form) are intrinsically better than others, the excellence standard gives little guidance as to how funds should be allocated among programs.

Table 1 compares NEA's allocation of funds among program areas to state arts agencies' allocation of their grants among different disciplines. (Data are from 1987, the most recent year for which state and NEA data are available.) The comparison is imprecise: NASAA's figures classify state grants on the basis of the kinds of artistic work the funds support. By contrast, NEA's figures are based on the agency's program categories: some of these, like NASAA's categories, are disciplinary; but others, like "museums" or "local test" are based on the kinds of organizations that receive the grants (a separate taxonomy in the NASAA scheme); and others (like "advancement" or "expansion arts") are based on administrative distinctions peculiar to the Endowment.

TABLE 1. 1987 NEA and State Arts Agency Grant Making Compared[1]

Field	Percentage of NEA Excluding State Programs and Research ($127.00M)		Percentage of SAA Grants by Discipline Excluding Humanities and "Non-Arts/Human-ities ($170.99M)
Dance	7.2	(8.8)[2]	8.2
Design Arts	3.5	(4.9)	1.5
Expansion Arts	5.3		
Folk Arts	2.4		2.1
Inter-Arts	3.2		
Literature	4.0		2.8
Media Arts	10.2	(10.9)	4.7
Museum	9.2	(13.8)	
Music	11.9	(15.6)	18.8
Opera/Musical Theater	4.9	(5.9)	4.3
Theater	8.5	(10.0)	12.4
Visual Arts	4.9	(5.5)	12.6[3]
Arts in Education	4.4		
Local Test Program	1.8		
Challenge	16.4	(1.3)[4]	
Advancement	1.9		
Other	0.4		
Crafts			0.9
Photography			0.5
Interdisciplinary			1.4
Multidisciplinary			29.7

[1]NEA figures calculated from material in FY 1987 NEA Annual Report. Percentages in parentheses include related challenge grants. State arts agency figures are calculated from National Assembly of State Arts Agencies, *Summary of State Arts Agencies Grantmaking Activities for Fiscal Year 1987.*
[2]Figures in parentheses in NEA column are percentages of total with challenge grants included within related program categories.
[3]Includes grants to museums for visual arts exhibitions.
[4]Grants to arts centers and presenters, not classifiable within NEA program scheme.

The NEA totals exclude the state programs category, which consists primarily of basic state grants and major grants to regional agencies. Because the Endowment's other programs also make grants to state and regional arts agencies, eliminating this category (which accounted for about 16 percent of total NEA grant making) does not eliminate double-counting; but it does restrict the endowment funding base to monies over which the agency has effective control. (Also removed from the NEA base is $430,000 budgeted for research.) The percentages in parentheses in column 1 indicate patterns of funding if challenge grants, the largest NEA program category serving organizations in many disciplines, are allocated to re-lated program categories.

The base for state grants excludes grants to the humanities, which constituted 3 percent of all state grant making in 1987, and a "non–arts/humanities" category, which accounted for 1.5 percent. Some states have councils for "the arts *and* humanities," though the latter are always junior partners. The "non–arts/humanities" category is more mysterious; NASAA believes that much of it consists of technical assistance (e.g., marketing or management aid) to arts organizations.

Let us look first at the categories for which the Endowment's programs and the states' discipline taxonomy are roughly comparable: music, theater, dance, opera–musical theater, de-sign arts, literature, folk arts, and media arts. Federal and state allocations among most of these categories are similar. Dance appears to do slightly better at the federal level, but that may be because NEA allocated an unusually large share of chal-lenge funds to this discipline in 1987. The states appear to spend somewhat more of their funds on music and theater, but if the musical portion of the expansion and advancement cate-gories were included in the Endowment breakdown, the pro-portions would be closer. The NEA appears to make more of its grants in support of opera–musical theater and literature than do the state arts agencies, but, given the lack of compara-bility, the differences are too small to draw firm conclusions. Because the states have a "crafts" category, which consists of grants to both fine arts and folk craftspersons and organiza-tions (which would be counted under visual arts and folk arts, respectively, in the NEA scheme), the apparent small Endow-ment edge in folk arts is misleading. Design arts play a more important role in federal grant making, but are small parts of both budgets. In other words, with respect to the allocation of funds among many of the most important artistic disciplines, patterns of state and federal grant making appear rather similar.

Grants to museums are harder to compare because the state disciplinary taxonomy divides them among the art forms that they support (predominantly visual arts). Fortunately, the National Standard includes a separate classification scheme based on the type of organization receiving grants, with a separate category for museums. This helps a great deal, although comparability remains imperfect because some state grants to museums support the humanities rather than the arts, the NEA museum program makes some grants to organizations that are not museums, other NEA programs provide some support for museums (for example, for programing in the performing arts), and data for NASAA's recipient-type categories are not as complete as for the classification by discipline. Nonetheless, we can arrive at a rough approximation.

In 1987 the Endowment's museum program accounted for 9.2 percent of the agency's grant budget, excluding state programs. If one adds challenge grants to museums to the total, the proportion rises to 13.8 percent. Of $106.6 million accounted for by NASAA's organizational category scheme, art museums received 7.5 percent (most of it in the "visual arts" category of the discipline classification), galleries and exhibition spaces 1.3 percent, and "other museums" 4.2 percent. If one eliminates about one-third of the latter that supported programs in the humanities rather than in the arts, the share of state funds granted to museums and exhibition spaces for arts programs was roughly 12 percent, about the same (given the imprecision of the comparison) as the NEA.

The most striking apparent difference in Table 1 is the presence of "multidisciplinary" programs as the largest category of state expenditure, with about 30 percent of the total. (An additional 1.4 percent of state grant funds support interdisciplinary programs.) By contrast, the NEA's "inter-arts" category, which assists both interdisciplinary (collaborations) and multidisciplinary activities (series including several art forms), accounts for just 3.2 percent of the Endowment total.

Part of the difference is illusory, in that almost one-third of the state "multidisciplinary" category reflects grants to local arts agencies (comparable to the 16 percent of the NEA grant budget that went to state and regional agencies for general purposes). An additional quarter was granted to arts centers, performance facilities, and "cultural series organizations"; most of this supported the presentation of work in several disciplines. Arts service organizations receive an additional 8 percent and universities and colleges just over 4 percent of the multidisciplinary total, with the remaining share (almost one-third) scattered widely.

NEA support for presenters and service organizations is divided among inter-arts, a variety of areas within disciplinary programs (for example, dance program grants for dance series to presenters who also sponsor theater and musical programs), and assistance to regional organizations that coordinate multidisciplinary touring series. NEA relies on its disciplinic programs to channel such funds because it is larger than the state agencies and can thus afford the division of labor involved in having many such programs. If the states supported presenters by discipline, their disciplinary allocations might appear to be even closer to those of the Endowment. Thus it is unclear to what extent the large multidisciplinary category in the state taxonomy reflects actual differences in the allocation of funds by discipline or simply differences in the way that the states and the Endowment make and keep track of their grants.

A marked difference *does* appear in the share of funds allocated to the media arts. The Endowment spends a considerably higher proportion of its funds (10.9 percent) on media than do the states (4.7 percent). The difference reflects the national scope of most film, radio, and television projects, as well as the NEA's ongoing relationship with the American Film Institute.

This review has revealed little evidence that the Endowment and the state agencies (taken as a group) allocate their funds—either between "major" and "emerging" organizations or among artistic disciplines, aside from media arts—in markedly different ways. Although more systematic analysis of more fine-grained and comparable data might yield different conclusions, the evidence reviewed here is consistent with the hypotheses that stereotypes are misleading and that similar political environments lead to similar funding patterns.

Differences within Fields

It is possible of course that within the broad categories we have discussed, there *are* systematic differences in the activities funded by the federal government and the states. It would be possible, but costly, to classify NEA grants in a manner that would permit comparison of this kind. Moreover, although NASAA asks the states to classify grants by recipient type and purpose, as well as by discipline, data include many fewer grants for the two former classification schemes than for the latter.

Grants to Artists. We can, however, use what data are available to look at a few kinds of grant support of particular interest. One such category is direct support for artists. Summing the fellowship categories in the 1987 NEA Annual Report (including fellowships provided through subgranting organizations) yields a total of $8.4 million in direct or delegated support for artists, or 6.6 percent of 1987 grants (not counting state programs and research). By contrast, the National Standard classification of state grant making by purpose reports that sums totaling 4.8 percent of state grants go toward artist fellowships or for the creation of new works of art. (The recipient-type scheme indicates that 3.8 percent of state grant money goes directly to individual artists.) We cannot make much of these figures because state responses in such categories were considerably less complete than for the "discipline" taxonomy, and because state totals omit grants to organizations that subgranted to individual artists. (According to NASAA's *State Arts Agency Profile 1987,* at least ten states, including New York and Massachusetts, avoided legal or political impediments to grants to individuals by funneling artist fellowship funds through associated private foundations or similar agencies.) Without data on Endowment and state grants to organizations for the purpose of supporting artist fellowships or commissions, we can do little more than pose the question of relative emphasis on artist support.

Support for Producing Organizations. One might also ask whether, within fields, the NEA or the states spend more on direct support for producing organizations in the performing arts, as opposed to presenters, service organizations, or other ancillary contributors to the disciplines. As usual, comparison is complicated by the differences in the way the NEA and the states report their grants and by nonresponse in the recipient-type field for the states. But, again, rough comparisons may be of some interest.

"Dance company grants" constituted 60 percent of the NEA's 1987 dance program expenditures; grants to performing groups amounted to the same proportion of state dance funding. (I have omitted state grants to "community" performing groups in this and the comparisons that follow, because such groups are usually amateur and thus outside the Endowment's scope of activity.) Three categories—grants to choruses, ensembles, and orchestras (of which the latter accounted for about 90 percent)—represented 67 percent of the NEA music program's budget; grants to performing groups represented 68 percent of expenditures in the state "music" discipline category. In opera–musical theater the comparable figures were 70 percent for the NEA ("professional companies") and 76 percent for the states. Only in theater did the Endowment focus more on direct grants to professional companies (80 percent of theater program funds were spent in the "professional theater company" and "artistic advancement: ongoing ensembles" categories) than the states (62 percent), which devoted almost 9 percent of their grants to "community" performing groups.

As usual, however, numerous caveats apply. The NEA proportions would be higher if grants to presenters for series that included several disciplines were classified as "multidiscipli-

nary" (as in the state calculations) and if support for performing organizations from challenge and advancement grants and
from a few other areas within discipline programs had been
included. State proportions would be somewhat higher if, like
the NEA, they reported support for school projects as a separate education program category.

Support for Amateur or Service Oriented Activities. In general,
the NEA restricts its grant making to professional organizations. By contrast, some state arts agencies provide support for
amateur community groups or applications of the arts in the
fields of health, criminology, or gerontology. Is this difference
a major one?

According to the National Standard data, the states made 3
percent of their 1987 grants to "community performing
groups," most of which were predominantly amateur theater
groups and musical ensembles. Such organizations receive little if any direct aid from the Endowment, so the difference,
though small, appears to be real.

The states also granted 2.2 percent of their funds to "community service organizations" (CSOs), correctional institutions, health care facilities, and senior citizens organizations,
of which more than 95 percent went to CSOs. The Endowment
made a few grants to such organizations through its Office of
Special Constituencies, but the amount ($54,000) was trivial.
The Endowment's expansion arts program (and a few others)
made a number of grants to organizations that might be classified as CSOs (e.g., New York's Henry Street Settlement) in the
state taxonomy. Rather than representing support for ama-
teurs, many of these grants reflected the fact that some small
professional organizations with little access to private donors
take advantage of administrative and fund-raising efficiencies
of being part of multipurpose (i.e., "community service") um-
brella agencies. The greater share of state funds going to
CSOs may also reflect higher levels of state support for small,
fragile professional organizations for which separate incorporation is not a desirable option. In any case, the differences
between NEA and state patterns are marginal at best.

Do the NEA and the States Support the Same Organizations? Of 244 art museums surveyed by the National Center for Educational Statistics on behalf of the IMS in 1980 (including all art museums with budgets of more than $795,664, and a random sample of one in four smaller museums), slightly more (59 percent) received state funds than had grants from the NEA (46 percent). Nonetheless, museums that received funds from the Endowment were much more likely than others to receive grants from the states, and vice versa. More recently, in a study of its twelve member states (reported in NASAA's 1989 report on *The State of the State Arts Agencies*), the Western States Arts Federation found that 89 percent of organizations with NEA funding also received grants from state arts agencies. Many more organizations received funds from the states than from the federal agency, however.

Summary. In the previous section, we focused on how the states and the Endowment allocate their funds across disciplines, and could find little evidence (except for the NEA's greater emphasis on media arts) of major differences. In this section, we asked how different types of applicants—artists, professional performing organizations, community and service oriented organizations—fared at the federal and state levels, with special attention to differences within discipline categories.

Again, few differences were visible and these were marginal. The states provide some support to amateur groups, but this represented a very small proportion of their total expenditures. The NEA may spend more of its money on performing organizations in a few fields (especially theater), but the evidence is weak. The major allocational differences between the states and the NEA are the most obvious ones. First, the state agencies spend about 3 percent of their funding on the humanities due to differences in their mandated missions. (A tiny proportion of NEA funding—e.g., a challenge grant to the Field Museum—also assists the humanities.) The states passed approximately 13 percent of their funds on to local arts agencies in 1987, some for operating support and regranting and some for specific projects. The NEA spent less than 2 percent of its grant total on local arts agencies in 1987, although this proportion has risen somewhat since then. The implications of the difference, however, are hard to grasp because we have no systematic information about what local arts agencies do with their funds.

Perhaps more fine-grained analyses of better data would reveal other differences. If the states and the NEA allocated their grant budgets in *dramatically* different ways, however, this should have been apparent in the evidence reviewed here. Thus we must conclude, until more detailed analyses demonstrate otherwise, that the Endowment and the state agencies are in very much the same business: both are primarily oriented to assisting professional arts organizations; both devote small proportions of their budgets to direct grants to artists; the states spend a little more on amateur and community oriented activities and, perhaps, a little less on the largest producing organizations; and the Endowment and the states allocate funds among disciplines in very similar ways.

Stability, Equity, and Policy

If this were all there was to it, then one might argue (provisionally, of course, while waiting for better data) that devolution does not matter very much: that whether public arts funds are spent by the Endowment or the state arts agencies, they will end up, more or less, in the same pockets.

Even if this is the case, however, several other factors suggest the need for caution in the face of proposals for further devolution of funds from the Endowment to the states. Considerations of stability of funding, distributive equity in geographic terms, and policy making with respect to national, as opposed to regional, artistic needs must all be taken into account.

Stability of Funding and
Political Vulnerability

From the standpoint of arts organizations that receive government funds, the predictability and stability of funding may be as important as its amount. The debates of 1990 made stability a more pressing issue, because they appeared to call into question, once again, the survival of the NEA.

In a hostile political environment, federal funding is more politically vulnerable than state support because a federal agency poses a larger, more visible target for nationally organized political movements. In other words, insofar as the NEA is vulnerable to attack, state appropriations represent a good portfolio diversification strategy.

From the standpoint of individual arts organizations, NEA grants may be more predictable. This is not a matter of policy: the Endowment has been less willing than most states to view its grants as operating support, although in practice it has provided ongoing funding to many organizations. By contrast, many states provide operating assistance to their major constituents, almost as a form of entitlement; and some have explored multiyear commitments as a way to further reduce uncertainty for grantees.

But state agencies have been more vulnerable than the Endowment to radical reversals. According to NASAA's 1989 report, *The State of the State Arts Agencies,* "Budgets vary greatly from year to year and from state to state. Depressed regional economies and state revenue shortfalls have contributed in the past 20 years to 28 agencies experiencing at least one 5-year period of declining budgets." Insofar as individual state budgets are more volatile than the NEA's, federal funding represents a source of stability.

Whether the states or the NEA are more politically vulnerable in the long run is another question. For many years, the Endowment demonstrated exemplary political independence; although political pressures grew with its budget during the 1970s, the agency was largely successful at withstanding them, until 1990 at least. By contrast, anecdotal information suggests that state agencies found it more difficult to maintain arms-length relationships with political leadership in the early days, but that growth has been accompanied by professionalization and increased agency autonomy. State agencies still vary in their relationship to political authority, however. Because they are smaller than the Endowment, their council members are often more directly involved in panel decisions, providing greater opportunity for political leverage. In sum, individual state agencies may be more vulnerable to political pressure than the Endowment, but because there are many of them, the effects of such pressure have usually been isolated.

Another standard of political independence is the extent to which legislatures pass special line items for particular institutions. According to NASAA, eighteen states and territories passed internal line items earmarking portions of arts agency budgets to specific institutions. These represented nearly $33 million (or 12 percent) of state and territorial agency appropriations. (The amounts involved ranged from trivial to substantial—less than 2 percent of appropriations for the state arts agency in Montana but more than two-thirds of agency appropriations in Florida, Hawaii, and Puerto Rico.) Moreover, many states passed line items *outside of* arts agency budgets, which are not included in the total.

If one takes into account the BSGs and, more important, regular appropriations for the Smithsonian Institution and other beneficiaries of congressional favor, the proportion of federal funds that are line-itemed inside and outside the NEA budget may be even higher than for the states. But it is also more predictable, and, with a few notable but unsuccessful exceptions (the Martha Graham Company, for example), organizations have been less ready to seek special lines at the federal than at the state level.

Geographic Equity

Most people would agree that arts funding should be distributed equitably from place to place. The point is not that every state should receive the same volume of federal grants or legislative appropriations, but that consistent principles should determine the allocations to each. Insofar as the Endowment makes its grants on a consistent basis (weighing quality or professional reputation with a concern with diffusion of access, so that programs in places with few artistic resources have better chances of being funded than equally strong programs in arts-rich areas), its grant making would seem to meet this test. By contrast, insofar as state legislative appropriations vary according to factors other than the quality and quantity of artists and arts organizations requiring support (e.g., local economies, traditions of government activism), they may collectively depart from equity principles: that is, arts organizations may be penalized for residing in states with stingy legislatures or poor economic conditions, quite apart from their merits or the services they provide.

A 1982 study by researchers John Urice and Richard Hoffcibert, then at the State University of New York at Binghamton, investigated factors influencing legislative appropriations to state arts agencies.[5] Population, of course, had a major effect: states with lots of people spent more on everything than states with just a few. States varied substantially in arts spending per capita, however, and the authors tried to understand why. According to their statistical analyses, the major predictor of per capita arts appropriations was the amount of money spent on social and human capital: states that appropriated a lot of funds for education, health, highways, and natural resources invested more in the arts.

A subsequent study by J. Mark Davidson Schuster[6] of MIT employed more direct measures of artistic activity to explain variation among the fourteen most populous states in both legislative arts support and the dollar volume of grants the states' arts organizations (including its arts agency) received from the NEA. In Schuster's analyses of 1985 data, the best predictor of legislative appropriations to state arts agencies *and* NEA grant dollars per state was the number of museums and nonprofit performing arts organizations located there. The density of artists also had a strong positive association with appropriations and NEA grants, but not so strong as the number of organizations. The rate of attendance at arts events (a measure of audience demand) had a relatively weak effect on each kind of funding. NEA grant levels appeared somewhat more responsive than state legislative appropriations to each form of demand: just what one would expect if NEA policies were relatively consistent, and unaffected by economic conditions and political traditions that vary from state to state.

Because the first study lacked measures of artistic demand and the second study was conducted on only fourteen large states, neither lends itself to bold generalization. Yet if we cannot be certain *why* some states spend more on the arts than others, we can, at least, ask if NEA grant making is more or less evenly distributed across states than are legislative appropriations to state arts agencies. Columns 1 and 2 of Table 2 list FY 1989 NEA grants by state (including and excluding the basic state grants required by law). Column 3 of Table 2 lists FY 1989 state legislative appropriations to state arts agencies. (Line-item appropriations are excluded.)

Surprisingly, state appropriations were on balance slightly more evenly distributed than were Endowment grants. The evidence for this is in the last line in Table 2, the oddly-named Herfindahl Index, a statistical measure of dispersion that could range from .02 (if each of the fifty states received the same share of the total) to 1 (if one state got it all). The index for state appropriations is .08. By comparison, the NEA index is .10 with the BSGs included, and .13 without them, indicating that the mandated pass-through does serve to equalize appropriations among states. Although the higher NEA figures reveal that Endowment funding is more concentrated by state than are legislative appropriations (largely due to New York's share of the total), the differences are small and the indices fall much closer to the theoretical minimum of perfect equality than to the maximum possible degree of inequality.

A bit of added purchase can be derived by inspecting the shares of funding received by the five and ten states that are highest and lowest in their respective columns. The five states with the highest totals of Endowment funding received 52 per-

TABLE 2. 1989 NEA Grants and Legislative Appropriations by State

	NEA inc. BSG ($M)	NEA exc. BSG ($M)	SAAs Apps ($M)
Alabama	1.23	.85	1.48
Alaska	.88	.53	1.70
Arizona	1.57	1.19	1.55
Arkansas	.45	.08	1.02
California	16.03	15.37	14.60
Colorado	1.26	.88	1.31
Connecticut	2.98	2.60	2.12
Delaware	.54	.19	.79
Florida	1.86	1.37	20.84
Georgia	2.88	1.93	3.25
Hawaii	1.07	.72	6.75
Idaho	.46	.11	.34
Illinois	4.83	4.36	7.51
Indiana	1.49	1.09	1.97
Iowa	1.03	.66	.82
Kansas	.90	.50	1.07
Kentucky	2.05	1.67	2.37
Louisiana	1.07	.68	.73
Maine	.82	.47	.62
Maryland	3.41	3.02	5.97
Massachusetts	5.60	5.19	19.54
Michigan	2.15	1.70	12.43
Minnesota	8.04	7.10	3.18
Mississippi	.56	.19	.50
Missouri	2.43	2.03	4.91
Montana	.74	.39	.73
Nebraska	1.06	.70	.89
Nevada	.57	.24	.27
New Hampshire	.79	.44	.47
New Jersey	1.68	1.25	22.76
New Mexico	2.53	2.17	.71
New York	40.09	39.54	55.96
North Carolina	1.60	1.19	5.01
North Dakota	.48	.13	.21
Ohio	3.50	3.04	10.02
Oklahoma	.72	.34	2.67
Oregon	1.51	1.24	1.43
Pennsylvania	6.07	5.59	12.75
Rhode Island	.80	.44	1.44
South Carolina	1.98	1.58	3.12
South Dakota	.47	.11	.34

TABLE 2. *(Continued)*

	NEA inc. BSG ($M)	NEA exc. BSG ($M)	SAAs Apps ($M)
Tennessee	1.04	.64	3.51
Texas	4.64	4.10	3.31
Utah	1.93	1.57	1.60
Vermont	.71	.36	.46
Virginia	1.65	1.24	3.77
Washington	2.23	1.83	1.76
West Virginia	.54	.18	1.78
Wisconsin	1.93	1.54	1.88
Wyoming	.88	.54	.206
5 highest states receive	52.0	58.3	52.6
10 highest states receive	65.3	72.0	69.5
5 lowest states receive	1.7	0.6	0.6
10 lowest states receive	4.0	1.8	1.8
Herfindahl index	.10	.13	.08

Sources: NEA raw data provided by the Endowment; State raw data from NASAA, *State of the State Arts Agencies.*

cent of agency grants made in the fifty states during 1989. (Territories are excluded from these calculations.) This is almost exactly the same as the share of legislative appropriations derived by the five states with the most open-handed legislatures. (If the BSGs are excluded, NEA grants are more concentrated in the top five.) The same is true of the ten most fortunate, except that the share of NEA grants (including BSGs) going to this group is somewhat lower than the share of state appropriations commanded by the ten agencies ranking highest in column 3.

By contrast, Endowment funding appears to provide a cushion for arts organizations in states with very little professional arts activity. The ten states with the lowest appropriations accounted for 1.8 percent of total legislative appropriations; by contrast, the ten states receiving the smallest sums from the NEA (including the BSGs) received 4 percent of the Endowment total. (If BSGs are excluded, the five and ten bottom states in NEA funding received almost exactly the same shares of the pie as the five and ten lowest-ranking states in legislative appropriations.)

In other words, if one takes into account the BSGs, NEA funding is about as concentrated on the most fortunate states as is state legislative funding, but somewhat more generous to least favored. Although more detailed analyses would be required to be certain, a plausible interpretation is that, with some exceptions, the Endowment and state legislatures provide relatively large sums to states with lots of arts organizations and lots of artists; the Endowment focuses somewhat more support on arts-poor states, through its BSGs, than do their own legislatures; and the arts in states with moderate levels of artistic activity (and organizations of the middle rank) receive a somewhat greater share of state legislative appropriations and a somewhat smaller share of NEA grants.

Policy Making

In discussing policy making at the federal and state levels, we must abandon the comfort of even inadequate data and engage in more speculative inquiry. Nonetheless, the issue is so important that it cannot be neglected.

The Arts Endowment has been reluctant throughout its history to admit that it makes cultural policy: its policy, so the NEA's chairs have argued, is to support the arts, not to play favorites among them. In practice, this means that the NEA has usually reacted to the pressures upon it rather than boldly articulate visions concrete enough to serve as bases for action.

Nonetheless, if the Endowment's leadership has been reactive in its allocation of funds among disciplines and purposes, Endowment programs have often been creative in identifying and meeting needs in their fields. The ability of the federal agency (or, more accurately, experienced staff and panelists within it) to take a national perspective permits it to exercise a unique function in the U.S. system of arts support. Thus, for example, the NEA helped to build the dance field with its touring grants in the mid-1970s and encouraged the marriage of opera and musical theater later in the decade; in the 1980s, it highlighted assistance to ongoing theater ensembles and worked with the states to advance support for folk arts. Unlike the majority of state arts agencies that are too small to employ the full gamut of specialized staff, the NEA has routine access to men and women who have devoted their professional lives to particular disciplines, both as employees and as members of specialized grant review and policy panels. The Endowment is particularly well equipped to act with respect to fields, like media arts or design arts, and functions, like research on public participation in the arts, that are national in impact; and on issues, like conservation and museum indemnification, that have small, geographically scattered constituencies.

By contrast, the state arts agencies, with their smaller staff, are restricted to an overview of their states (and increasingly, through regional organizations, neighboring states) and less able to place concentrated effort on issues that affect only a few of their constituent organizations. On the other hand, the states are better equipped to take the lead in addressing art forms and issues that have a big impact in a few places. This has been especially true with respect to art forms with roots in particular, regionally concentrated, ethnic or racial communities: The New York State Council on the Arts, for example, has pioneered programs in jazz, and several western arts agencies have been in the vanguard with respect to support for Native American or Latino arts. Similarly, state agencies are better equipped than the NEA to exert leverage on public school systems and to develop programs with local arts agencies. These advantages explain why the NEA channels relatively high levels of its education, local agency, and folk arts budgets to the states.

Conclusion

The most striking findings of this review have to do with the dogs that did *not* bark: by and large, comparisons of the funding patterns of the NEA and the state arts agencies failed to find strong, reliable differences. On the basis of these admittedly rough comparisons, the Endowment and the states (taken together) appear similar in the relative emphases they place on different artistic disciplines and on the needs of producing organizations and artists. (Because the NEA and the state arts agencies are public institutions operating under similar political constraints, this should come as no surprise.) Moreover, the grant making of the Endowment's panels and the budget making of state legislatures yield similar distributions of funds across the states.

Throughout this chapter, attention has been called to the need for more reliable and thorough data. Classification of Endowment grants according to the National Standard used by the states and more complete recording of state grants in the purpose and recipient-type fields would be a good place to start. Comparable data on the programs of local arts agencies is an increasingly pressing requirement for intelligent policy making. And special studies of issues about which little evidence is currently available—state support for non–Euro-American art forms and artists, the functions and dynamics of state and federal grant making and policy panels, and the extent of indirect fellowship support to artists are three examples—would also be most useful.

Nonetheless, existing data document that grant making by the states and by the NEA is less different than common stereotypes suggest. It follows that no particular kinds of artists or arts organizations obviously stand to lose or benefit from increased devolution from the Endowment to the states.

It does *not* follow from this that devolution does not matter, however. Certain kinds of policy leadership can only be exercised by a strong federal agency. Other forms of leadership can best be exercised by the states. If the resources of either were permitted to fall below some threshold level, the arts would be considerably worse off.

Moreover, a division of labor between a strong Endowment and strong state arts agencies, even if it is indistinct, has all the virtues that engineers, communications theorists, and systems analysts attribute to other forms of redundancy. The coexistence of federal and state grant making makes errors less costly by giving worthy artists and organizations an extra door on which to knock. It also represents a form of risk pooling in an era of political vulnerability. Perhaps most important, it provides a flexibility that permits experimentation and leadership to emerge at different levels, enhancing opportunities for learning by the system as a whole.

It is particularly important that devolutionary proposals be considered with an eye toward historical and political context. Because it occurred as the outcome of many separate decisions rather than explicit federal policy, the dramatic *de facto* devolution of arts funding and responsibility from the federal government to the states during the 1980s is too often overlooked, both by those who call for more funds for the states and by their critics who argue that the states could not handle the responsibility. As Nathan and Doolittle note in their book on the Reagan era,[7] the federal government and the states seem to change roles from time to time. When the former is dynamic, the latter tend toward passivity. When conservatives control the executive branch, reformers organize and find their greatest successes in the state capitals. The fact that the NEA was particularly dynamic during the late 1960s and early 1970s, when most of the action in American politics was at the federal level, and that the state agencies seemed to many especially vigorous and progressive during the conservative (and prosperous) 1980s, is both unsurprising and a poor guide to the future. If there is a lesson to be learned, it is that neither centralization nor devolution is a satisfactory substitute for the suppleness and responsiveness that a mixed system affords.

Notes

[1] Larson (1983).
[2] Nathan, Doolittle, and associates (1987).
[3] This figure was created by Francie Ostrower and updated by Lee Miller.
[4] Arian (1987).
[5] Urice (1982).
[6] Schuster (1988).
[7] Nathan, Doolittle, and associates (1987).

Bibliography

Arian, E.. 1987. *The Unfulfilled Promise: Public Subsidy of the Arts in America.* Philadelphia: Temple University Press.

Banfield, E.C. 1984. *The Democratic Muse.* New York: Basic Books.

Becker, C. 1989. "Private Fantasies Shape Public Events: And Public Events Invade and Shape Our Dreams." In Raven 1989.

Bolcom, W. 1988. "Trouble in the Music World." *Michigan Quarterly Review* 27 (4).

Burns, J.S. 1975. *The Awkward Embrace: The Creative Artist and the Institution in America.* New York: Alfred A. Knopf.

Choksy, L., R. Abramson, A. Gillespie, and D. Woods. 1986. *The Teaching of Music in the Twentieth Century.* Englewood Cliffs: Prentice-Hall.

Cremin, L. 1969. *The Transformation of the School: Progressivism in American Education, 1876-1957.* New York: Alfred A. Knopf.

Cummings, M.C. 1982. "To Change a Nation's Cultural Policy: The Kennedy Administration and the Arts in the United States, 1961-1963." In Mulcahy and Swaim 1982.

Cummings, M.C., and R.S. Katz. eds. 1987. *The Patron State: Government and the Arts in Europe, North America, and Japan.* New York: Oxford University Press.

Danto, A. 1990. "From Pollock to Mapplethorpe: The Media and the Artworld." *Gannett Center Journal* IV (1).

DiMaggio, P.J. 1984. "The Nonprofit Instrument and the Influence of the Marketplace on Policies in the Arts." In Lowry 1984.

Efland, A. 1990. *A History of Art Education: Educational and Social Currents in the Teaching of Visual Arts.* New York: Teachers College Press.

Eisner, E. 1972. *Educating Artistic Vision.* New York: Macmillan.

Erb, D., H.W. Johnson, T.W. Leavitt, et al. 1984. "A Symposium: Issues in the Emergence of Public Policy." In Lowry 1984.

Feld, A., M. O'Hare, and J.M.D. Schuster. 1983. *Patrons Despite Themselves: Taxpayers and Arts Policy.* New York: New York University Press.

Gates, T. ed. In press. *Music, Society and Education in the United States.* Tuscaloosa: University of Alabama Press.

Getty Center for Arts Education. 1985. *Beyond Creating.* Los Angeles: J. Paul Getty Trust.

Ginsberg, A. 1987. "Nazi Pillage of Art in World War II: The Dreams, the Methods, and the Restitution." Paper prepared for the Research Seminar on Government and the Arts, Johns Hopkins University, May 12, 1987.

Goodnow, J. 1977. *Children Drawing*. Cambridge: Harvard University Press.

Hargreaves, D. ed. 1989. *Children and the Arts*. Milton Keynes, UK: Open University Press.

Harris, J.S. 1970. *Government Patronage of the Arts in Great Britain*. Chicago: University of Chicago Press.

Harris, N. 1966. *The Artist in American Society: The Formative Years*. Chicago: University of Chicago Press.

Hobbs, R., and F. Woodward. eds. 1986. *Human Rights/Human Wrongs: Art and Social Change*. Iowa City: The University of Iowa Museum of Art.

Hughes, R. 1986. "Art and Politics." In Hobbs and Woodward 1986.

Jeffri, J. ed. 1986. *The Artists' Work-Related, Human and Social Services Questionnaire I*. New York: Research Center for Arts and Culture, Columbia University.

―――. ed. 1988. *The Artists' Work-Related, Human and Social Services Questionnaire II*. New York: Research Center for Arts and Culture, Columbia University.

―――. ed. 1989. *Information on Artists*. New York: Research Center for Arts and Culture, Columbia University.

―――. ed. 1990. *The Artists' Training and Career Project*. New York: Research Center for Arts and Culture, Columbia University.

Keens, W., and N. Rhodes. 1989. *An American Dialogue*. Report of the National Task Force on Presenting and Touring the Performing Arts. Washington, D.C.: The Association of Performing Arts Presenters.

Kermode, F. 1957. *Romantic Image*. New York: Routledge & Kegan Paul.

Kernochan, J.M. 1989. "The Distribution Right in the United States of America: Review and Reflections." *Vanderbilt Law Review* 42 (5).

Kramer, H. 1990. "A *Times* Critic's Piece about Art Amounts to Political Propaganda." *The New York Observer*. August 13–20, 1990.

Lacy, S. 1989. "Fractured Space." In Raven 1989.

Larson, G.O. 1983. *The Reluctant Patron: The United States Government and the Arts 1943–1965*. Philadelphia: University of Pennsylvania Press.

Lesnick, H. 1986. "Artists, Workers, and the Law of Work." *Journal of Arts Management and Law* XVI (2).

Levine, E. 1982. "Artists in Society." *The Public Interest* 66.

Lippard, L. 1989. "Moving Targets/Moving Out." In Raven 1989.

Love, J., S. Bigley, and B. Klipple. 1990. *Summary of State Arts Agencies' Grantmaking Activities for Fiscal Year 1987.* Washington: National Assembly of State Arts Agencies.

Lowenfeld, V. 1957. *Creative and Mental Growth.* New York: Macmillan.

Lowry, W.M. ed. 1984. *The Arts and Public Policy in the United States.* Englewood Cliffs: Prentice-Hall.

Madsen, C. ed. In press. *Research in Music Behavior: Applications and Extensions.* Tuscaloosa: University of Alabama Press.

Mayhew, K., and A. Edwards. 1966. *The Dewey School: The Laboratory School at the University of Chicago.* New York: Appleton Century Co.

McKinzie, R. 1973. *The New Deal for Artists.* Princeton: Princeton University Press.

Miller, L.B. 1966. *Patrons and Patriotism: The Encouragement of the Fine Arts in the United States, 1790–1860.* Chicago: University of Chicago Press.

Morison, S.E. 1965. *The Oxford History of the American People.* New York: Oxford University Press.

Mulcahy, K.V., and C.R. Swaim, eds. 1982. *Public Policy and the Arts.* Boulder: Westview Press.

Nathan, R.P., F.C. Doolittle, and Associates. 1987. *Reagan and the States.* Princeton: Princeton University Press.

National Assembly of State Arts Agencies. 1988. *State Arts Agency Profile 1987.* Washington, D.C.: NASAA.

———. 1989. *The State of the State Arts Agencies, 1989.* Washington, D.C.: NASAA.

National Endowment for the Arts. January 12, 1987. "ARTISTS" (draft). Washington, D.C.: NEA.

———. 1988. *Annual Report 1987.* Washington, D.C.: NEA.

———. January 1989. "ARTISTS" (draft). Washington, D.C.: NEA.

Netzer, D. 1978. *The Subsidized Muse: Public Support for the Arts in the United States.* Cambridge: Cambridge University Press.

Phillips, P. 1988. "Out of Order: The Public Art Machine." *Artforum* 12.

———. 1989. "Waste Not." *Art in America* 2.

Piaget, J. 1962. *Play, Dreams, and Imitation.* London: Routledge & Kegan Paul.

Purcell, R. 1956. *Government and Art.* Washington, D.C.: Public Affairs Press.

Raven, A. ed. 1989. *Art in the Public Interest.* Ann Arbor: UMI Research Press.

Roxan, D., and K. Wanstall. 1964. *The Rape of Art: The Story of Hitler's Plunder of the Great Masterpieces of Europe.* New York: Coward-McCann.

Schuster, J., and M. Davidson. March 1988. *An Inquiry into the Geographic Correlates of Government Arts Funding.* Monograph prepared for the Research Division, National Endowment for the Arts. Cambridge: Massachusetts Institute of Technology.

Scott, P., and W. Cohen. 1984. "An Introduction to the New York Artists' Authorship Rights Act." *Art and the Law* VIII (3).

Smith, N. 1982. *Experience and Art.* New York: Teachers College Press.

Speiller, W.M. 1980. "The Favored Tax Treatment of Purchasers of Art." *Columbia Law Review* 80 (2).

Stalker, D., and C. Glymour. 1982. "The Malignant Object: Thoughts on Public Sculpture." *The Public Interest* 66.

Straight, M. 1979. *Twigs for an Eagle's Nest, Government and the Arts: 1965–1978.* New York: Devon Press.

Swaim, C.R. 1982. "The National Endowment for the Arts, 1965–1980." In Mulcahy and Swaim 1982.

Taylor, J.C. 1979. *The Fine Arts in America.* Chicago: University of Chicago Press.

Throsby, D., and D. Mills. 1989. *When Are You Going to Look for a Real Job?* North Sydney, Australia: The Australian Council.

Tschopik, H. 1991. *Los Angeles—A Multicultural Handbook.* The 2000 Partnership.

Urice, J.K. 1982. *State Legislative Funding of, and National Endowment for the Arts Grants to, State Arts Agencies.* Binghamton: Center for Social Analysis, SUNY-Binghamton.

Webster, P. In press a. "Refinement of a Measure of Creative Thinking in Music." In Madsen.

———. In press b. "Creative Thinking in Music: Approaches to Research." In Gates.

Weil, S. 1983. "The Filer Commission Report: Is It Good for Museums?" In *Beauty and the Beasts: On Museums, Art, the Law and the Market.* Washington, D.C.: Smithsonian Institution Press.

Wolf, D. 1989. "Artistic Learning as Conversation." In Hargreaves 1989.

Woodard, T. 1990. "Harlem Renaissance." unpublished.

Wygant, F. 1983. *Art in American Schools in the Nineteenth Century.* Cincinnati: Interwood.

Ybarra-Frausto. 1986. *Lo del Corazon: Heartbeat of a Culture.* San Francisco: The Mexican Museum.

Final
Report of
The American Assembly

A t the close of their discussions, the participants in The
American Assembly on *The Arts and Government: Questions
for the Nineties,* at Arden House, Harriman, New York, November 8–11, 1990, reviewed as a group a draft of the following
statement, which was then revised in the light of their comments. This statement represents general agreement; however, no one was asked to sign it. Furthermore, it should be
understood that not everyone agreed with all of it.

Preamble

This American Assembly on *The Arts and Government* met in
the immediate aftermath of the most serious challenge to direct federal support of the arts in the twenty-five year history
of the National Endowment for the Arts (NEA). An eighteen-
month public and congressional conflict had been provoked
by two exhibitions assisted in part by the NEA. They included
works of art that some members of Congress and several private organizations seized upon to forward the argument that
public funds were being misapplied to support obscene and

blasphemous materials. NEA grant procedures, some asserted, were obviously not working and needed to be overhauled. Some of the opponents carried the argument a step farther, maintaining that the episode proved the federal government has no legitimate role in funding the arts.

This initial phase of the argument in 1989 led the Congress, for the first time, to impose content guidelines on NEA grant-making procedures. The controversy that followed soon became a lightning rod that exposed the wide variances among the American people in political, social, religious, and aesthetic values, and raised anew basic questions about the rationale for public arts support and the processes for its administration. The unfettered artistic freedom envisaged in the original NEA legislation could no longer be assumed inviolable.

That government-aided art was not more widely supported by the general population came as a shock to many arts supporters. The realization grew that a much more concentrated effort was needed to convey the positive achievements of the NEA to a far wider spectrum of the population, and that the arts programs themselves were still reaching only a minority of the population. The content restrictions in the legislation raised their own set of constitutional questions and brought about the direct involvement of a great many individual artists, along with others, in political action to oppose the new provisions.

When The American Assembly planned its meeting in the fall of 1989, the full extent of the challenge to federal funding was yet to unfold. It was clear only that further battles loomed and that significant issues were at stake. The spring and summer of 1990 witnessed a chain of dramatic and unpredictable events that left the outcome in constant doubt. The Assembly developed an agenda that sought to accommodate the fluid situation in Washington, but also to look ahead to issues of arts policy that would endure beyond the immediate crisis. As the calendar would have it, the legislative resolution of the controversy occurred only two weeks before the Assembly met. The House and Senate agreed on a bill reauthorizing the

NEA for three years and appropriating funds for the coming year at approximately the current level.

Understandably, therefore, the topicality of this Assembly, which included participants who were almost all directly involved in some aspect of the drama just concluded, resulted in a lively and sometimes contentious meeting. Even so, a degree of consensus emerged, most prominently expressed in a statement of basic principles that reflect many of the discussions and underlie this report's Findings and Recommendations.

Principles

- A flourishing artistic life is in the best interests of a democratic society. The arts and the artist contribute to the nation's identity and to the education and happiness of its citizens. It is, therefore, appropriate that government at all levels join with the private sector to further the nation's artistic life and to provide access to the arts to all citizens.
- Excellence and the defining standards of excellence, which exist for every culture and for every art form, must be the touchstone of all government funding for the arts and artists.
- Constitutional principles of freedom of expression, essential to a democratic society, are of special importance to a thriving artistic climate. Government policies and private actions that threaten to curb artistic "speech" or to constrict in any way the marketplace of ideas for the arts have no place in American society and must be vigorously opposed.
- Government arts programs should support new work of promise that may prove risky or unpopular. Some art has always been controversial and will continue to be, especially as cultures and art forms become more diverse and the boundaries of art continue to expand.
- Public funding policies must be administered according to the principle that no artist's work may be compromised, suppressed, or unrecognized because of race, ethnicity, gender, sexual preference, or political or religious beliefs.
- With public support goes public responsibility. Artists fulfill

this responsibility by pursuing the highest quality work of which they are capable; arts organizations fulfill it by carrying out their stated missions and by developing broader and more critically aware publics for their work.

Findings and Recommendations

The National Endowment for the Arts

The National Endowment for the Arts, in its twenty-five years of operation, has proved an effective vehicle for promoting the support and appreciation of the arts in the United States. It has broadened access, bringing the arts for the first time to millions of Americans. It has provided encouragement and support to institutions old and new, large and small, and has become the largest single source of support for the creative work of individual artists across the land.

The NEA, from its inception, has emphasized excellence in artistic achievement and the promise of achievement as the armature that connects all of its activities. The central mechanism for judgments of quality and promise has been the grant advisory panels of peers and other professionals. The system has generally worked well to identify changing needs and develop new programs. Proposals for the improvement of the panel system to make it more responsive deserve attention and should be examined. But care must be taken that the NEA's integrity as an institution be maintained and efforts resisted that would weaken its role as the central vehicle for direct federal support for the arts and artists. At this particular time, the NEA has a specially compelling responsibility to protect freedom of expression, not only for the artists it supports but for every artist.

This Assembly believes the NEA should:

• Strengthen the institutions through which the arts are produced and presented to the public, reflecting in all its actions the full range of traditions and artistic forms that comprise this country's cultural vitality.

- Promote greater access to the arts by new and underserved communities and assist them in their efforts to build and stabilize their own institutions.
- Continue to support, through grants, fellowships, and other assistance, artists of accomplishment and promise, whether working in traditional, nontraditional, experimental, or innovative forms.
- Work to increase appropriations to the NEA so as to restore, at a minimum, the real purchasing power of its budget at the beginning of the 1980s.
- Exercise leadership in exploring and developing the central issues of cultural policy by strengthening the NEA's research program, funding private research efforts, and convening conferences on major policy issues.

Of particular concern to all those who participated in this Assembly was the role of the NEA and other levels of government in furthering the arts in education. Because of the special importance of the subject, it is addressed in a later section of this report.

State and Local Arts Support

As the NEA developed, arts agencies in every state and territory became significant partners, encouraged in many instances by the NEA's example. In addition, local arts agencies, both public and private, grew rapidly. They now number more than 4,000, and are receiving more than $100 million a year in tax funds. Their contribution to promoting cultural pluralism and nurturing individual artists has become increasingly significant.

While federal appropriations to the NEA stagnated in the 1980s, state arts agencies experienced dramatic growth. Today total state appropriations are 60 percent greater than the NEA's. The statutory allocation to state arts agencies of at least 20 percent of NEA program funds has substantially aided the efforts by other levels of government to support the arts.

In the reauthorization of the statute in 1990, a new provision was adopted to increase the allocation of NEA program funds to state and local arts agencies to 35 percent by Fiscal Year 1993. The long-term consequences of this action by Congress, part of a last-minute compromise, were not adequately examined. The action carries the risk of diminishing the national leadership role of the NEA and producing adverse results for artists and arts institutions. State and local arts agency funding should continue to be increased, but not at the expense of the NEA's important national role. This Assembly recommends that:

- The new provision increasing the NEA allocation to the states should be carefully reviewed by the next Congress and modified, if necessary.
- Any increased federal allocations to the states must not be allowed to replace existing state arts agency funds. Consideration should be given to requiring states to match any increase in federal funds with new appropriations.

Advocacy and Political Action

To keep the arts on the public agenda, a broader constituency must be found and developed. The events of the past eighteen months forced supporters of the arts to confront the political process head-on, but the arts community as a whole was not prepared to compete on equal terms with its adversaries. The controversy also revealed vast differences among many Americans about the nature of art and the role of the artist.

The steady overall increase in funding in the 1970s and 1980s from the private and public sectors had tended to obscure the need to bring about better understanding among arts supporters, artists, and the public. In addition, it became clear that arts supporters had to become more politically sophisticated in the techniques used by successful claimants to public support.

It was also the case that fractures occurred in the arts community itself as a result of differing objectives and perspectives. Arts advocacy can only succeed if all participants in the process refrain from asserting their interests at the expense of others. Every group must benefit in an equitable way. Advocacy is stronger to the extent that coalition is complete.

In future, while differences within the arts community must be acknowledged, ways must be found to coalesce around commonly shared goals and to pursue them in a spirit of cooperation.

To improve the case for the arts and its presentation to the public, this Assembly recommends that:

- Arts advocates improve communication to the public about ways that government-supported arts programs and projects are benefiting the economies of, and enhancing the quality of life in, cities, towns, and other localities.
- Arts supporters explore more effective ways to involve citizens at the grassroots level in articulating and working for cultural policies that benefit everyone.
- Arts communities closely monitor proposed federal, state, and local legislation and regulations that have potential application to the arts. Artists and arts institutions should be prepared to support or oppose specific measures, as appropriate.
- Arts communities, including the for-profit arts and entertainment industry, forge working alliances with other groups that intersect with the arts, including labor unions, educational and religious organizations, chambers of commerce, and economic development councils.
- Arts advocates initiate a coalition with corporate chief executive officers who understand the central role of the arts in communities and are prepared to serve as advocates for the arts with all levels of government.
- Arts professionals develop a network of institutions devoted to the basic research, rigorous analysis, and continuing exchange of information needed to define and reinforce advocacy objectives.

Cultural Diversity and Government Support

This country's artistic life has always been distinguished by the remarkable range of cultures from which its artists have drawn their inspiration. In recent years, these cultures have been expanded and enriched by new waves of immigrants. The historic problems of adaptation and community acceptance are as challenging and difficult now as they have ever been. Our best imagination and understanding is required to minimize the social dislocations and conflicts that always accompany immigrations from other cultures.

In the clash of cultures, artists have always had a special capacity to illuminate the differences among peoples and expose the reasons for conflict. They may not provide solutions, but their insights can be crucial in helping us understand and accommodate diversity and change.

If the arts and artists from the many specific cultures contributing to this country's extraordinary diversity are to make their full contribution to national life, they need help. Aided by a variety of tax incentives to giving, the arts as a whole in the United States receive their primary financial support from the private sector—individuals, foundations, and corporations. However, because private giving is voluntary, there is no assurance that every deserving need in the spectrum of need will be addressed.

Some communities, despite the richness and quality of their cultural achievements, have yet to gain equal access to many private sources of funding. Public agencies, on the other hand, are often in a position to identify and assist underserved populations. For communities still seeking to share in the private philanthropy that is directed primarily toward larger and better known institutions, public agencies have a responsibility to address their unmet needs. Government recognition and support may also have the effect of encouraging private giving and improving access to private sources. If the cultural requirements of underserved communities are to be effectively addressed by government, this Assembly recommends that:

- Public arts agencies take the steps necessary to ensure recognition for every culture in our society. The statutory definition of the arts must be revised, if necessary, to embrace activities, forms, and expressions that may not be eligible for assistance according to current definitions.
- Guidelines of public funding agencies be developed, and staff and panel members selected, to ensure that the criteria of quality and excellence applied to the art of all cultures reflect an understanding and awareness of their specific values and traditions.
- Public arts agencies encourage opportunities for the professional development of artists and arts administrators from communities with a history of unequal access. Programs should also be developed within such communities that reflect their special character and needs.

International Cultural Policy

In the wake of the Cold War, the United States must adopt new international cultural policies for a transformed world. New needs and opportunities exist for the arts as a means of representing this country's national character, its diversity, ideals, and objectives to the rest of the world. A broad range of initiatives by the appropriate federal agencies is required. This Assembly recommends:

- Expanded cooperative public and private programs for the full and free exchange of art and artists with other countries.
- Developing exchange programs that tap the abundant cultural resources brought by the waves of new immigrants in the past two decades, as well as those of African Americans, Latinos, Native Americans, and Asian Americans.
- A comprehensive study of international cultural policy by the appropriate federal agencies, drawing on private as well as public sector resources and experience and recommending specific actions.
- Careful consideration by the administration of the advantages to the United States of rejoining the United

Nations Educational, Scientific and Cultural Organization (UNESCO).

Tax Policies

Tax policies are critical to the stability of the arts in the United States. Exemptions, deductions, and other special rules affecting taxable income, property, customs, and other taxes are indirect forms of aid that dwarf direct support in overall amount. Tax provisions that benefit the arts, as well as education and other social needs, constitute an enlightened approach to public policy that is distinctive to this country. Tax law can provide valuable incentives to private giving, decentralize decision making, and establish a desirable counterweight to direct support.

Changes in the tax law often come about in response to broad political forces. Frequently the impact on arts and culture of such changes is not given sufficient attention. For example, the effect on charitable giving of the dramatic reduction in the top marginal tax rate is still unclear. By contrast, it soon became evident that changed provisions in the 1986 tax code affecting the full deductibility of the market value of gifts of appreciated personal property had caused a sudden and serious decline in gifts of art and manuscripts to museums and other institutions. Vigorous advocacy by a coalition of museums and charity federations has managed to restore, in part, the prior provision, though for only one year.

A variety of proposals for special tax treatment of the arts continues to be advanced, including some new ideas such as special assessment districts. More than other forms of aid, however, tax based assistance may set the interests of the arts against those of a larger society.

In light of the above considerations, this Assembly recommends that appropriate research bodies:

• Analyze the advantages and disadvantages for the arts of present and proposed tax provisions.
• Identify successful examples of the creative use of tax laws by arts institutions and public agencies.

The Arts in Education

To those who have worked in the field of arts education, the relevance of the arts to human development is unquestionable. Only in recent years, however, has systematic research established that the arts are, in fact, special ways of knowing— ways that are as essential to basic education as the mastery of verbal and numerical skills. It is also the case that for many children, school based arts programs provide them with their first direct arts experiences and are the beginning of a lifelong commitment. Arts education, therefore, must be a priority for both the arts and education communities and should actively engage federal, state, and local arts and education agencies. Sequential arts education must be encouraged, and such programs should be supported by careful research and adequate resources. This Assembly recommends that:

- The National Endowment for the Arts initiate action to achieve a consensus around national goals for arts education.
- The NEA play an expanded role in the advocacy of arts education, using the authority of the chairman's office to raise awareness at the federal, state, and local levels.
- Federal, state, and local agencies identify and fund exemplary arts education models and recognize outstanding individual leadership in every area of achievement.
- All government arts education support be based on equal access, especially to people of color and in less privileged communities, and reflect an awareness of this country's range of cultures and art forms.
- Government programs at all levels be prepared to protect the work of artists, teachers, and other educators as they involve students in making and thinking about works of art that will sometimes be at variance with community values.

A Final Word

The Assembly adjourned to an uncertain domestic and international climate. At home, a period of economic stringency was underway and hard choices to deal with compelling social needs would be required by the country. Abroad, the crisis in the Gulf and its potential consequences were casting an ominous shadow.

Throughout their discussions, Assembly participants were well aware that in such a climate of scarcity, the structures that sustain the arts will need to be stretched even farther if current levels of service to the public are to be maintained. Imagination and ingenuity will be in particular demand. But the seriousness of the outlook only served to reinforce the conviction, evident throughout the discussions, that the arts' power to heal and help, teach and question is needed now more than ever.

Participants

GEORGE H.J. ABRAMS
Special Assistant to the
    Director
National Museum of the
    American Indian
Smithsonian Institution
New York, NY

MARIE ACOSTA-COLON
Director
The Mexican Museum
San Francisco, CA

ALBERTA ARTHURS
Director for Arts &
    Humanities
The Rockefeller Foundation
New York, NY

J. THOMAS BACCHETTI
Executive Director
Atlanta Symphony Orchestra
Atlanta, GA

STEPHEN BENEDICT
Founder and Former
    Director
Graduate Program in Arts
    Administration
Columbia University
New York, NY

SUSAN S. BLOOM
Vice President
Worldwide Cultural Affairs
American Express Company
New York, NY

◁ JOHN BRADEMAS
President
New York University
New York, NY

CAROL R. BROWN
President
The Pittsburgh Cultural
    Trust
Pittsburgh, PA

MARY BURGER
Research Assistant
Harvard Project Zero
Graduate School of
    Education
Harvard University
Cambridge, MA

CORA CAHAN
President
42nd Street Entertainment
    Corporation
New York, NY

LUIS R. CANCEL
Executive Director
The Bronx Museum of the
    Arts
Bronx, NY

○ SCHUYLER G. CHAPIN
Vice President
Worldwide Concert
    & Artist Activities
Steinway & Sons
New York, NY

EUGENE V. CLARK
Representative of the Vatican
    Museums in the United
    States,
    Washington, DC
Archdiocese of New York
St. Agnes Church
New York, NY

DUDLEY COCKE
Director, Roadside Theater
Appalshop, Inc.
Whitesburg, KY

JAN COLLMER
President
Collmer Semiconductor, Inc.
Dallas, TX

◁ KINSHASHA CONWILL
Executive Director
The Studio Museum in
    Harlem
New York, NY

MILTON C. CUMMINGS,
JR.
Professor of Political
    Science
Department of Political
    Science
Johns Hopkins University
Baltimore, MD

GORDON DAVIS
Lord, Day, & Lord, Barrett,
    Smith
New York, NY

LEON B. DENMARK
Executive Director
Newark Symphony Hall
Newark, NJ

VISHAKHA N. DESAI
Director
The Asia Society Galleries
New York, NY

JOAN DILLON
Board Member
American Arts Alliance
Kansas City, MO

† PAUL J. DIMAGGIO
Associate Professor
    Department of Sociology
Yale University
New Haven, CT

◁ DORIS DIXON
Professional Staff Member
Senate Labor and
    Human Resources
    Committee
(Senator Thad Cochran)
Washington, DC

x JOHN E. FROHNMAYER
Chairman
National Endowment for the
    Arts
Washington, DC

DONALD H. GAREIS
Trustee
Robert W. Woodruff
    Arts Center, Inc.
Atlanta, GA

▷ JACKIE GOLDENBERG
Editor
Independent Commission
    Report
New York, NY

xx GUILLERMO
    GOMEZ-PENA
Performance Artist
San Diego, CA

◁ ROY M. GOODMAN
New York State Senate
New York, NY

◁ WILLIAM D. GRAMPP
Professor of Economics
University of Illinois
Chicago, IL

VICTOR MASAYESVA, JR.
Filmmaker-Artist
Is Productions
Hotevilla, AZ

RUTH R. MAYLEAS
Program Officer,
Education & Culture
Program
The Ford Foundation
New York, NY

▷ TIMOTHY J. MCCLIMON
Vice President
AT&T Foundation
New York, NY

VAL A. MCINNES
Director of Development &
Director of Judeo-Christian
Studies
Tulane University
South Dominican Foundation
New Orleans, LA

CHARLES L. MEE, JR.
Playwright and Historian
New York, NY

◁ DAVID MENDOZA
Executive Director
Artist Trust
Seattle, WA

RICHARD MITTENTHAL
Partner
The Conservation Company
New York, NY

▷ ELIZABETH MURFEE
President
EMC Company
New York, NY

◁ CHARLOTTE MURPHY
Executive Director
National Association
of Artists' Organizations &
National Campaign for
Freedom of Expression
Washington, DC

○ RAYMOND D. NASHER
President's Committee
on the Arts and the
Humanities
Dallas, TX

◁ MICHAEL O'HARE
Lecturer in Public Policy
John F. Kennedy
School of Government
Harvard University
Cambridge, MA

◁ ROBERT PEASE
Executive Director
Allegheny Conference
Community Development
Pittsburgh, PA

◁ BERNICE JOHNSON
REAGON
Curator
National Museum of
American History
Smithsonian Institution
Washington, DC

† REBECCA RILEY
Director
Special Grants Program
John D. and Catherine T.
MacArthur Foundation
Chicago, IL

PEDRO RODRIGUEZ
Executive Director
Guadalupe Cultural Arts
    Center
San Antonio, TX

STEPHEN L. SALYER
President &
    Chief Executive Officer
American Public Radio
Minneapolis, MN

▷ SUZANNE M. SATO
Associate Director for
    Arts and Humanities
The Rockefeller Foundation
New York, NY

†◁J. MARK DAVIDSON
SCHUSTER
Associate Professor
Department of Urban
    Studies & Planning
Massachusetts Institute
    of Technology
Cambridge, MA

RUTH SHACK
President
Dade Community
    Foundation
Miami, FL

† RICHARD E. SHERWOOD
Partner
O'Melveny & Myers
Los Angeles, CA

○ WILLIAM STRICKLAND
Executive Director
Manchester Craftsman's
    Guild
Pittsburgh, PA

◁ KATHLEEN M. SULLIVAN
Professor
Harvard Law School
Cambridge, MA

† BARBARA L. TSUMAGARI
Executive Director
The Kitchen
New York, NY

MARTA VEGA
President & Executive
    Director
Caribbean Cultural Center
New York, NY

◁ JOEL WACHS
Second District
Los Angeles City Council
Los Angeles, CA

LEWIS WALDECK
Director, Symphonic
    Services Division
American Federation
    of Musicians
New York, NY

◁ STEPHEN E. WEIL
Deputy Director
Hirshhorn Museum
    and Sculpture Garden
Smithsonian Institution
Washington, DC

◁ DENNIE PALMER WOLF
Senior Research Associate
The Development Group
Harvard Project Zero
Graduate School
    of Education
Harvard University
Cambridge, MA

◁ MICHAEL WOO   †◁ GERALD D. YOSHITOMI
Thirteenth District   Executive Director
Los Angeles City Council   Japanese American
Los Angeles, CA   Cultural & Community
                                         Center
                                     Los Angeles, CA

† Discussion Leader
▷ Rapporteur
◁ Panelist
○ Panel Moderator
x Delivered a Formal Address
xx Presented a Performance Piece

About the American Assembly

The American Assembly was established by Dwight D. Eisenhower at Columbia University in 1950. It holds nonpartisan meetings and publishes authoritative books to illuminate issues of United States policy.

An affiliate of Columbia, with offices in the Helen Goodhart Altschul Hall on the Barnard College campus, the Assembly is a national, educational institution incorporated in the state of New York.

The Assembly seeks to provide information, stimulate discussion, and evoke independent conclusions on matters of vital public interest.

American Assembly Sessions

At least two national programs are initiated each year. Authorities are retained to write background papers presenting essential data and defining the main issues of each subject.

A group of men and women representing a broad range of experience, competence, and American leadership meet for several days to discuss the Assembly topic and consider alternatives for national policy.

All Assemblies follow the same procedure. The background papers are sent to participants in advance of the Assembly.

The Assembly meets in small groups of four or five lengthy periods. All groups use the same agenda. At the close of these informal sessions participants adopt in plenary session a final report of findings and recommendations.

Regional, state, and local Assemblies are held following the national session at Arden House. Assemblies have also been held in England, Switzerland, Malaysia, Canada, the Caribbean, South America, Central America, the Philippines, and Japan. Over one hundred sixty institutions have cosponsored one or more Assemblies.

Arden House

Home of The American Assembly and scene of the national sessions is Arden House, which was given to Columbia University in 1950 by W. Averell Harriman. E. Roland Harriman joined his brother in contributing toward adaptation of the property for conference purposes. The buildings and surrounding land, known as the Harriman Campus of Columbia University, are fifty miles north of New York City.

Arden House is a distinguished conference center. It is self-supporting and operates throughout the year for use by organizations with educational objectives. The American Assembly is a tenant of this Columbia University facility only during Assembly sessions.

Index